Digital Sports Journalism

Digital Sports Journalism gives detailed guidance on a range of digital practices for producing content for smartphones and websites. Each chapter discusses a skill that has become essential for sports journalists today, with student-friendly features throughout to support learning. These include case studies, examples of sports journalism from leading global publications, as well as top tips and practical exercises. The book also presents interviews with leading sport and club journalists with wide-ranging experience at the BBC, Copa90, Wimbledon, the *Guardian* and BT Sport, who discuss working with new technologies to cover sports stories and events.

Chapters cover:

- live blogging;
- making and disseminating short videos;
- working for a sports club or governing body;
- finding and transmitting stories on social media;
- podcasting;
- longform online journalism.

The job of a sports journalist has altered dramatically over the first two decades of the 21st century, with scope to write content across a new variety of digital platforms and mediums. *Digital Sports Journalism* will help students of journalism and professionals unlock the potential of these new media technologies.

Charles M. Lambert spent two decades as a television journalist, covering news and sport for the BBC and ITV. He has run the sports journalism degree courses at the University of East London and the University for the Creative Arts, UK, where he is now in charge of the journalism and media cluster.

Digital Sports Journalism

Charles M. Lambert

Routledge
Taylor & Francis Group

LONDON AND NEW YORK

First published 2019
by Routledge
2 Park Square, Milton Park, Abingdon, Oxon OX14 4RN

and by Routledge
711 Third Avenue, New York, NY 10017

Routledge is an imprint of the Taylor & Francis Group, an informa business

British Library Cataloguing-in-Publication Data
A catalogue record for this book is available from the British Library

Library of Congress Cataloging-in-Publication Data
A catalog record for this book has been requested

ISBN: 978-1-138-29620-6 (hbk)
ISBN: 978-1-138-29621-3 (pbk)
ISBN: 978-1-315-10014-2 (ebk)

Typeset in Berling and Futura
by Apex CoVantage, LLC
Printed by CPI Group (UK) Ltd, Croydon CR0 4YY

Contents

Major projects: longer pieces of sports journalism 149

Figures

Tables

Acknowledgements

This book would not have come about but for Niall Kennedy, the former editor of Media and Cultural Studies at Routledge. It was Niall's enthusiasm for my initial idea that persuaded me to explore the idea of a book about smartphone-era sports journalism in more detail and his persuasiveness that convinced me I was the person to write it.

I doubted my qualifications because I am not a digital native but rather someone who learnt his trade working on very traditional BBC and ITV news programmes. But, as I began to explore the digital landscape, I began to realise that there was no one out there with a complete understanding of social media, live blogging, match reporting, video and podcasting making, data-journalism and everything else covered in this book. My job was to find experts and persuade them to share some of the skills of their craft with my readers.

So, I am immensely grateful to everyone who agreed to be interviewed for this book, namely Neil Atkinson, Emily Brammeir, Mark Coyle, Steve Gibbs, Phil Harlow, Paul Hassall, Rebecca James, Nishant Joshi, Jim Mansell, Ben Milne, Andy Naylor, Jean Octavian Popescu, Stewart Power, Ian Singleton, Neil Smythe, Simon Wear, Alexandra Willis and Jonathan Wilson.

I am also indebted to friends, colleagues, former colleagues and former students who helped me track down some of the people on that list, as well as offering their own advice: Lesley Adams, Mark Coyle, Russell Fuller, Adrian Hobart, Barnaby Slater and Robyn Wallis.

The book is also the result of discussions with current and former students. Like most academics, I learn as much from my students as I teach them. It seems invidious to single out just a few individuals but Tom Cann and Alex Dinnadge both worked on projects which have influenced the book; Zoe Burke, Freddie Harding, Elliott Heath and Rebecca James have all given me advice, based on their experiences of working as digital journalists. Alex Lambe has advised on how he built up a Twitter following. Alex Antzara and Tom Cann have allowed me to use their pictures.

My thanks to work colleagues for their support and tolerance during this book's gestation, in particular Jacob Crowley, Simon Clarke, Kathryn de Vries, Claire Griffiths, Yuwei Lin, Sophie Miller, Adam Powley, Adrienne Rosen and Nathalie Wiedhase.

Special thanks are due to Kitty Imbert, the editorial assistant at Routledge Media and Cultural Studies, for putting up with all my stupid questions about the publishing process and to Niall's successor Margaret Farrelly.

This is my first attempt at writing a book and I would value any feedback. You can write to me at charleslambertsouth@gmail.com or via the publisher.

Finally, my biggest debt of thanks goes to my family, Kalpana, Anjali, Rahul and Anya who had to put up with me during the process of writing this book.

Charles M. Lambert, December 2017

Introduction

I'm exponentially happier than I have ever been at my place of work, exponentially. One, it's much more exciting because you're on the edge of your seat; you've got to make decisions much more quickly. Two, managing businesses with explosive growth is a lot more enjoyable than managing businesses in decline. (Wear, 2017)

      – Former magazine publisher Simon Wear, now chief executive of the Play Sports Network, which runs three YouTube channels

It's 1990. You are working as a sports reporter on a regional daily paper in a big northern city. You get a tip-off from a contact at your local, top-flight football club, who says that the manager is interested in signing a player called Paul Johnson from a lower league club in the Midlands.

Who is Paul Johnson? What position does he play? How old is he? Where's he played before? Your source doesn't know. You reach for your trusty *Rothmans Yearbook*, the only place to find this kind of information, but Paul Johnson doesn't appear in it. Perhaps he's only joined his current club since the most recent edition was published. Or maybe he's a youth team player who wasn't on the radar when it was being compiled.

You call your opposite number at the paper in the Midlands town. But he's out at the club's training ground conducting interviews. He has recently been supplied with a mobile phone, someone on the news desk explains exasperatedly, but he keeps it switched off because he hasn't worked out how to use it. So, you call the club itself. It doesn't have a press officer; media enquiries are dealt with by the club secretary and he's out too – at a Rotary Club business breakfast. He'll call you when he gets back – probably lunchtime.

Back to the local paper. You persuade your new friend on the news desk to put in a request to the library for clippings on Paul Johnson. Half an hour later, she gets back to you; it turns out there are two Paul Johnsons at the club. You quickly deduce that your club is more likely to be interested in the promising 18-year-old winger who's recently broken through from the youth ranks rather than 36-year-old recruited from a local non-league club to cover a goalkeeping crisis.

Eventually the secretary and the sports reporter get back to you and you are able to stand the story up by speaking to someone else at your local club. You manage to scramble 150 words together just in time for a 3pm deadline.

Within a dozen years, this mode of working had gone forever. The arrival of the internet meant that you could find out Paul Johnson's position, date and place of birth, former clubs and number of appearances, goals and assists at the touch of a few buttons. In the process, you'd also discover the name of the soap star he was going out with, his favourite grime artist and which players are in his team on *Football Manager*.

Move on another five years and the news that United are interested in signing Johnson is all over Twitter by 7.30 in the morning. You can forget about writing a back-page lead on the story unless you can get an exclusive interview with him. And both the player's new agent and the Media and Communications department at the Midlands club are making it pretty clear that won't be happening.

Even those of us who worked throughout the technological changes of the late 20th and early 21st centuries sometimes forget how much the job of a sports reporter has changed. It is important to emphasise that the changes outlined above were not simply a result of technology but of changing audience demands and expectations. Sports fans are no longer prepared to wait until you the journalist see fit to publish the news of a transfer – they want to know about it as soon as possible and to have the opportunity to discuss it with fellow fans of their club.

It's easy to assume that every change that sports journalism has undergone in the past quarter of a century has been the result of the internet. In fact, journalism has always been evolving, ever since it emerged as a distinct craft sometime in the 18th century. Using technology is nothing new either; in the 19th century, Reuters built its preeminence on its use of the cable and staff had to use code – Morse code. Being a good journalist has always been not just about being able to use technology but being able to use technology to find and tell great stories.

It has been a challenge to write a book about digital journalism because practices are constantly changing in response to technological change and audience behaviour. But, in many areas, some norms or conventions are emerging. Many podcasts have been running, and following broadly the same format, for more than a decade. A BBC live blog covering a day at the 2016 Olympics didn't look all that different to a BBC live blog covering a day at the 2012 Olympics. There are generally accepted dos and don'ts to writing an online quiz. The scheduling of social media posts has been commonplace for at least five years. It is now increasingly hard to imagine a new social media company challenging the main existing players. Change is continuing – and is unlikely to stop – but a new media landscape is beginning to settle down.

WHAT IS DIGITAL SPORTS JOURNALISM AND WHO DOES IT WELL?

In this book, I use the term "digital" to refer to types of journalism that have been made possible by:

- the invention of the world wide web,
- the prevalence of smartphones, and
- the ability to collate and manage large amounts of data.

Digital doesn't fully capture this, but it seems better than the alternatives.

Around the turn of the century, organisations like the BBC would talk about TV, radio and website or TV, radio and *online*. Today, these terms don't feel quite right. For a start, as we shall see, a lot of modern journalistic practice is not based around a website anymore but, rather, tries to get content out on social media. Secondly, increasingly people are watching TV and listening to radio via an internet connection rather than via traditional broadcast methods so "TV, radio and online" is confusing and inaccurate.

We could use the term "multimedia journalist". The problem here is that the word doesn't clearly explain which media we are referring to. In the 1990s, I thought of myself as a multimedia journalist because I worked in TV and radio (and, occasionally, a slow-moving text-based news service called Ceefax).

I also considered "smartphone journalism", as almost all the journalism featured in this book was designed to be consumed on a phone; but this term risks confusion with journalism actually *produced* on a smartphone (which is true of some but not all of the examples we'll be looking at).

Most of the exponents I spoke to for this book use "digital" as a shorthand for the wide range of new forms of journalism that emerged in the wake of Tim Berners-Lee's invention of the world wide web in 1989. (Note, not the internet – that's quarter of a century older. Google it: thanks to Sir Tim's invention, you can.) It's not perfect – and it may become superfluous as older forms of journalism become less popular – but it seems to be the most commonly understood term in current use.

I have consciously adopted a broad definition of the word *journalism*. A former colleague once showed me his National Union of Journalists card from the late 1970s. On it, he had to sign a declaration that he had never worked in any form of public relations; it was important to the union that journalism remained pure and unsullied by commercial considerations. But sports journalism has always had a complex relationship with marketing as, by simply covering a sports event, you are unavoidably drawing attention to sponsors, equipment manufacturers and the clubs themselves, which tend to be businesses that sell shirts, scarves, posters and all sorts of other paraphernalia. The expansion of so-called "club journalism" has muddied the waters further. Today, there is a large grey area between journalism and marketing in which native advertising, branded content and contract publication all sit. Many freelance journalists, including several interviewed in this book, move seamlessly between working for clubs, businesses and governing bodies and producing unfettered journalism. This book is not the place to debate the rights and wrongs of these developments; my approach has been that if a technique appears to be journalistic, or could be of use to sports journalists, then it should be covered.

The range of techniques explored is also deliberately broad. There are very few individuals who are likely to be skilled story-finders, storytellers, presenters, subject knowledge specialists, planners, photographers, videographers, sound recordists, graphic designers, illustrators, animators, coders, data experts and picture editors. The more of these disciplines you can include on your CV, the stronger a position you'll be in when it comes to looking for work. Equally, just as some of the best TV journalists are those who gel well with camera crews and picture editors, so some of the best digital journalists are those who understand what, say, animation or data visualisation can bring to a story and appreciate the most effective ways of working with specialists in those fields. In my experience, not many sports journalists are good at drawing – but if you are, then it's a valuable skill you can bring to your journalism.

The examples chosen come from both legacy and new media companies and from individuals who are not working for companies at all. Legacy is a term applied to organisations like newspapers, magazines and radio and TV stations which have ventured into the digital realm while still producing print or broadcast output. New media companies are those that were set up specifically to meet the demands of the digital world. Many of these, such as Joe, Unilad, Clickon, Goal, Squawka, Copa90 and Football Republic, have made sport a significant part of their efforts to win audiences and all of these feature in this book. Equally, at the time of writing, the three most popular digital news providers in the United Kingdom, by some distance, are legacy publishers: the BBC, the Mail Online and the *Guardian*. I make no apology for the focus on the BBC (my former employer) and the *Guardian* as both have been at the forefront of innovation in the way sport is covered. Other examples concern individuals. One of the distinctive features of digital journalism is that you do not need to be some kind of media organisation to practise it. It is possible to set up a blog, a podcast or a fan TV channel and build an audience without any official backing, as several of the interviewees and case studies in this book demonstrate.

ABOUT THIS BOOK

Writing in *The Spectator*, Roger Alton describes a scene a few years ago when a well-known actor arrives, looking frustrated, at the door of a church for a wedding:

> "What's up?" asked the small boy patrolling the entrance. "Newcastle are playing this afternoon and I can't find out what's happening." "Give me your phone," said the lad, who clicked a few clicks before handing it back. The match was now live on the screen, via some pub in Oslo.

I have been teaching sports journalists for a decade. This book grew out of conversations with former students who went on to work as journalists. I asked them what they would have liked us to have taught them at university – but didn't. Social media was the most common answer, while some said we were teaching video-making for television, not the internet. We had focussed a lot on match reporting but our teaching didn't reflect the methods that are now commonplace in the industry.

In most cases, their employers assumed they would be good at using mobile technologies and social media. There is a widespread presumption that anyone aged under 30 is a digital native and, like the small boy in Roger Alton's (2017) story, highly adept in using tech and in modern methods of communication. Generally, this is a fair assumption: millennials tend to have much better digital literacy than my generation. But, as teachers, we could still offer more guidance in knowing what tools are out there and how to make the most of them.

These new digital skills won't replace traditional journalistic ones, as Mark Coyle explains below. New sports journalists will still need to build contacts, spot great stories persevere in their pursuit of those stories and write well. I strongly believe there will always be a place for a stirring report of a great event and for revealing interviews or investigative features. But you won't be asked to interview Serena Williams on your first day in your new job; in fact, you probably won't be asked to interview the tennis champion at the tennis club in your local town. You'll most likely be asked to manage your employer's social media platforms.

Chapters 2–10 of this book each look at a different skill or task that someone starting out in sports journalism might be asked to do: live blogging, match or event reporting, making and disseminating short videos, working for a sports club or governing body, finding and transmitting stories on social media. The final two chapters, on podcasting and longform online journalism, deal with skills that a novice probably won't be asked to undertake but which may help in their development as journalists.

I have deployed a variety of styles to show how sports journalists use the various tools at their disposal. Each chapter includes one or more of the following:

- The back story, which looks at how the particular form emerged and developed. I hope that an understanding of how practices evolved in the past will help readers understand how they may progress in the future.
- Case studies: examples of stories or series which I feel will prove instructive.
- The schedule: an insight into sports journalists' working lives.
- Top tips: Advice from a specialist in that particular area.
- Your turn, which suggests some ways that you can practise these skills in the classroom, in your living room or at a local sports club.

All the chapters, of course, include advice on how to practise the skill in question. This section includes a look at some of the tools you'll need. It's not this book's place to promote any particular piece of software, hardware or application. This would be foolish, as new apps come out weekly claiming to perform better than existing ones so some of my recommendations might be out of date before the ink has dried. Some readers may find that their university wishes them to use particular software for good reasons. Having said that, it would be difficult to write a book of this kind without reference to, for example, Facebook, Twitter or WordPress and, at times, I will direct readers towards particular apps which are especially useful.

There are two areas that, after much deliberation, I decided not to tackle in this book.

The first is coding. In my view, the next generation of journalists will learn to code, just as previous generations learned to use shorthand and my generation learned to film and edit pictures. These are necessary ancillary skills for those of us who want to tell stories to mass audiences. But, if someone wants to learn a coding language then I would expect them to buy a book devoted to that language rather than one that only touches on it briefly.

The second is eSports. At my university we recently started teaching students to report on sports video games and these sessions were hugely popular. It's clearly an area that is growing. But, at the time of writing, very few conventions or accepted practices have evolved. So, I would encourage readers to experiment with different ways of covering this area.

THE BACK STORY: SPORTS JOURNALISM IN THE EARLY 21ST CENTURY

There are already four excellent textbooks aimed at students on Sports Journalism courses or young people in the early stages of their careers. The aim of this book is not to compete with these texts or replace them; all four address long-established journalistic practices that are not covered in depth in this book. Rather this book seeks to complement existing texts by looking at particular aspects of sports journalism that are unique to the digital age. These include:

- Sports Journalism is now a conversation
  Journalists are accustomed to talking to their sources and passing what they glean onto their audience. Today, their sources and their audience may be one and same. In Chapter 3, for example, we look at a story involving the British and Irish Lions which emerged from social media and was later disseminated through social media. Audiences are now able to react instantly to anything a journalist publishes and the best sports journalists are those who can respond with similar speed.

TIP: Be prepared to join the conversation.

- Sport Journalism is a great laboratory
  Sports events are excellent opportunities to experiment with new storytelling techniques. If you wanted to try out 360° photography or live blogging or reporting on Snapchat for the first time, it probably wouldn't make sense to use them during a hostage siege or plane crash. The great advantage with sport is that it happens at a prearranged time in a prearranged venue – so you can plan your approach in advance.

TIP: Be prepared to experiment; be prepared to fail; be prepared to try something different.

- Sports Journalism is embracing data
  Of all the technical changes of the computer era, the one least remarked upon concerns our ability to make use of data.
  In the first Ashes test of 2013, England appeared to be in a strong position: Australia were 117 for 9 in their first innings. Teenage spin bowler Ashton Agar came to the crease and unexpectedly took the attack to the hosts. Records began to fall: highest score by a number 11 at Trent Bridge, highest score by an Australian number 11 in England, highest score by an Australian number 11 in tests, highest score by a number 11 of either side in an Ashes test, record tenth wicket partnership etc. Eventually, Agar overtook West Indies' Tino Best's 95 against England – the previous record for a last man in – before falling two runs short of an improbable century. In the past, checking these records would have taken hours of painstaking research in books (or microfiches). Today, you can use a basic spreadsheet, set the filters so you are looking at just number 11 batters and order the data by score. Provided, you have the data to hand, you can answer all these questions in seconds.

TIP: Don't be put off by data. The numbers themselves may not be interesting; you're after the stories hidden within them.

- Sports Journalism is fun
  Most business journalists weren't fascinated by the FTSE100 when they were ten years old. Political journalists didn't rush home from school to hear what the Chancellor of the Exchequer had announced in his budget. Even music and fashion journalists probably didn't find their callings until their mid- to late-teens.

Today, more than ever, the best sports journalism seems to embody the passion of fans. I put this down to the influence of fanzines. What all fanzines had in common was an irreverent writing style. Typical content might include lists of the best club songs or elevens composed of the finest bald or ginger players to don the club shirt. Cricket, rugby, speedway and other sports all found ways of replicating this. It was a far cry from the rather flat content found in most club programmes and most sports journalism of the time, which took sport much more seriously. It's relatively easy to trace a direct line from the fanzine writing of the 1980s to a lot of today's online sports writing such as the kind found in *The Fiver* or *The Blizzard* (Chapter 10).

TIP: Your writing has to be fun to read. You might be the first with the story but, if someone else is telling it in a more entertaining way, audiences will go to them in two clicks.

- Sports Journalism covers a topic that is now regarded as having great economic value
  In the 1990s, sport began to appreciate the growing commercial value of its *product*. British football started receiving tens (later hundreds) of millions of pounds from BSkyB television and the big clubs became global brands with supporters in every corner of the planet. So, there was more demand for stories about these clubs and more openings to write about sport. The new fans, many of whom might not ever visit their club's home ground, had an insatiable appetite for stories. And, when there weren't any stories to be had, they would happily make do with opinions, discussion and prediction. This phenomenon was not limited to football; the value of rights to major tennis, golf, cricket and rugby tournaments have all sky-rocketed – and that's before we come to boxing.
  This has led to a host of new websites (Chapters 1 and 2), podcasts (Chapter 11) and fan channels (Chapter 10). It's also meant clubs have tried to exercise more control over the way news about their players is managed (Chapter 9).

TIP: The more people there are writing about sport, the more important it is for you to stand out.

- Sports Journalism covers a topic that is now regarded as having great political value.
  For a long time, it was widely accepted that sport and politics do not mix. Two developments in the 1980s changed that. The first was the boycott of South African sport because of the country's apartheid policy, which divided people based on their race. The boycott is widely regarded as one of the most effective tactics that helped bring apartheid to an end. The second was the Hillsborough disaster, in which 96 Liverpool fans were killed in a crush at the start of an FA Cup semi-final at Sheffield Wednesday's ground. The tragedy forced thousands of football fans to sit up and take notice of the way the game was being run.
  Meanwhile, politicians realised sport had the potential to improve national morale and our health and well-being. Millions of pounds of public money went into sport – particularly those sports where Great Britain had the chance to do well in the Olympics. For journalists, this meant a whole new field opened up – that of sports news.

TIP: Sports journalism is no longer just about the 90 minutes on the pitch or what happens in the velodrome or the boxing ring. You need to understand the bigger picture.

TOP TIPS: WHAT MAKES A GOOD DIGITAL SPORTS JOURNALIST?

Mark Coyle was at the forefront of changing the BBC into a digitally-focussed broadcaster including taking on the role of editor, BBC London 2012 Online. He launched BT Sport's digital operation and then moved to become head of media for Velon, an organisation that represents some of the main road race teams in cycling.

1 A good journalist is a storyteller – only the medium changes

The ability to have an interest in finding and telling a story is at the heart of what a journalist should be. The fundamental journalistic requirement is to have an interest in your surroundings and the people around you, the world around you, be it politics, sport, news. My current staff have a core specialism in cycling, but they are journalists – that's what they do.

2 Perseverance

Sometimes we journalists have to pursue things that somebody else just doesn't want to tell you and often they are the most interesting things. If you don't get it from them, you have to be inventive enough to consider how else you can get the information.

3 Fleet of foot

You have to be creative about where you get the information from. Especially in the world we live in now. It could be crowd-sourced, it could be UGC (user-generated content), it could be the internet.

4 The ability to be flexible

By this, I mean the ability to change course. Is this person able to spot they've got an intersection in the road coming up and to say "do I go right, do I go left? Not sure, but I'm going to take account of all the circumstances and keep ploughing on"?

5 World experience

I am looking for people who've shown nous, who've put themselves out there. People who've done service in a restaurant – that's a good door opener for dealing with people, for dealing with difficult situations. So, I could ask that person "tell me about something difficult that's happened in the restaurant? What happened when a diner sent back a meal?" So I'm looking for examples of them dealing with people and dealing with difficult situations.

(Coyle, 2017)

What is notable about these tips is that they are very traditional journalistic skills. The first person to employ me as a journalist, nearly 30 years ago, might have said the same thing. Maybe an employer 30 years before that would have concurred. The core skills of journalism remain the same – only the tools we use have changed.

Having said that, it would be odd to try to secure a job at a digital media company if you haven't already spent a lot of time experimenting with social media and film or podcast-making. "I probably wouldn't see a candidate who said they were interested in digital media but had never bothered to shoot or edit because it's practically free nowadays", reckons Neil Smythe (2017), who has worked at some of the biggest names in digital sports media, including Copa90 and the Football Republic. "We can get free edit software, we can shoot on your phones. If someone says they are interested in editing and they've never done it – that's a real sign for me."

Simon Wear, who runs three YouTube-based cycling channels agrees:

> "We look for people who are incredibly inquisitive because every single day [social media] changes so unless you are inquisitive in what you are looking at, what you are playing with, every new platform that comes out, then your mind is not geared up in quite the right way to be successful."

> "[We employ] True Digital natives. What I mean by true digital natives is people who spend a huge amount of time in their lives communicating via social platforms. And I use the word communicating very deliberately because it's understanding how to use those channels, not just consuming those channels."

> Does that mean he'd have studied applicants' digital footprint (ie what they'd posted online and on social media) before he interviewed them?

> "I'd have done that sort of research beforehand and if they weren't on it already they wouldn't be sitting there in front of me."

> "You're not necessarily looking for someone who's got all the right answers, you're looking for someone who has got all the right answers or who agrees with me, but the mere fact that they are thinking about it and processing that information is what you are looking out for in a candidate."

> (Wear, 2017)

FINALLY: DON'T FORGET TO ENJOY YOURSELF

I began this introduction with an upbeat quote from Simon Wear. This is a man who rose to the top in his chosen profession, magazine publishing. And yet, he says he's much happier today working in digital media, producing more than a thousand hours of sports content every year, constantly "on the edge of his seat".

This is a valuable corrective to those who see journalism as being in decline and bemoan the changes that we've seen over the past 20 years. There have never been more opportunities to get yourself published, to record and post commentaries or podcasts and to build a name for yourself. The range of sport, particularly women's sport, that is covered is greater than ever before – and certainly far broader than the days when our main source of sports news was papers who devoted eight out of nine pages to football. Ordinary fans can exchange opinions with leading sports writers and athletes and even set up their own channels. There may be fewer staff jobs on the sports desks of local newspapers but, at many legacy publishers, it is sport that is sustaining their titles and keeping them afloat while they transition into digital organisations. The quality of writing is as strong as it's ever been, from the witty one-liners you might find in a live blog, through to the sophisticated story telling of *The Blizzard* or the *New York Times*.

Right. Let's get started.

FURTHER READING

I would strongly recommend that this book is read alongside one or more of these classic texts. The first three are written by experienced UK-based sports writers; the fourth is a useful alternative perspective from the US.

Andrews, P. (2014) *Sports Journalism, A Practical Introduction* (2nd ed.). London: Sage

Steen, R. (2014) *Sports Journalism: A Multimedia Primer* (2nd ed.). London: Routledge

Toney, J. (2013) *Sports Journalism: The Inside Track*. London: Bloomsbury

Stofer, K., Schaffer, J. and Rosenthal, B. (2009) *Sports Journalism: An Introduction to Reporting and Writing*. Lanham: Rowman and Littlefield

REFERENCES

Alton, R. (2017) *If you can see top games for free where will footie's millions come from?, The Spectator* magazine at www.spectator.co.uk/2017/01/if-you-can-see-top-games-for-free-where-will-footies-millions-come-from/

Coyle, M. (2017) Interview conducted by the author on 18/7/2017

Newman, N. (2017) *Digital News Report 2017* at www.digitalnewsreport.org/survey/2017/overview-key-findings-2017/

Smythe, N. (2017), iInterview conducted by the author on 21/7/2017

Wear, S. (2017) Interview conducted by the author on 7/9/2017

DIGITAL CONTENT

First principles

CHAPTER 1

Digital storytelling

When print journalists move to jobs in television, they sometimes find it hard to adjust to working with pictures. They've been accustomed to relying on their ability to tell stories with words, so they find it hard to now share this role with sounds and images. There's a tendency to assume the words should be "in charge" – even though it's often powerful pictures that will grab the audience's attention.

When newspapers first set up websites, there was a similar tendency to simply take the print version of a story and plonk it online without giving much thought to the particular requirements of the new medium. This is sometimes referred to as "shovelware", an IT term which means taking something designed for one system and applying it, without any changes, to another: sometimes it works, more often it doesn't (Koci Hernandez and Rue, 2016 p 4).

THE INGREDIENTS OF AN ONLINE STORY

Online storytelling presents a challenge. You are not simply juggling words and moving pictures but a whole range of different media. Your ingredients might include:

Text: Your words
Text: Someone else's words, maybe an expert analyst or a player who's missing the game through injury
Photographs: Still images, possibly arranged as galleries
Video: Films that you have shot and edited yourself – or ones made by other people
Social media posts: Most commonly from Twitter or Instagram – possibly including video
Graphics: Maps, timelines, graphs, league tables and other data representation techniques, including, possibly interactive graphics.
Quizzes and polls: Effectively games that encourage people to remain on the site. In some cases, these may be designed to be shared with friends.
Standalone audio clips: These are used fairly rarely nowadays. If you have a short audio clip, the tendency is to add some images to it.
Page furniture, eg side bars providing background information.

"I usually choose the picture or graphic before I've even started writing" – Elliott Heath, online writer at Golf Monthly (Heath, 2017)

The balance between the different ingredients will depend on what kind of dish you are making. This is how four different organisations covered the same story:

Saints sack manager Claude Puel after one season in charge
Peter Howard, sports reporter
Saints have this evening announced that they have sacked manager Claude Puel after just one season in charge.
DailyEcho.co.uk 14 June 2017
www.dailyecho.co.uk/sport/15348071.Saints_sack_Claude_Puel/

Ingredients: Text (eight paragraphs), a picture gallery (27 images)
This was a breaking news story – one that caught a lot of Southampton fans by surprise. The author wanted his story to appear in people's social media feeds before anyone else's coverage of the same story. Text – words – can be produced quickly, so long as you have the facts at your fingertips. The only other ingredient used is a picture gallery showing some highlights of Puel's time in charge at St Mary's which could be quickly assembled; it might even have been prepared in advance in case of an announcement.

Le Tissier: Puel sacking was right
No reporter named (Jeremy Langdon appears in video clips)
Matt Le Tissier has backed Southampton's decision to sack manager Claude Puel after the club took a "backwards step" last season.
SkySports.com 15 June 2017
www.skysports.com/watch/video/sports/football/10916387/le-tissier-puel-sacking-was-right

Ingredients: Text (one paragraph), video (five minutes)
Sky had already reported the Puel sacking, so there's very little need for any explanatory text, graphics or tweets; now they are after reaction so they just go straight into their interview with Le Tissier. Everyone knows the news – they're now waiting to hear what Southampton's greatest former player, Matt Le Tissier, has to say about it. Fortunately, for Sky, he works as a pundit for them, so he would have been easy to contact. The company often makes use of this approach, reflecting the fact that it has better access than most to leading players and ex-players. Note, there is still some text because search engines need words to pick up on.

Again, time is an issue here. The interview has simply been "topped and tailed" and posted online. Later in the day, Sky assembled a longer story which includes speculation on Saints' next manager and a tribute to Puel from current player James Ward-Prowse.

Claude Puel sacked after just one season in charge of Southampton
Tashan Deniran-Alleyne
Southampton have confirmed they've parted company with manager Claude Puel after just one season in charge.

Squawka.com 14 June 2017
*www.squawka.com/news/claude-puel-sacked-after-just-one-season-in-charge-of-southamp
ton/959929*

Ingredients: Text (nine paragraphs), one photograph, two interactive graphics
Just as Sky's unique selling point is their access to players and pundits, so Squawka has
built a reputation for using statistics to better inform readers. The key elements here are
the two graphics. The writer uses an interactive tool which Squawka has developed, its
Comparison Matrix, to highlight Southampton's lack of goals at home compared to other
clubs and to compare the side's performance under Puel with how Saints fared the previous season.

**Southampton sack Claude Puel despite run to the EFL Cup final as club plan for the
"long term"**
Tom Farmery

- Southampton have sacked Claude Puel after just one season in charge
- Saints run to the EFL Cup final somewhat masked a poor campaign
- Puel is understood to have fallen out with players, who didn't like rotation policy

MailOnline 14 June 2017
www.dailymail.co.uk/sport/football/article-4605158/Southampton-sack-Claude-Puel.html

Ingredients: Text (eight paragraphs), three photographs.
"After three paragraphs you need to have a picture; that's the norm", explains MailOnline's consultant sports editor Jim Mansell:

> Online has unlimited space whereas the newspaper has limited space so if
> you're interested in the story you probably want as many pictures as possible.
> That's a key element: putting pictures in the right place to make sure the
> reader carries on through them. You can't have too many in a block because
> otherwise they might not get beyond those pictures and might not read fur-
> ther down the story. But it's essential to provide breakers from time to time
> so the text is broken up.
>
> (Mansell, 2017)

The story itself is photo-heavy but has no video or graphic content – again possibly
reflecting the need to publish quickly.

The mix of ingredients is broadly the same as DailyEcho.co.uk's. What is interesting
about Mail Online's coverage is way it's presented. The headline is twice as long and contains three distinct ideas: (1) Puel's been sacked; (2) this is despite Saints reaching the EFL
Cup final; (3) the club is planning long term.

The three bullet points which follow (some *Mail* stories can have six or eight) effectively encapsulate the whole story. The story itself is photo-heavy but has no video or
graphic content.

"The essence is to tell the story as briefly as possible to lure the reader into reading it further. The summary of the headline is the key to ensure we capture the readers' attention and try to make them read further on" (ibid).

The summary won't just capture the readers' attention – it's also designed to capture the attention of Google's search engine. We'll come to that in Chapter 6.

"Our research indicates that people want to know very quickly what the story is beyond the headline. This is a skill that the operators on Mail Online are taught and they use on a daily basis," Mansell adds.

The summary is well-crafted. Even if you feel it effectively tells you the whole story, many fans will be tempted to read on. Was it a poor campaign? Which players has he fallen out with? How do we know they didn't like his rotation policy?

Plenty of other organisations, particularly other tabloid newspapers, have tried to copy the *Mail* style but few achieve its success, proving it's quite hard to pull off.

WHO MAKES UP THE AUDIENCE?

Who are you reporting on sport for? No journalist knows exactly who is reading, watching or listening to their work but it helps to have a rough idea. Mansell, for example, says the Mail Online audience is "the opposite end of the age scale to those who read the newspaper".

The first point to note is that a large proportion of your audience will be consuming sports journalism on their phones. Mobile consumption of news recently overtook laptop and desktop computers and looks set to grow. The balance in favour of mobile is probably even greater among sports fans because they'll often check their phones on the way to or from matches or events. The Reuters Institute for the Study of Journalism produced the fascinating statistic that 56% of UK adults access news websites in "personal spaces" such as bedrooms, bathrooms and toilets (Newman, 2017). A significant minority of your audience will probably be so-called SYBAWs (smart, young, bored at work) looking on their office computers but, if you don't make your work accessible on a mobile phone, you'll be really limiting the number of people it reaches.

There is a widespread assumption that the main readership of sports stories is male. One of the main reasons that companies such as Joe and Unilad have gone big on sport is that they are trying to target young men. Having said that, it doesn't seem a good strategy to produce content that alienates 50% of the potential audience.

Both Joe and Unilad also show a very good understanding of what not to cover. Few new media companies have succeeded in taking on legacy companies head on. Instead, they recognise that they have something different to offer and expand on those things that the legacy companies do not do well. I shall expand on this point in the next chapter.

Media companies spend a lot of money on analytical packages that try to tell them who their audiences are, so they can work out which sections of the community they are under-serving.

Let's have a look at some more examples of online writing – for very different audiences.

Rob Burrow Will Retire From Leeds and Leave Legacy For The Little Guy
Adam Bower
The diminutive 34-year-old is to retire from playing at the end of the season and will long be remembered as one of the Rhinos' finest players.
theGuardian.com 19 July 2017
www.theguardian.com/sport/2017/jul/19/rob-burrow-retire-leeds-rhinos-rugby-league

Ingredients: Text (12 paragraphs), two photographs
This begins as a news story, but the main body of the piece is an appreciation of Burrow's career in rugby league by one of the sport's most knowledgeable specialists. This isn't a story that we'd expect someone to simply read in a hurry while flicking through other sports news; League fans might be expected to spend a bit of time absorbing Bower's reflections. So, it makes sense to focus heavily on text supported by a photograph of Burrow's try in the 2011 Grand Final.

Paulie Malignaggi Reacts With Total Class To Conor Mcgregor's Cocky Sparring Post
Darragh Murphy
Paulie Malignaggi knows the score.
What goes down in sparring, stays in sparring.
Joe.co.uk 22 July 2017
www.joe.co.uk/sport/paulie-malignaggi-reacts-with-total-class-to-conor-mcgregors-cocky-sparring-post-134765

Ingredients: Text (nine paragraphs), one photograph, three tweets
This story is about a conversation that's taking place on social media. Mixed martial arts fighter Conor McGregor has recruited boxer Paulie Malignaggi to help him train for his bout with Floyd Mayweather. He then posted a tweet showing him appearing to taunt Malignaggi by sparring with his hands behind his back. In this case, the tweets *are* the story. All the writer needs to add is a bit of context explaining the background to the tweets.

Elise Christie Could Lead Great Britain To Best Medals Haul Ever at 2018 Pyeongchang Winter Olympics
Kevin Coulson
Great Britain are on course to achieve their best ever medal haul at the Winter Olympics in PyeongChang.

Eurosport.com 1 November 2017
www.eurosport.co.uk/olympics/pyeongchang/2018/elise-christie-could-lead-great-britain-to-
best-medals-haul-ever-at-pyeongchang-winter-olympics_sto6393452/story.shtml

Ingredients: Text (eight paragraphs), one photograph, one table, two videos.
The curious thing about this story is that it isn't really a story. Eurosport had the rights to the 2018 Winter Olympics and so they were keen to develop interest in the event. The only story here is a piece of analysis by a company called Gracenote Sports who have predicted the winners of each event and, based on this, drawn up a notional medals table.

Speed skater Elise Christie was, at the time, Britain's best-known and most successful Winter Olympian, so the headline references her and there is a large photo of her in an attempt to draw readers in. Neither of the videos actually have very much to do with either Gracenote's survey or Christie. One is an explainer about the sport of skeleton, the other marks 100 days to the start of the Games.

The approach recognises the fact that most Eurosport readers won't know very much about winter sports but will be interested in the UK's prospects at an event with the word "Olympics" in its title.

Adam Peaty sets second 50m breaststroke world record in day
No reporter named
Britain's Adam Peaty broke the 50m breaststroke world record for the second time in a day as he reached the World Aquatics Championships final.
bbc.co.uk/sport 25 July 2017
www.bbc.co.uk/sport/swimming/40714957

Ingredients: Text (16 paragraphs), two videos, one tweet, one chart, expert analysis (five paragraphs)
This does not include the section at the bottom about other swimmers in action on the same day.
This is perhaps the perfect situation for a journalist. He or she or, more probably, *they*, as this appears to be a team effort, have:

- the right to use the footage of Peaty in action,
- tweets from the man himself,
- two experts (former Olympians Rebecca Adlington and Steve Parry) to provide analysis, and
- a simple graphic showing the ten fastest ever times in the world for breaststroke.

It enables them to produce a very rich, mixed media online report.

SUMMARY

The factors that will determine the balance of ingredients include:

- **Urgency:** If you are keen to get the story out there as soon as possible before your rivals, then writing text tends to be quicker than editing audio or video. If you've filmed an interview that can run without very much editing, then you can also use that when you're up against the clock.
- **Audience:** the length of a typical story on Joe is about 200 words. They know that their readers normally won't stick around to read anything much longer. By contrast, the *Guardian* and Squawka both know they are addressing readers who have an appetite for a more in-depth look at sport.
- **What the story is actually about:** the Peaty story was about his record-breaking swim; the Le Tissier story was about his reaction to Puel's sacking; the Malignaggi story was about the exchange of tweets. So, in each case it made sense to put those elements – the clip of the swim, the interview, the tweets – at the centre of the story. If your piece is about a piece of breaking news, as in the Echo's reporting of the Puel story, then text is usually the clearest, most unambiguous form of communication.
- **Rights to pictures:** Sky has better access to Premier League footage, and player interviews; Squawka doesn't, but has developed data visualisation tools to help analyse players. It makes sense for both outlets to play to their strengths. In the same way, if you managed to interview someone who had played in the 1953 FA Cup final and he gave you some black and white photographs of players relaxing before the game, then you'd want to make the most of them.

USING A MIX OF INGREDIENTS: ANALYSIS OF AN ONLINE STORY

As we've seen, the Adam Peaty story is a rare example of when the journalists have all the components they could possibly need at their disposal: pictures, video, tweets, experts and graphics. So, let's have a look at how the BBC handled it in more detail.

As you read this next section, it might be useful to have the story open on a computer or on a phone. It's at bbc.co.uk/sport/swimming/40714957.

The headline: **Adam Peaty sets second 50m breaststroke world record in day**
Like all good headlines this explains what's happened – he's broken the same record twice in a day. It also contains some key search terms that someone might use if looking for a story about the swimmer: Peaty, breaststroke and world record. You don't need to include "swimming" because the story's in the swimming section of the BBC website – and, besides, search engines know that breaststroke is a type of swimming.

When I started out as a reporter, I'd have been tempted to try out a pun. Perhaps "Peaty swims a blinder" (a reference to the TV programme *Peaky Blinders*). While you do still see these in print versions of the tabloid newspapers, this seems to be a dying artform.

You might object that "Adam Peaty sets second 50m breaststroke world record in the same day" might read a bit more fluently. But that pushes up the character count (the number of letters). It's currently 57 characters. Search engine optimisation (SEO) is constantly changing and there are a lot of different theories about what works best but the current thinking is that 60 characters is ideal for a headline; most headlines on the BBC Sport website are around about this length. We'll look at SEO in more detail in Chapter 6.

The video: Before we come to any more text whatsoever, we're shown video of Peaty's most recent race. There are good reasons for this. Firstly, the story is all about Peaty's world record-breaking swim, so we want to see it. Secondly, it helps emphasise that the BBC has the broadcast rights to the World Aquatics Championships.

Links to other BBC content: The next thing we read is "World Aquatics Championships on the BBC. Hosts: Budapest, Hungary. Dates: 23–30 July. Coverage: Live across BBC Two, BBC Red Button, Connected TV, online, BBC Sport mobile app and BBC Radio. Click for full times." So, the BBC is using this story to promote its coverage of the Championships.

The intro text: "Britain's Adam Peaty broke the 50m breaststroke world record for the second time in a day as he reached the World Aquatics Championships final." If this were a print story, you'd probably try to avoid repeating the words in the headline. This is less of an issue online. This intro explains the story very clearly and adds a bit of context by explaining that Peaty has now reached the final of the competition.

The second paragraph: "The defending champion, 22, won the semi-final in 25.95 seconds, becoming the first person to break 26 seconds and eclipsing his 26.10 in the heats." Notice how we've already managed to answer all the key questions expected of a news story:

- **Who?** Adam Peaty
- **What?** Broke the world record twice in a day
- **Why?** To reach the final of the World Aquatics Championships 50m breaststroke
- **Where?** Budapest
- **How?** By covering 50 metres in 25.95 seconds, eclipsing his 26.10 in the heats
- **When?** Today (unless you're informed otherwise, we normally assume an online story relates to the day of publication)

Paragraphs 3–5: Now the author has answered all those questions, we can weave in a quote from Peaty.

> "I honestly can't believe it. I can't even think. I just went out there and did what I do", he told BBC Sport.
> Peaty retained his 100m breaststroke title in Budapest, Hungary on Monday.
> He added: "The hard work has gone on in the gym. I am looking for areas of where I can improve and hopefully get down to mid-25."

Traditionally, journalists were taught to get a quote in around about the fourth or fifth paragraph. There were two good reasons for this. Firstly, it breaks up the writing and introduces a new voice so it's not just a reporter lecturing you. Secondly, it adds authenticity or verification to the story: Peaty himself is saying "it's happened so it must be true".

Once again, the BBC is underlining the fact that it's the broadcaster on site at the Aquatic Championships. He "told BBC Sport" because BBC Sport was there – supporting a sport that, outside of the Olympics, tends not to get much coverage.

Note the phrase "retained his 100m breaststroke title" is underlined. This indicates that it's a hyperlink: click on it and it will take you to the BBC coverage of the previous race on Monday. This is an important feature of online journalism. However you arrived on a particular site, be it via a search engine or a social media post, the publisher wants you to stay there for as long as possible. So they will regularly offer you the opportunity to jump to other content that might interest you.

So far, the longest sentence in the story is 27 words; the shortest just four. Short sentences make sense when you consider someone may be reading this on a phone, on a busy bus or train on their way to work.

There then follows another hyperlink – taking us to a longer profile of Peaty. This is followed by a tweet from Peaty himself. Both of these elements help split up the text; a large block of uninterrupted words can be off-putting for a reader.

The tweet itself shows us a bit of Peaty's personality. While the quotes in the earlier paragraphs have the feel of the kind of official comments that a successful sportsman should make, the tweet, with its "big love to you all" and Union flag seems to come from the heart.

After the tweet there are another six paragraphs of text which help wrap up some important loose ends, such as who he was racing against. Because this story is very much about Peaty, the swimmer who came second, Felipe Lima, doesn't make his first appearance until halfway down the story.

The next video is a clip of Rebecca Adlington – probably still the swimmer best known to the British public – commenting on Peaty's achievements. At 54 seconds long it's an ideal length for reposting on social media.

This is followed by a chart summarising the records that Peaty now holds. Bullet points are popular in digital journalism – because they are easier to read than blocks of text.

Next up – a graphic listing the ten fastest times recorded for the 100 metre breaststroke – all held by Peaty. (The BBC might be reusing an old graphic here because the race he's just competed in is the 50 metres.) If this table appeared in print, one might expect dates and competitions – Olympics, Commonwealth Games etc – to be added but that might be hard to read on a phone.

The piece ends with more expert analysis and then a short summary of how other British competitors got on in the pool. The experts probably won't sit down and write 50 words themselves. If you were part of the BBC team on site, one of your roles might be to sit down and interview Rebecca Adlington for five minutes and then convert her comments into the two or three pithy paragraphs.

YOUR TURN

The purpose of this exercise is to get you searching for the ingredients of a digital sports story and to encourage you to experiment with different ways of mixing them together.

First, get a few recent copies of a local newspaper. A weekly freesheet is ideal as it will probably have coverage of relatively low-level sport – local cricket leagues, gymnastics competitions or equestrian events, for example.

Choose a story. Ideally a fairly obscure topic that hasn't been widely covered elsewhere. What we're going to do is recreate that newspaper story as a digital story.

Online, try to find as much content for your version as you can. This will involve tracking down some of the participants on social media. Twitter is the most obvious place to look but there may be good pictures on Instagram; some friends and family may have posted video on YouTube. Try to make contact with some of them directly so you can get your own quotes and you can ask them if it's okay for you to use their pictures. The club involved will probably also have its own website.

If there's no video, you can always make your own. It's easy to record some interviews and add still images. More ambitious video making is covered in Chapter 7.

As you assemble your story, bear the following in mind:

- Try to mix up your ingredients. Avoid long chunks of text or sequences of videos one after the other.
- Apply the normal rules of good news writing. Start with the most important facts and make sure you answer the questions who, what, where, when, why and how (or, in sport, how fast, how high or by how much).
- Put the strongest content first. This will normally be video.
- Write clearly and concisely. Avoid sentences with more than 25 words.
- Embed social media to break up your text.
- Use hyperlinks.
- Try to use at least one graphic. Use Excel or PowerPoint to experiment with what you can do (more on this in Chapter 8).

Once you're happy with your story, try retelling it using the Mail Online style.

As we haven't looked at posting content online, just write it on a Word or Pages document for now. We'll look at websites in the next chapter.

SUMMARY

- Try to mix up your ingredients. Avoid long chunks of text or sequences of videos one after the other.
- Apply the normal rules of good news writing. Start with the most important facts and make sure you answer the questions who, what, where, when, why and how (or how fast, by how much).
- Put the strongest content first. This will normally be video.
- Write clearly and concisely. Avoid sentences with more than 25 words.
- Embed social media to break up your text.
- Use hyperlinks to keep readers on your site.
- Promote your organisation's other media. Eg if it holds the TV or radio rights to the event make sure you draw attention to that.
- Use graphics – especially if you don't have broadcast rights.

FURTHER READING

Bradshaw, P. and Rohumaa, L. (2018) *The Online Journalism Handbook* (2nd ed.). London: Routledge

Bull, A. (2016) *Multimedia Journalism a Practical Guide* (2nd ed.). Abingdon: Routledge

REFERENCES

BBC (2017) *Adam Peaty sets second 50m breast stroke record in one day* at www.bbc.co.uk/sport/swimming/40714957. Last accessed 26/11/2017

Daily Echo (2017) *Saints sack Claude Puel* at www.dailyecho.co.uk/sport/15348071.Saints_sack_Claude_Puel/. Last accessed 25/11/2017

Eurosport (2017) *Elise Christie could lead Great Britain to best medals haul ever at 2018 PyeongChang Winter Olympics* at www.eurosport.co.uk/olympics/pyeongchang/2018/elise-christie-could-lead-great-britain-to-best-medals-haul-ever-at-pyeongchang-winter-olympics_sto6393452/story.shtml. Last accessed 26/11/2017

Guardian (2017) *Rob Burrow will retire from Leeds and leave legacy for the little guy* at www.theguardian.com/sport/2017/jul/19/rob-burrow-retire-leeds-rhinos-rugby-league. Last accessed 26/11/2017

Heath, E. (2017) Email to author, 29/06/2017

Joe.co.uk (2017) *Paulie Malignaggi reacts with total class to Conor McGregor's cocky sparring post* at www.joe.co.uk/sport/paulie-malignaggi-reacts-with-total-class-to-conor-mcgregors-cocky-sparring-post-134765. Last accessed 26/11/2017

Koci Hernandez, R. and Rue, J. (2016) *The Principles of Multimedia Journalism*. New York: Routledge

Mail Online (2017) *Southampton sack Claude Puel* at www.dailymail.co.uk/sport/football/article-4605158/Southampton-sack-Claude-Puel.html. Last accessed 26/11/2017

Mansell, J. (2017) Interview with the author, 14/08/2017

Newman, N. (2017) *Digital News Report 2017* at www.digitalnewsreport.org/survey/2017/overview-key-findings-2017/

Sky Sports (2017) *Le Tissier: Puel sacking was right* at www.skysports.com/watch/video/sports/football/10916387/le-tissier-puel-sacking-was-right. Last accessed 25/11/2017

Squawka (2017) *Claude Puel sacked after just one season in charge of Southampton* at www.squawka.com/news/claude-puel-sacked-after-just-one-season-in-charge-of-southampton/959929. Last accessed 26/11/2017

CHAPTER 2

Getting set up

Later in this chapter, we'll look at setting up a website and identifying sites which will host your content; but, first, let's think about what you are going to write *about*.

FINDING YOUR NICHE

In the early 1990s, Filippo Maria Ricci decided to become a freelance African football correspondent. At that time there were hardly any African players at the big European clubs, only two African sides had ever progressed past the group stages of the World Cup and the African Cup of Nations was largely ignored outside its home continent.

Based in Rome, Ricci came up with the novel idea of sourcing stories by visiting embassies (Ricci, 2008 pp 11–13). The staff there, he reasoned, probably had plenty of time on their hands to chat and there was a fair chance they'd be football fans. The strategy produced mixed results – but even at those embassies where the staff weren't prepared to sit around chatting calcio, he'd normally be directed to a pile of old newspapers with substantial sports sections.

As the profile of African football, and footballers, rose during the 1990s, so Ricci's expertise came to be increasingly in demand from newspapers, magazines, radio stations and even the sticker company Panini. (He recruited the Milan striker George Weah to help him identify the Liberian squad; Weah played a practical joke on him by giving him the wrong names.)

Today, there are thousands of people in Europe who can talk intelligently about African football. There'd be no point in trying to repeat what Filippo Ricci did. But you can go out and find your own specialism whether it be in a particular sport or a particular aspect of that sport. You may, for example, have a love of tactics or building stories around data.

Let's take another example – cycling. The growth of interest in both road and track cycling in the United Kingdom has grown exponentially since the start of this century. As the gold medals and tour wins started coming in, media companies urgently needed people who understood the sport and had plenty of contacts in it. If you knew even a bit about cycling and had good journalistic skills, you'd be in demand.

Legacy media companies, those who were around before the internet like the BBC, BSkyB or the *Guardian*, tend to be better resourced than newer ones. However, these older, established companies need to cover all major sporting events – the Grand National, the Boat Race, the Six Nations, Wimbledon etc – which means they can be very stretched. That often means that niche areas open up for freelance journalists to write about.

CASE STUDY: CONOR MCGREGOR

He's gone from a fighter that nobody outside of the hardcore MMA fan-base in Ireland could even recognise to the biggest pay-per-view star in sports entertainment, inside of four years.

– Nick Peet, presenter of award-winning podcast *Fight Disciples* (BBC Radio Five Live in July 2017)

No sport encapsulates the difference between legacy media and new media in the way that Mixed Martial Arts (MMA) does. If you were a keen sports fan who, each day, checked your BBC sports app, it's quite possible that you might not have even heard of the Ultimate Fighting Championship's (UFC) biggest star, Conor McGregor, at least until 14 June 2017 when he announced that he was going to take on Floyd Mayweather in a boxing bout. (The BBC did cover McGregor's fights, but they rarely made the front page of the app.) If, on the other hand, your main source of sports news was Joe.co.uk or Unilad, you'd think McGregor is one of the biggest sports stars in the world: maybe second only to Cristiano Ronaldo.

Talk of a fight between McGregor and Mayweather, the most successful boxer ever in financial terms, began to surface in January 2017. In that month alone, Joe ran ten stories about McGregor, while the far better-resourced BBC and *Daily Telegraph* both ran just two. Another new media company, LADBible, which barely covers sport at all, ran six.

As the rumours intensified, legacy publications began to realise they'd missed a trick. MMA, which had been dismissed as "grotesque" or a "circus", is hugely popular among teenagers – largely because of social media. McGregor's style of fighting is perfect for a world of 15-second video clips. While a tee-shot in golf or a wicket in cricket requires some understanding of those sports, even someone who has never seen MMA before is likely to be impressed by the Dubliner's extraordinary speed, power, reach and ability to conjure up the unexpected. Clips of his fights regularly clock up tens of millions of views on YouTube, which puts him a bit behind Cristiano Ronaldo and Lionel Messi, but comfortably ahead of Sebastian Vettel and Lewis Hamilton.

What Joe and Unilad do well is understand their audiences. During July 2017, when Unilad published 25 stories about McGregor, it did not carry any news about the Tour de France, the England v South Africa test cricket series, the Women's European Football Championships, the Women's Cricket World Cup, the Open Golf or the World Para Athletics Championships. Joe, which has a strong football focus, did cover Euro 2017 and the golf, but not the other events. This was not a failure on their part – it simply reflects an understanding that these stories are all better covered by legacy publications. Unilad and Joe do not try to offer the kind of comprehensive sports coverage that the BBC or Sky do.

In late 2017, the BBC did launch its own MMA podcast – not surprisingly they recruited Nick Peet from *Fight Disciples* to present it.

TIP: Think about what the big boys are *not* covering, or under-serving. What are your friends talking about that the BBC, *Guardian* and Mail Online are not?

OPINIONS

> The article was designed to get clicks, likes and get people talking about things. That's new age journalism. That's what you do nowadays.
>
> – Nigel Yalden of New Zealand Radio Sport commenting on
> a piece in the NZ Herald which argued that the All Blacks
> needed a defeat in rugby's Autumn Internationals as a
> "wake-up call" (BBC Radio Five Live, November 2017)

When I was training as a journalist, I was taught to avoid expressing my own opinion at all costs. "Wait until you're qualified to express it," I was told, meaning wait until I'd covered 400 games and interviewed 600 players. Then, my opinion would carry more value – I could charge for it.

Today, with far more sport on television, the journalist's job is less about reporting *what* happened and far more about explaining *why* something happened or speculating on what *might* happen. This means providing background, context and, yes, opinions.

With the arrival of social media, it was clear that people were more likely to respond to an outspoken opinion than to a post that merely conveyed facts – especially if you aren't the first person to report those facts.

Nonetheless, I think my lecturer's advice still has some value. You don't want to lay into a player and then find yourself trying to get an interview out of them a week later. Ill-informed opinions can damage your credibility. And there are few pieces more boring than those that either state the obvious (eg Rovers have conceded 20 goals in five games so they need to sort out their defence) or repeat what scores of other writers are saying (eg overseas players in the Premier League are having a damaging effect on the England national team).

When you start out as a sports journalist, I think it's important to decide what kind of writer you are. Are you someone who prefers to diligently and conscientiously report on sport or are you the kind of person who can regularly come up with interesting and challenging opinions that you can defend when you face a barrage of criticism on social media?

TOP TIPS: OPINION PIECES

Andy Naylor (2017) is chief sports reporter at the Brighton Argus. As he's been covering Brighton and Hove Albion for 25 years, he's well-qualified to express his point of view. He writes an opinion column for the paper called *Nailed On*; the online version is called *Talking Point* (puns don't lend themselves to online headlines).

1   Go with what comes into your head. I watch a lot of Premier League games. One week, I thought "a lot of the supposed top teams have conceded three goals" and it evolved into a piece about the standard of Premier League defending.

2   Don't end up writing something that's been done to death elsewhere. So much stuff goes out now about analysis. If you're not careful it can look a bit dated. The way I make it different is I give it an Albion slant. For example, the story came out about the transfer window possibly changing so that it closes before the start of the season. That story's gone out widely but, if I were to write about that, I'd do an Albion angle on it and look at when they've done their signings.

3   Allow time for it. It takes a lot longer than you might imagine.

4   It's meant to be an opinion column – you need to say something. So, if you don't have an opinion, if you're just sitting on the fence and just presenting two sides of the argument, it defeats the object. So, I've said Gary Cahill is overrated. People might turn around and say "what's he talking about? Gary Cahill is the best centre half in England." So, you're creating a talking point. People might say 'I agree with him about that' or they might say he's talking utter rubbish.

5   Don't let it bother you if you get it wrong. It's an opinion; that doesn't mean you're always going to be right. If it ends up being wrong, so be it.

WEBSITES

OK, so you're setting up as a digital sports journalist. First of all, you're going to need a website. Right?

Well, maybe. Since 2010, journalists have tended to focus less on producing content for websites and more on producing content for *audiences*. If the audiences are not going to come to your website then it makes sense to find out where they *are* going – and that's generally social media.

You may have visited the websites of some quite well-known sporting publications and noticed that they haven't been updated very recently. That's because they don't regard them as much of a priority as other channels.

Now This News is one of the most successful producers of online short video, attracting billions of views for some of its pieces. Until autumn 2017 its website was just a single page directing you to its Facebook, Twitter, Snapchat, Instagram and YouTube feeds. The company assumes that people no longer have a series of favourite websites, which they visit each day or each week. Instead, they rely on social media to bring them the most interesting stories. It's hard for 30-somethings to understand that young people today don't use the world wide web in the way they do. Instead, many receive content entirely through a single social media channel. "Personally, I'm of the view that websites are dying and have been since 2008", reckons Simon Wear of the Play Sports Network, whose content is mainly distributed over YouTube. "It's a consumer behaviour point. DO people wake up in the morning, turn on a computer and go to a set of bookmarks? I don't think any of us do that anymore. It's all driven by supply, consumer behaviour, distribution" (Wear, 2017).

So, there are some fairly good reasons for not setting up a website (or blog):

1   No one will visit it. At least not as many people as watch your videos on YouTube or Facebook.
2   It's time-consuming to maintain. A blog that isn't updated regularly is very dull and soon falls behind other sites in terms of search engine optimisation.
3   It can be pricey. You may have to pay to register your site, pay for someone to host it and for someone to protect it from nasties like malware and viruses. That can easily come to a thousand pounds a year. If you do get hit by some kind of attack, you can spend twice that getting the site cleaned up.
4   Increasingly, your audience will be using phones to access sports journalism. That's fine if you have the resources to produce an app. If not, when did you last use a web browser to read a piece of journalism on your phone?

If you want your work to be seen, then it makes sense to publish on an existing website that already has an audience rather than setting up a website from scratch. There are several sites that will pay for sports articles, albeit not a fortune (there's no minimum wage in cyberspace). Some of these sites have been criticised because they only pay contributors a small fraction of what they make in advertising; I would still argue that it's better to be on a site that gets read than on one that doesn't. Things to look out for include whether you are paid per article or per page view and whether the site allows you to include links to your other work.

You might also consider posting material on sites such as Reddit or Medium, where users submit content which is then voted up or down by other members. Reddit has sub-sections devoted to, for example, NBA and soccer. Medium has a monthly subscription but it also attracts good writing; I made contact with designer Jean Octavian (see Chapters 3 and 9) through Medium.

However, there are some distinct advantages to having your own site, particularly if you are job-hunting:

1   It's useful to have a single place where all your best stories can be found and which allows you to direct readers to content you've created for other outlets. The head of media at one sports organisation told me he now thinks of their website as a kind of "brochure" which explains what they do, rather than being something that has to be updated every day.
2   Some forms of journalism will need a website if you wish to practise them – most obviously the kind of sophisticated multimedia storytelling that we'll be looking at in Chapter 12.
3   It may make you more attractive to an employer if you can demonstrate some understanding of layout, navigation and a reader's journey.
4   Some experienced pros, such as the former BBC sports editor Mihir Bose, have websites which act as a kind of repository for their best writing. The word "magazine" derives from a medieval French word *maguesin* which means "storehouse". (The modern French word *magasin* means both a shop and a warehouse.) That's how Bose uses his website – it's his magazine, storing all the best journalism he does.

5   It may be useful to have a place where you can explore a particular specialism, independently of your employer or university work.

Alexandra Willis of Wimbledon enjoys the fact that, when you control a website, you aren't at the mercy of other people:

> The reason why "owned channels" are important is that they are the audience that you truly own. People are trying to understand that audience, for example through personalised experiences. You have complete control over what that platform does. Facebook could change the way that their platform works tomorrow and all the best practice that we've tried to employ would go out of the window whereas it's totally up to us what we make the Wimbledon homepage looks like or how we choose to enable people to consume video and so on and so forth.
>
> (Willis, 2017)

In this book, we're going to assume you do have your own website; but most of the exercises can be practised without one.

SETTING UP A WEBSITE

Several companies – Blogger, Tumblr, Squarespace, Weebly, Wix and WordPress are probably the best known – enable you to set up your own website.

You'll need to decide whether you want to pay for your own domain or whether you are happy with your site being a (free) sub-domain.

Your own domain

- You own your website. You have to buy a domain name (from companies such as 123-reg or GoDaddy) and pay rent to a hosting company, eg Bluehost, to store your content.
- You'll have more control over the design and appearance of your site, particularly how content is organised and the side bars.
- You can add plug-ins to enable you to design quizzes or personality tests and run live blogs.
- You're responsible for keeping your site virus-free. This means regularly updating both the main website software and individual plug-ins.

A sub-domain

- You don't own your site. It belongs to Blogger or WordPress or whoever and their name appears in the url (uniform resource locator – the link that leads someone to your site).
- They'll also put ads on your site that you have no control over.

- You're likely to have fairly limited control over the look of the site.
- You may not be able to add plug-ins.
- You will probably get very little storage.
- The site is free and the owner of the main domain is responsible for keeping it safe.

Of the six companies named above, WordPress is the most popular; it's been estimated that 25% of the web is made up of WordPress sites. Wordpress.org provides websites that users manage themselves; wordpress.com provides free sub-domains which it manages.

You can upgrade from .com to .org fairly easily. It's much harder to travel in the other direction because some of your content may rely on technology that doesn't exist on the simpler version. So, it may be worth starting off with a. com site and upgrading if and when you need to.

Website providers have a habit of making frequent changes to the dashboards for their free sites, which makes it difficult to provide precise advice in a book. Before you sign up for a site it's worth researching (by looking on message boards) what functionality you'll be getting.

Whether you opt for a free or paid-for site, you'll be asked to come up with a url. This should be the same as the name of your website, which will appear at the top of each page. This can be tricky. You're looking for one which:

- hasn't been taken already;
- is also available as on Twitter, Facebook, Snapchat etc – so you have a consistent brand;
- is not too similar to an existing account name;
- doesn't limit you. For instance, if you were setting up a Bristol Rovers fansite, then the url Roversforever might be ideal. But, if you are planning a more general sports site then it's going to restrict you. It might be difficult to approach a Bristol City player for an interview.

Note that, if you host your own site, you'll need to buy your domain name. This can be a fiendishly complicated process and the prices can go up and down quite a bit. As a rule, domains ending. com tend to be more expensive than .site or .club.

WEBSITES AND BLOGS

Although the terms are now used interchangeably, the words "website" and "blog" mean slightly different things.

The word blog (a shortening of "web log") originally referred to a particular kind of website, a diary where postings were simply added one on top of the other, without any navigational system. Twitter is sometimes referred to as a micro-blogging site because posts simply pile up, most recent first.

Blog:

FIGURE 2.1 Typical structure of a blog

Professional website:

A professional website typically has a homepage explaining the purpose of the site from where the visitor can follow a clear route to specific areas that interest them. A site specialising in winter sport, for example, might have a navigational bar with links to skiing, luge, ice-skating, ice hockey etc.

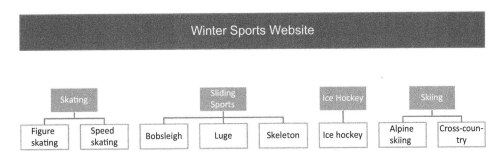

FIGURE 2.2 Typical structure of a professional website

Most free websites were designed as blogging platforms and don't give you very much freedom to create a navigational structure. You can, however, create links between pages. So, you can assign a page called "Winter Sport Headlines" to be your home page so that it's the first thing visitors see when they land on your site. On that page you write a list of brief headlines and include hyperlinks to each of the stories you're referring to. Of course, it does mean the home page must be regularly updated.

If you opt for a paid-for site, then, when you post a story, you'll be asked what category you want it to go in. Note that a story can go in more than one category. If you don't select a category, the story might not be visible at all.

PICTURES AND VIDEOS: LEGALITIES AND PRACTICALITIES

Because it is easy to cut and paste photographs, graphics and even videos from one website to another, there is a temptation to think that it is legal. It's not.

Photographers are professionals doing a challenging job. They are entitled to earn a living – just as journalists are. Taking and reusing their work without permission is theft. Some people seem to be under the impression that Getty Images, one of the largest providers of sports imagery, allows free use of its library. This isn't the case. Getty decided, a few years ago, to permit access to some of the library provided proper credits are used. The scheme does not cover print reproduction of pictures, nor does it allow you to use all Getty's images.

Broadcasters pay vast sums of money for sports rights and, so, you are on very risky ground if you help yourself to football or F1 footage. Simply sticking on a caption crediting the original broadcaster isn't going to help much. In 2016, the England and Wales Cricket Board (ECB) and broadcaster BSkyB took action against the makers of an app that allowed users to record an eight-second clip of a test match, add commentary and then post it on Twitter. The court came down on the side of the ECB and BSkyB, deciding that even an eight-second excerpt constitutes a breach of copyright (England and Wales High Court, 2016).

Students sometimes tell me they can't see what they are doing wrong as "everyone's doing it". They are right; it is difficult for even well-staffed organisations to keep tabs on everyone who is reusing copyrighted content online. But if you start making money out of their pictures, then they probably will come after you. A fellow lecturer told me that one of his students received a "cease and desist" letter after a short film that incorporated Champions League footage had been viewed six million times on Facebook.

Furthermore, if an employer sees your website full of pictures that don't belong to you, they may well think "well, this youngster shows potential but I don't think I can take a risk on someone who could land me with a big fine".

However, there are ways that you can use copyrighted material without paying a small fortune:

- As mentioned above, Getty Images allow limited use of their library, provided the work is properly credited. Let's imagine we're looking for a photograph of Cristiano Ronaldo. Simply visit gettyimages.co.uk and enter the name of what you're looking for in the big search bar. From the results, pick your preferred image and hover over the embed logo </> if it's there (if not you can't use the picture). Clicking on the embed button will generate an embed code; on a story page on your website you simply have to select "Add Media" and paste in this code. This will put the picture with the correct attribution on your site.
- You can also use Creative Commons. This is a website where artists are encouraged to share their work freely, sometimes with restrictions on how they can be reused. Go to CreativeCommons.com and select what kind of search you wish to do – you're given 12 options, including YouTube (video) and SoundCloud (audio); I normally select Google Images. Once you've found the image you wish to use, it's not quite as

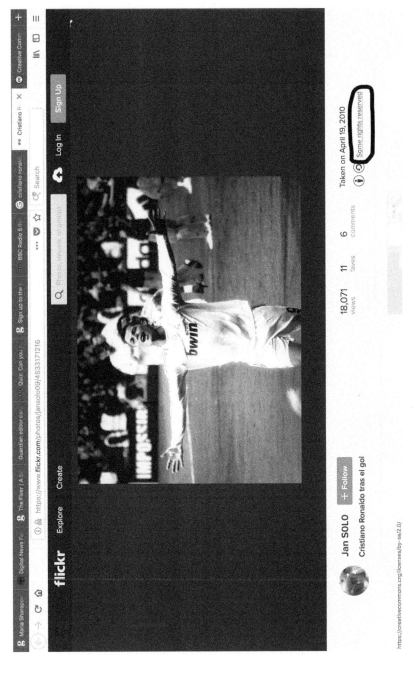

FIGURE 2.3 Screenshot from flickr, image courtesy of Jan Solo

simple as using Getty's site. You'll need to read the licence under which the owner of the image is offering to share it. Note, I've circled this in the image, above, where it says "some rights reserved". Normally this will involve a picture credit but it may also include other stipulations or restrictions. In the example below, the photographer, Jan Solo, has requested I credit him and indicate if changes were made. Some photographers request that an email be sent to them when their images are used. In my experience, 90% of free-to-use photographs come from flickr, which is a site where photographers post albums of their work and make them available to share. I would advise setting up a flickr account so that you can quickly and easily source pictures.

- Other media companies also allow you to use their content. For example, the *Guardian* allows you to use video from its site so long as you abide by certain conditions, such as not removing the logos, branding or any advertisements, not trying to pass the work off as your own, not changing its meaning and not charging visitors for access to it (*Guardian*, 2010).

- You can, in certain circumstances, embed other people's work on your website or social media feeds. For example, returning to the case involving test match cricket referred to above, the ECB itself now tweets short clips of wickets and boundaries which you can embed in a live blog. YouTube gives people who upload video to the site a choice whether to enable embedding – so if this option is switched on it could be interpreted as a sign that the maker is happy to share it (Bradshaw, 2013).

- In 2014, the UK government created an exemption to the copyright law enabling individuals to use footage for the purpose of "parody, caricature and pastiche" without having to obtain permission from the original author. This, technically, is the loophole that allows people to create mash-ups of politicians' speeches set to music or sped up or slowed down – and you can find plenty of similar videos on YouTube involving the likes of Cristiano Ronaldo or LeBron James. It has yet to be tested in the UK courts and several legal commentators have suggested there are a lot of blurred lines. For example, it is unclear how much of the original work can be adapted.

- Why not just ask the rights holder? Plenty of photographers would probably be happy to support an upcoming sports journalist particularly if it means their work gets shared with a wider audience. Contact details of most photographers should be fairly easy to find online; if not, the National Union of Journalists' photographers' branch may be able to help.

USER-GENERATED CONTENT

News organisations increasingly make use of pictures taken by members of the public who are not professional journalists or photographers. Some of these people might be regarded as "citizen journalists"; the BBC refers to their contributions as UGC which stands for "User-Generated Content".

UGC has clearly transformed the way stories like the civil war in Syria are reported or coverage of disasters where it may take professional news crews an hour or more to get to the scene.

Its role in covering sport is more limited as sports events are scheduled and the right to film at an event often proscribed. There will, however, be some great opportunities to use UGC. For example, if you are trying to build the atmosphere ahead of a live blog of an overseas rugby, cricket or football match involving a British team, then you could use photos of fans enjoying themselves in local bars before kick-off.

Occasionally, pictures from sports events that are not filmed by professional broadcasters can "go viral". A great example of this is the "Knuckey Try" (Knuckey, 2016). Alan Knuckey, who plays rugby for amateur side Charlton Park, was behind his own try line when he dropped the ball behind his back, flicked it over his head and then ran the whole length of the pitch to score. The footage was picked up by ITV, BBC and even overseas media in the United States and New Zealand. It's worth keeping an eye out for these quirky stories.

There have also been attempts to deploy networks of citizen journalists to cover mega-events such as the Olympic Games. For example, people in London were able to relate stories about communities displaced to make way for the 2012 Games in ways that would not have been possible for previous Games.

ADD MEDIA OR EMBED MEDIA?

As shown above, there are situations when you are not allowed to download pictures or videos and *add* them to your website, but you may be able to *embed* them on your site. In this latter case, you're not helping yourself to someone else's footage; you're providing a link to it.

Another advantage of this approach is that you are not using up your site's data storage. Whether you use a free service like Wordpress.com or one where you pay for hosting, you will have a data limit and, if you regularly post large videos, you'll eventually find yourself coming up against it. So, if you can get YouTube or Twitter to host the clip for you it saves you space.

There are, however, downsides to this:

- You can't choose to embed just *part* of a video that's on another site. For example, let's say you've filmed a great interview with a member of the Nottingham Forest side of the 1980s. You want to illustrate the interview with two or three goals, taken from some archive footage of an entire match you've found online. To do so, you'll need to contact the rights holder to get permission, download the footage and re-edit it with your interview.
- If you're embedding a video that you've uploaded to YouTube, you have no control over the adverts they'll add.
- You can't guarantee that the url will always take you to the footage "link rot".

Professional sports media organisations, like Sky or BT, try to avoid embedding because:

- They make money from the adverts at the start of their clips. An advertiser might pay $25 (around £19) per 1,000 views of an ad (Lipschultz, 2017 p 73). That's around 10 times more than YouTube would pay for the same number of views.
- They want to create the impression that they are a one-stop shop for sports coverage – you don't have to go off somewhere else.

If you're starting out, however, embedding is a great way to get interesting, dynamic content onto your site quickly without going over your storage limits.

SUMMARY

- It's a good idea to try to develop a specialism; try to identify an area of sport where you can become an expert – one where there aren't already lots of pundits.
- Strong opinion pieces can deliver a lot of clicks. But be realistic: are you the kind of writer who can deliver interesting, well-informed opinions week in, week out?
- Sophisticated websites can be time-consuming and expensive to maintain. But you can achieve a reasonably professional look by using a blogging platform such as Blogger or Weebly.
- Do not help yourself to other people's work without asking permission; it's illegal to cut and paste pictures and put them on your website. There are legal ways of using other people's material – there's normally advice on how to do it on their website.

REFERENCES

Bradshaw, P. (2013) *Test your online Journalism Law 2* at https://onlinejournalismblog.com/2013/11/19/copyright-law-celebrity-picture-online-journalism/. Last accessed on 25/11/2017

England and Wales High Court (Chancery Division) (2016) *England and Wales Cricket Board Ltd & Anor v Tixdaq Ltd & Anor* at www.bailii.org/ew/cases/EWHC/Ch/2016/575.html. Last accessed on 25/11/2017

Guardian (2010) *Embedding Guardian videos on third party sites: Terms of use* at www.theguardian.com/global/2010/jun/08/1. Last accessed on 25/11/2017

Knuckey, A. (2016) *Best rugby try ever* YouTube at www.youtube.com/watch?v=7Xfth-l6dw4. Last accessed on 25/11/2017

Lipschultz, J. (2017) *Social Media Communication* (2nd ed.). New York: Routledge

Naylor, A. (2017) Interview conducted by the author, 16/8/2017

Ricci, F. (2008) *Elephants, Lions and Eagles: A Journey through African Football*. London: WSC Books

Wear, S. (2017) Interview conducted by the author on 7/9/2017

Willis, A. (2017) Interview conducted by the author on 15/9/2017

CHAPTER 3

Social media

Twice a year, German sports marketing experts RESULT Sports produce a league table showing which clubs have the most fans, followers or friends on social media (RESULT Sports, 2017). Their 2017 table appears on the next page.

There are some interesting details to note here:

- The numbers involved are astronomic. In the case of Barcelona, its digital community is more than 2,000 times the capacity of Camp Nou. In fact, it's four and a half times the entire population of Spain. Manchester United's 111 million-strong digital community equates to roughly twice the population of England while, at number 38 in the table, AS Monaco boast a digital community 179 times greater than the number of people living in the principality. So, the numbers of people that can be reached through social media vastly exceeds the numbers that can attend matches, join membership schemes, visit your website or any other currently existing form of communication. (It should be pointed out that, in many cases, the *same* people are following clubs on several platforms. So, Barca's 206 million followers includes some duplication.)

- Facebook's reach dwarves everyone else's. At the top end of the table, Facebook accounts for about half of Barca, Real Madrid and Manchester United's digital community, as much as the rest combined. Once you get past the top seven clubs, that figure is often up to two-thirds – though Twitter seems to perform well in Brazil. Some young people I speak to claim to be bored of Facebook, but its growth shows no sign of slowing. And remember: in the first ten years of its existence, Facebook didn't show very much interest in cultivating sports fans. It does now.

> Facebook is the priority because it's the biggest one, it's got the most people on it, and it's got the most engagement in terms of people liking or commenting. Twitter has to be frequently updated and, in terms of driving people to your website, it's not that effective.
> – Phil Harlow (2017) of Livewire Sport

> The Sport on Facebook page has 15 million followers, so that ticks our box straight away.
> – Mark Coyle (2017), head of Media for cycling group Velon

GLOBAL DIGITAL
FOOTBALL BENCHMARK 1 – 25

#	Team	League, Country	Digital Community	Facebook	Instagram	Twitter	Periscope	Google+	YouTube
1	FC Barcelona	La Uga, Spain	206,711,621	102,660,473	50,763,512	40,895,642	326,754	8,990,205	3,075,035
2	Real Madrid	La Uga, Spain	204,968,920	104,620,981	50,905,304	39,123,730	262,476	7,652,403	2,404,026
3	Manchester United	Premier League, UK	111,821,507	73,677,207	18,186,213	13,145,001	0	6,813,086	0
4	Chelsea FC	Premier League, UK	76,852,804	48,013,399	9,622,836	11,342,866	0	7,241,068	632,635
5	Arsenal	Premier League, UK	63,373,961	38,028,720	9,753,692	10,381,425	115,389	4,449,974	644,761
6	FC Bayern München	1 Bundesliga, Germany	61,217,243	42,434,659	10,207,705	4,880,320	52,619	2,935,657	706,283
7	Liverpool FC	Premier League, UK	48,972,373	30,052,037	4,334,917	8,906,639	88,724	4,981,094	608,962
8	Juventus	Serie A, Italy	45,469,736	30,139,745	7,354,799	5,565,162	65,399	1,781,459	563,172
9	Paris St. Germain	Ligue 1, France	45,304,170	29,659,877	8,171,550	5,529,517	130,814	1,374,390	438,022
10	Manchester City	Premier League, UK	43,416,925	25,014,587	4,971,021	8,202,774	94,194	4,212,302	922,047
11	AC Milan	Serie A, Italy	39,464,252	24,779,533	3,358,191	5,082,039	0	5,898,752	345,737
12	Galatasaray Istanbul	SuperLig, Turkey	25,270,812	13,192,362	3,600,467	7,313,072	223,799	729,048	212,064
13	Borussia Dortmund	1 Bundesliga, Germany	23,835,466	15,427,297	4,205,377	2,758,286	55,963	1,166,625	221,918
14	Atlético de Madrid	La Uga, Spain	21,795,977	13,797,583	3,400,682	3,353,648	0	1,129,846	114,218
15	Corinthians	Brasileiro Serie A	19,619,992	11,355,021	1,874,181	5,164,773	66,454	819,394	340,169
16	Fenerbahce Istanbul	SuperLig, Turkey	19,124,522	9,890,007	2,504,640	5,959,058	214,301	397,208	159,308
17	Flamengo	Brasileiro Serie A	18,636,443	11,395,971	2,043,319	4,489,034	36,459	90,507	581,153
18	Al-Ahli	Premiere League Egypt	16,862,565	11,268,858	2,671,003	1,883,577	0	864,118	175,009
19	Club América	Liga MX Clausura, Mexico	14,576,106	10,228,793	878,481	3,062,947	69,979	0	335,906
20	PERSIB Bandung	Liga 1, Indonesia	13,771,475	9,572,479	1,210,683	2,958,178	1,019	24	29,092
21	Boca Juniors	Primera Division Argentina	13,680,097	8,271,717	1,745,342	2,804,661	38,822	691,421	128,134
22	River Plate	Primera Division Argentina	12,831,627	8,349,663	1,401,229	2,261,651	21,568	689,875	107,641
23	Tottenham Hotspur	Permier League, UK	12,289,242	8,451,921	1,207,812	2,119,886	28,700	282,547	198,376
24	AS Roma	Serie A, Italy	12,166,714	8,910,400	1,112,932	1,681,786	12,761	236,240	212,595
25	Sao Paulo FC	Brasiloiro Serie A	12,156,304	6,808,487	1,190,219	3,612,475	45,003	10,785	489,335

- If clubs make an effort, they can significantly increase their social media reach. For example, Manchester United have roughly four times as many Instagram followers as Liverpool. That doesn't mean they have four times as many supporters; it just shows that they've made an effort with that particular platform.

WHAT IS SOCIAL MEDIA?

Lipschultz (2017 p 353) defines a social network as "any online platform that enables communication between site accounts". Hill and Lashmar (2014 pp 142–143) suggest that social *media* requires two distinct features:

- participation that allows communication to travel in both directions and the production and consumption of content;
- groups of people gathering in communities based on shared interests. Numbers of followers and of reposts enhances someone's status within their community.

This definition covers WhatsApp, Viber, Pinterest, Kik, Shots, Message boards, flickr, Reddit, Periscope, LinkedIn, Google+, Facebook, Twitter, Instagram and Snapchat.

In this chapter, and this book, we'll mainly be looking at the last four in that list. This is not say that other sites may not have their uses. Several organisations spotted a story when Italian World Cup winner Cristian Zaccardo offered his services on LinkedIn: "I'm still good physically, I could play two more years at high levels. Who will take me to make a deal? Serious and strong professional soccer player." And, if you were writing a piece about the changing fashions in kit design, the arts-focussed Pinterest might be helpful. But, in my conversations with professionals writing about sport, it's Facebook, Twitter, Instagram and Snapchat that pop up most. These have come to be known as the big four of social media.

Although there is constant speculation about whether one of the big four will need to merge with another media organisation, it is hard to see a new player entering this market. This is because, whenever a new idea emerges, one or more of the big four are likely to try to copy it. For example, when Snapchat's Stories function proved very popular, Instagram reacted by developing something very similar. When apps that allowed live video streaming emerged, Facebook, Twitter and Instagram all moved into that area. In Twitter's case, it actually bought Periscope before that app was even launched publicly.

Video sites like YouTube and Vimeo may also be regarded as social media. We'll be looking at online video later in the book.

A student recently asked: "I use Instagram, Snapchat and LinkedIn. Do I really have to use Twitter as well?" It's a good question. Most of us tend to use one or two social media regularly and feel comfortable with them. But, if you're a journalist trying to get content out to diverse audiences then you need to use whatever channels they are watching. If you say you're not going to use Twitter, then you can't communicate with the millions of people who only use Twitter and no other social media. Having said that, it is very difficult to serve four different social media platforms and a website; there's a risk you can spread yourself too thin. So, it makes sense to focus on the social media where you can develop the largest audiences and provide weekly updates on the others. Large organisations can afford to employ people who really understand how particular channels work. One way of coping if you are trying to manage several different social media streams is to use a tool called Hootsuite, which we'll be looking at below.

You may have also heard the term "dark social". This, seemingly sinister, phrase refers to content that is shared by email, text message or private messaging apps, such as WhatsApp, Facebook Messenger or Viber. The word "dark" refers to the fact that, as this kind of sharing is private; it cannot be measured in the way that exchanges on Twitter or Instagram can. One estimate suggests that 84% of outbound sharing is through dark social (Parker, 2017) while the Reuters Institute for the Study of Journalism has shown that "the use of WhatsApp for news is starting to rival Facebook in a number of markets including Malaysia (51%), Brazil (46%), and Spain (32%)" (Newman, 2017). The report authors argue that the appeal of dark social is that you know your shared content will be seen and won't be left to the vagaries of an algorithm.

To be a really effective communicator, it pays to spend time working out how people use social media and the kind of language they use. "I have taught myself by looking at what our fans like and want to see whilst ensuring that our messaging is reaching the right people," says Rebecca James, a Communications Officer at Arsenal FC (James, 2017).

TIP: Study people who command large numbers of followers or get lots of shares. What are they doing differently? Is it language? Is it timing? Is it use of pictures?

HOW JOURNALISTS USE SOCIAL MEDIA

Crudely speaking, there are two reasons to use social media:

- to find stories, facts, quotes, images etc;
- to publicise your stories.

This is a bit of a generalisation, but, because they are open platforms, Twitter and Instagram are better suited to finding things whereas, because of the enormous numbers involved, Facebook is better for publicising your work.

Until recently, social media was regarded as a means of drawing traffic to a website – and for big media organisations it still is. But, increasingly, it makes more sense to simply post your story or short film directly onto Facebook or Twitter. As we saw in Chapter 2, this saves a lot of time spent managing a website. You can even use these platforms to broadcast live.

A good example of a journalist using social media to find a story is provided by *Times* cricket writer Elizabeth Ammon, who tweeted: "Please do get in touch with me if your cricket club has been subject to vandalism of any kind this season. Collating the stats." Within two days, she'd had 120 replies and, clearly, had uncovered an under-reported issue. The beauty of Twitter is that it is so easy to re-tweet an appeal like this, so she wasn't limited to people who already followed her.

TIP: All the main social media channels put guidance on their websites, advising journalists how to use their platform most effectively. Their business models are all based on getting as many people as possible to use them, so it makes sense to court journalists who they regard as opinion formers. Make use of these help pages – they contain some great advice.

UNDERSTANDING SOCIAL MEDIA

Each form of social media behaves differently. There's no point anyone setting up a new social media application that simply replicates what an existing one is doing. The precursors to Google+ were simply alternative versions of Facebook, which is partly why they never took off.

So why might you choose to use one form of social media rather than another? For example, why do reporters typically put live updates during games on Twitter not Facebook? On Twitter you can post as many times as you want without diminishing the reach of each individual tweet. But Facebook only serves up one or two posts an hour to your newsfeed from any one author.

"You can post ten times in an hour but the majority of your followers will only see two or three of those because Facebook selects what it thinks are the best ones," (Gibb, 2017) explains Aldershot Football Club head of media, Steve Gibb, who does "moment-by-moment" match reports on Twitter.

"But Facebook can push our highlights out to a much bigger audience. If I post them on Saturday night, then, by the time you get up on a Sunday morning, you've had 20–30,000 views."

Instagram, meanwhile, is very picture-based; it will favour strong, square images.

In the section that follows, we'll look at the different channels individually. I am going to assume that you have a basic familiarity with each social medium and will focus on ways of using it to tell stories about sport. But, first, some general points that apply to all social media.

If you are following 500 people, your feed/timeline is going to get pretty busy and, unless you are glued to it 24/7, you'll miss a lot. The social media organisations know this and so they push the content they think you'll find most interesting to the top of your feed or send you a notification. Of course, this isn't done by human beings; it's done by a computer following a set of rules called an algorithm. It's important for journalists to have some understanding of these algorithms but they are all governed by two basic rules:

1 They want you to use their site – so they'll try to push the best content to the top. "Best" is determined by number of likes and shares, particularly among your community, by certain keywords that you've picked up on in the past, by the visual content of the post and by how quickly it loads.
2 They want you to stay on their site – so they'll try to push content that keeps you there. So, Facebook is now penalising content that takes you to an external website.

All social media channels reward engagement. If you never post then people won't follow you, you won't figure highly in news feeds and you'll struggle to get attention. But engagement doesn't simply mean posting – it means re-posting other people's content, ideally with a comment, it means initiating conversations with fellow journalists or sports stars and it means making good use of pictures. Unless you have a lot of followers, a stand-alone post may not get noticed; you're more likely to get a reaction if you comment on someone else's post.

An increasingly important question for people using social media is *when* to post. A lot of thought is being given to which times of day people are likely to be most receptive to your stories. And, of course, the more times you post a link to your story, the greater the chance of your followers spotting it. Most social media now enable you to schedule posts (in the case of Facebook, you can schedule them up to six months in advance). So, you might send out a short version of your story at 7am, to catch people as they are waking up and checking their phones, a slightly different version at lunch-time and a longer version in the evening when they might have more time.

Increasingly, there is an expectation that you should post pictures or video and not just words. If someone is scrolling through a feed, then pictures are going to jump out at the reader in a way that blocks of text won't. Most social media algorithms now push video higher on users' timelines.

GIFs (graphic interchange formats) are a particularly eye-catching form of video. They have been compressed so that they will load much more quickly than other videos – which is particularly useful to reach people reliant on 3G or 4G phone connections. Compressed video isn't very high quality but that doesn't matter if someone is viewing on a phone. The big advantage of a GIF over other kinds of video is that it will load automatically rather than waiting for someone to press play. So, someone scrolling through their Twitter feed will see a GIF playing whether they choose to or not. This also means that someone can't rewind to the start of a GIF; once it finishes, it goes back to the start, so they tend to be short (less than 10 seconds).

You can easily attach a GIF to your Twitter feed – Twitter has a stock of them that you can select from at any time. To turn an existing video into a GIF is also straightforward: a Google search will produce several pieces of free software that will do the job.

TIP: Have a few quirky all-purpose GIFs to hand so that you can add them to tweets at short notice.

BUILDING A FOLLOWING ON SOCIAL MEDIA

Most journalists want to build as big a readership as they can, and social media enables us to do that in a way that has never been possible in the past. I have become accustomed to students telling me they have very impressive followings on social media – often into five figures. Their secret? You follow me, I'll follow you.

For example, one of my students specialises in writing about rugby. Every so often he'll go visit the Rugby Football Union (RFU) Twitter page and systematically follow everyone who has liked one of their recent tweets. Each of these people will then get a notification saying that they've just been followed so they'll visit his profile and (and this is important) read his biography which explains that he covers rugby. They might also look at his tweets and see that he regularly tweets about the sport in a lively style. So, many of these users will then choose to follow him.

Others have developed large followings by working with other users – particularly those who support the same clubs as they do. There is quite a strong culture among some clubs' fan accounts – Arsenal's for example – of encouraging supporters to follow other fan accounts.

NEW ACCOUNTS OR OLD ACCOUNTS?

It takes time to build a following on social media so, if you already have an account with a few hundred followers, then it makes sense to carry on with that for your sports journalism.

This may, however, depend on what you've been posting up to now. An employer is unlikely to be too impressed with a timeline full of accounts of drunken nights out, or worse. It may also be worth separating your sports journalism from your social life. Most Facebook users happily link posts about their relationships or children's play dates with news and sports stories. But, if you are setting yourself up as an authoritative commentator on the Chinese Super League, does your audience also want to see pictures of your mother's 50th birthday party? So, it may be a good idea to set up a separate account for your professional posts.

Most social media now understand that some people are likely to be managing several accounts and so it is now easier to manage multiple channels (eg through TweetDeck).

You also need to think carefully about what you include in your posts. I recently spotted a former student at my university using quite an abusive term in a conversation on Twitter. It was directed at a friend and was probably not meant to come across as being quite as offensive as it seemed – but that subtlety tends to get lost in 140 or 280 characters. To make matters worse, this graduate was now employed by one of the UK's best-known sports media companies – something he proudly proclaimed in his profile. So, he was running the risk of bringing his employer into disrepute.

TWITTER

> Because it's short and sweet you can post regularly on Twitter but if you scroll through your personal feed on Facebook and someone's narrating every part of their day, it wouldn't be very interesting.
>
> – Emily Brammeier, content editor for cycling team Sunweb (Brammeier, 2017)

Despite the extraordinary reach of Facebook, Twitter tends to be the journalist's favourite form of social media communication. It's hard to find a leading sports journalist, or even a lower league one, who doesn't use the platform. Henry Winter of *The Times*, for example, had 1.25 million followers in November 2017 – three times as many as Prime Minister Theresa May. In this book, we'll be looking at it in more depth than we will for the other members of the big four as there are several tools which make Twitter especially useful.

Twitter is ideally suited to breaking news. Chelsea have signed a new player; Alastair Cook has resigned the England captaincy; Dylan Hartley has been left out of the Lions squad. Because posts are limited to 280 characters, it encourages immediacy rather than longer, thought-out pieces. If you discover a new piece of sports news, it makes sense to get it out there on Twitter first – possibly with the promise of updates to come on other platforms.

Tweets were originally limited to 140 characters, which really forced writers to be concise. In 2017, this went up to 280. But, if Twitter permitted limitless tweets, there is a risk that it would lose its special appeal as a source of breaking news. Sometimes, clubs and other organisations that want to put out lengthy statements get round the character limit by attaching the whole statement to a tweet as a photograph.

Hashtags

In the aftermath of a breaking story, such as the ones cited above, there will be a lot of chatter on Twitter. This is where hashtags are important. If you have something interesting to say about, say, the decision to appoint Joe Root as England test match captain, there's no point beginning a tweet "Re the story about Joe Root being given the England captaincy . . ." because, by the time you've written that, you've used a fair chunk of your 280 characters. There's also no way of making sure that other people who are interested in the story get to see your pearls of wisdom.

The hashtag is a means of addressing both these problems. Twitter users will quickly identify a, usually short, word that can be used to indicate which current story they are talking about. In this instance, for example, it might be #Root or #CaptainRoot.

This indicates that the story is *about* Root. Otherwise a search might locate tweets claiming that money is the root of all evil or that root ginger is the secret of a good punch. If you are interested in a particular story, you can search using the hashtag, and Twitter will filter out all the other tweets – you just get the conversation about the story that you are interested in.

Hashtags also enable you to find people who share your perspective on a story. For example, football fans might include #COYS (Come on you Spurs), #COYB (Come on you Baggies) or #PUSB (Play up Sky Blues – a line from Coventry City's club song). These hashtags are being used to indicate loyalty or shared values as well as being a filtering device. When Brazilian Formula One driver Felipe Massa retired from the sport, fans discussed the story using the hashtag #ObrigadoMassa. (*Obrigado* is Portuguese for "thank you".) On a more negative note, when some West Bromwich Albion fans were calling for the sacking of manager Tony Pulis, many would include #PULISOUT in their tweets. Others responded with #PULISIN. If you had wanted to catch the attention of both sides, you could have included both hashtags in your tweet.

"I include #KeepChallenging in most of our content", says Emily Brammeier (ibid), who runs the social media channels for cycling team Sunweb. There's no *need* for her to do this as anyone who is interested in Sunweb stories will be able to find her tweets easily. Instead, the use of the hashtag acts as a form of branding for the team. People who do not support the team would not use it, even if they are talking about Sunweb.

Brammeier also uses hashtags to distinguish particular strands of content. "We have a #InsideOut feature that's been going for three years. We use that for behind-the-scenes pictures. One of our photographers does arty, behind-the-scenes on the bus things so when we get that footage we'll use #InsideOut" (ibid).

Television programmes also make good use of hashtags. For example, by using the hashtag #MOTD, you can join in a conversation with other Match of the Day viewers while the programme is taking place.

In football, a clear convention has now developed for referring to games. This involves using three-letter abbreviations of clubs' names, bolted together, home side first, eg: #TOTCRY indicates you're referring to Tottenham's home game against Crystal Palace. In this case, tweeters can use the first three letters of the clubs' names without risk of ambiguity. This isn't always the case: #MANWES could refer to either of the Manchester clubs playing West Bromwich Albion or West Ham United. So, Manchester City are MCI, United are MUN, West Brom are WBA and West Ham are WHU. It's normally fairly easy to guess, or spot, the abbreviation being used.

In rugby, a "v" is normally inserted, eg #WASvHAR for Wasps v Harlequins (a search using #WASHAR brought news of the Dutch amateur football match between Waskemeer and Harkemase Boys). In cricket there doesn't appear to be a consistent pattern: both #ENGWIN and #ENGvWIN were used during the 2017 test series. Boxing tends to use the full names of both fighters #ParkerFury.

Competitions have also come to evolve their own hashtags. Tennis beat golf to #usopen; the latter has to make do with #usopengolf. Tweeters will sometimes use #usopen when referring to the competition in general terms or #usopen2012 when referring to a particular championship. The United States Olympic Committee wrote to companies that used the hashtags #TeamUSA and #Rio2016 warning them to desist or face legal action. No cases were brought and, in any event, the letters were designed to discourage businesses from pretending to be official sponsors rather than putting off journalists from using hashtags as filters.

For sporting events that don't attract mainstream media coverage, either on TV or radio or via local papers' online services, Twitter is vital, as Emily Brammeier of the cycling team Sunweb explains: "We have a men's, a women's and a development team. With the women's and the development team, the main way people follow races is with a race hashtag on Twitter" (ibid).

Note: when you enter a hashtag, Twitter, as a default, will bring up the Top Tweets about the subject, ie those which have been most liked or tweeted or those sent from users with big followings. To follow an event using Twitter, you'll need to switch to Latest or News in the bar along the top of your screen. This will bring up all tweets with that hashtag, most recent first. You also have the useful option of restricting your search to just tweets with photos or videos attached.

Hashtags often have a short shelf life. At the time of Alastair Cook's resignation, the hashtag #CaptainCook was in fairly common use. If you use it as a search term today, it's more likely to generate references to the 18th century navigator.

Lists

Lists are a useful way of assembling groups of people on Twitter. For example, imagine you're covering a local area which includes a couple of football teams, a couple of rugby teams, a county cricket side, a team that competes in British Touring Cars and a leading hockey club. You can divide up the people you follow on Twitter according to which of these sports sides they relate to.

You could also create a list of your most important sources. So, if you haven't time to scroll through your whole Twitter feed, you can look at just the ones that are most likely to provide new stories. Many journalists also keep lists of their main rivals so they can check they haven't gotten hold of any exclusive news ahead of them.

You can also group together people who took part in a particular Twitter debate or people who you met at a particular event. This allows you to keep these relationships warm.

Creating lists is really simple but it's easier to do on a computer rather than a phone. Click on your profile picture in the top right-hand corner. Then, on the drop-down menu, choose lists. This will take you to a new page which, on the right-hand side, gives you the option "Create new list".

Lists can be public or private. You'll probably want most of yours to be private – after all, you don't want your competitors to see where your stories are coming from (and you certainly don't want that list of rivals to be public). But some people might feel it's a compliment if they appear on your list of, say, Olympic Sailing Experts.

TIP: Look at how other journalists use lists. Elizabeth Ammon, mentioned earlier, is a good example of someone who makes extensive use of them.

TweetDeck and Hootsuite

TweetDeck is a device that allows you to view several Twitter feeds at the same time and is an essential tool for live blogging sporting events. Using hashtags at a game allows you to see *every* tweet about the game, but TweetDeck allows you to focus on three, four, five or six people whose views you are especially interested in, fellow journalists perhaps or former players.

It works on desktop or laptop computers rather than phones. It was originally produced by a separate company but is now owned by Twitter. It has, however, retained its own website, tweetdeck.com, or, if you're a mac user, you can download it as an app.

When you log in for the first time, you'll see four columns: your own Twitter feed (ie everyone you're following), notifications, messages and activity. To remove any of these, just click on the logo made up of two lines with circles at the top right of the column (I call it the "two swimmers" logo). This generates a drop-down menu which includes "remove". To create a new column, click the + sign in the side bar on the right. You'll see that you can add named users, lists or mentions (particularly useful if you have more than one account). If you choose "search" you can then enter a hashtag, eg #TOTCRY, to bring up all the tweets about the game you are covering.

It's worth spending a bit of time getting to grips with TweetDeck. You can use it, for example, to tweet from multiple accounts simultaneously or to schedule posts.

TweetDeck has several rivals, the best known of which is Hootsuite. This enables you to monitor Twitter, Facebook and Google+ etc all in one place. You can also post simultaneously on different networks, though bear in mind this isn't always a good idea as the different platforms often call for different approaches. Hootsuite also allows several people to have access to the same accounts and provides analytical reports which show, for example, the geographic spread of people who read your posts. It can also be used to schedule posts, though this is now a feature of all the main platforms.

While the fact that you can post to several different social media platforms on Hootsuite gives it a huge advantage over TweetDeck, I find the latter is less complicated to use – particularly for live blogging (Chapter 4).

Verification

When Twitter started, you had no way of knowing whether you were communicating with a real sports person or an impersonator. In a well-known instance, a spoof Andy Townsend account tweeted that the former Ireland footballer wanted to see more female officials in the sport, particularly "the attractive ones" (Lee, 2012). There are some very funny spoof accounts out there – @Vern_cotter which shares the supposed thoughts of the former Scotland rugby coach is a particular favourite.

So, Twitter came up with the idea of adding a blue tick to verify that accounts were genuine. If someone feels that their account is one of "public interest", then they can apply to Twitter for a tick next to their account name. "Typically this includes accounts maintained by users in music, acting, fashion, government, politics, religion, journalism, media, sports, business, and other key interest areas", according to Twitter's official support site. The introduction of the blue tick doesn't seem to have helped ITV presenter Piers Morgan, however. In November 2017, he got into a row with someone impersonating the former Ivory Coast footballer Kolo Touré (Daily Record, 2017).

Verification is not based on numbers – I know several sports journalists whose accounts were verified when their followings were still in the low hundreds – but, having a sizeable following does appear to make it more likely that you'll secure the prized blue tick.

Twitter gives verified users a second Notifications tab. While the normal Notifications list shows *any* tweets that mention you, this second tab only lists mentions by other verified users. This acts like a kind of press card; it filters out some of the dozens of comments from fans and trolls and makes it easier for journalists to contact well-known sports stars.

Even if the account is verified, do not assume you are always communicating with the named account holder. Many sports stars get other people to manage their accounts for them. This practice was exposed ahead of the third Ashes test in 2009. A tweet from Australian opener Phillip Hughes' account revealed that he'd been dropped several hours before the team captains took to the middle for the toss, the point at which team line-ups are normally released. It emerged that Hughes' account was being run by a manager who was in India during the test match and who had miscalculated the time difference. Spencer Owen, the founder of popular YouTube football team Hashtag United, used to run Belgian defender Vincent Kompany's Twitter account.

In any case, if you depended for all quotes on things that players say on Twitter, your coverage would be very bland. Few players tweet anything more imaginative than "great three points for the lads today – fans were amazing" – though Benjamin Mendy of Manchester City is a refreshing exception.

TIP: When it comes to interviews, it's hard to beat a face-to-face conversation. Phone interviews can be helpful – especially if you need facts in a hurry. There's also a place for email interviews – they allow someone the time and space to get their thoughts in order. Social media is great for tracking down interviewees but not the best medium for actually conducting them.

FACEBOOK, INSTAGRAM AND SNAPCHAT

Facebook

As we saw in the last chapter, there is a tendency to move away from hosting content on websites to pushing it out on social media instead. For that reason, many sports clubs concentrate as many resources on their Facebook page than on their official website: there's a bigger audience there. For many people, their entire internet activity is based on Facebook; they only occasionally leave to visit other sites. Result: you can build a far larger audience for your posts on Facebook than through any other mechanism.

This is especially true of video. Ian Singleton, editor of BBC Sport Online says:

> On Facebook there's a very specific eco-system that makes video work, and it's making short form, viral, social video work really well and when it cuts through it's a really good mechanism to help people find it. Individual websites don't have that eco-system set up for discovering content; it's a different space.
>
> There's a real demand on their platform for emotive, compelling, sharable short-form on-demand video. Facebook's algorithm is clever because when you engage with that with likes, comments and shares, it then takes that to a different audience because it takes it to your friends.
>
> (Singleton, 2017)

For sports publications, this presents a challenge. They may be able to reach a larger audience on Facebook but they sell advertising on their own sites. If readers access their content on Facebook, then it's Facebook, not Rugby World or Procycling, that benefits from the advertising revenue.

There is also concern about brand identification. If someone reads a story written by Mail Online's sports team on Facebook, will they remember that the story came from the *Mail*? Or will they think it's just another story they read on Facebook?

What tends to happen, therefore, is that publications try to take advantage of Facebook's massive reach to promote their brand, while keeping much of the best content for their own site. For example, Golf Monthly posted some footage of Tiger Woods practising ahead of his attempt to make a comeback and it accrued an impressive 300,000 views in one month. But the magazine probably wouldn't "give away" an interview with a star like Woods on Facebook.

They also pay close attention to comments on Facebook. It's the world's biggest message board so it makes sense to take notice of what readers are saying about Tiger Woods, Chris Froome or Marcus Smith. Comments can also be a source of great personal stories such as the wedding story, below. People are more likely to put stories about their lives on Facebook than on Twitter or Instagram.

Ian Singleton believes that individual websites and Facebook can co-exist:

> On our website, the best form of video that works is relating to our rights – action, singular compelling moments. People have chosen to come to view this content so we can make it slightly longer. What doesn't work as well is human interest that works really well on Facebook. You've got to know what's a Facebook video, what's the treatment, what's the drivers of that. Where people go wrong sometimes is they conflate everything as social video.
>
> (ibid)

There is some debate about the level of engagement that content on Facebook achieves. Yes, people may *see* your content; but do they really read it or watch it in any detail? The average viewing time for a Facebook video is just ten seconds (Saric, 2017). 96% of goal.com stories on Facebook achieved a "like" (Corcoran, 2017). But this may be a reflection of the fact that it runs a lot of stories about star names, like Lionel Messi or Wayne Rooney.

"It's probable that fans see the name and 'Like' as a casual gesture on the story, rather than engaging any further with the content", according to media analyst Liam Corcoran (ibid).

It's worth taking the time to experiment with what sort of video works best on Facebook. Maybe you've conducted an interview with a well-known athlete and you've put a three-minute version of your interview on YouTube and your own website. That's unlikely to have the viral quality that Ian Singleton refers to. But maybe she said something funny while you were setting up that you caught on camera. Perhaps a 20-second clip of *that* would get more shares?

As well as supporting pre-recorded videos, Facebook also allows you to broadcast using Facebook Live. As we'll see in Chapter 10, this has proved to be a very useful tool for fan channels. We'll also look at how you can use Facebook to transmit live programmes in Chapter 7.

One of the biggest, perhaps *the* biggest, development in sports media in recent years has been Facebook's move into sporting rights. So far, it's streamed baseball, cycling and cricket (launching an audacious, if unsuccessful, bid for the internet rights to the Indian Premier League) but more could follow. If it wanted to enter a rights auction, Facebook could outbid the likes of Sky, BT, ESPN or Star. But it may not have to: Facebook can reach an audience so much larger than any satellite broadcaster that sports governing bodies may be prepared to sell to the social media giant for less than they would to a traditional broadcaster and benefit from increased revenues from advertising and sponsorship.

Instagram

Like WhatsApp, Instagram is owned by Facebook so, if you have a Facebook account, you can automatically set up an Instagram one using the same passwords.

While Twitter started out as a text-based service which gradually came to add pictures and then video, Instagram was set up as an image-sharing site with room for short comments. It was born at a time (2010) when it was relatively easy to upload files of around five megabytes and, so, this was the obvious next step for social media.

> For an event like Wimbledon which is beautiful and that's one of our attributes, Instagram, when it first launched, was amazing because it celebrates beautiful imagery and beautiful photography and we could be very distinctive when you looked through a feed of different content.
> – Alexandra Willis, head of digital communications
> and content at Wimbledon (Willis, 2017)

So, perhaps the first major difference between Twitter and Instagram is that the latter is driven by images. It's a picture-first application. Even today, pictures are cropped on Twitter; because it's trying to show several tweets simultaneously, you normally have to click on a picture to see the whole of it. By contrast, pictures on Instagram fill most of the screen.

Emily Brammeier says that, for Team Sunweb, Instagram comes second in their "hierarchy"; after a race, she'll post first on Twitter, then Instagram, then Facebook:

> You have to go where the people are and then boost that and we've found a following on Instagram. If you look at any of our posts, on Twitter, Facebook or

Instagram, we'll post a gallery and it's always those that get more engagement so it's obvious that cycling fans would most like to see images.

(Brammeier, 2017)

This, in turn, makes Instagram popular with athletes. Search for Serena Williams, Cristiano Ronaldo or Simone Biles and you'll be shown a gallery of artful photography that emphasises their athleticism.

But if that was the only difference, then Instagram probably wouldn't have much application for sports journalism beyond events like Wimbledon, big bike races, the Olympic Games or National Hunt's Cheltenham Festival, which are intrinsically photogenic. It was when Instagram launched its "stories" function (or "posts with multiple photos and videos" as Instagram's own website calls them) that sports journalists and sports organisations really woke up to its potential. It meant that, by grouping a series of images together, you could tell the story of a sporting event from start to finish, show the development of a particular athlete or present a variety of perspectives ahead of a major event.

"It's rough and ready content, it's really easy to produce, it builds during the day, hence why it's called a story", Alexandra Willis (2017) explains.

There's preparation, then there's live, then there's putting everything to bed again – it fits perfectly. We see higher engagement on that kind of content than almost everything else because of the position someone is in during a day at Wimbledon. They're generally at work; they may have BBC Sport in the corner of their desktop but they don't have time to follow it properly.

The third important difference between Instagram and Twitter is that the former is very much adapted for a mobile phone. This may seem a strange observation: people tweet on their phones the whole time. But while Twitter, with its ancillary tools such as TweetDeck, is ideally suited to the journalist based on a laptop in a press box, Instagram favours the informal newsgatherer. "What they've done now with their live platform is allowed us to go behind the scenes and show off bits of Wimbledon that you'd never get to with a broadcast camera", Willis explains. "Because you're doing it with a phone, it fits in a very personal way."

Having said that, in Chapter 8 we're going to see some examples of Instagram posts that clearly have been created using more sophisticated software on laptop or desktop computers. Instagram has become popular for telling stories using data. Creative designers, such as Jean Popescu, have shown imaginative ways of condensing large chunks of statistics-heavy text into engaging info-graphics. "The best thing about Instagram is the story format", he says. "I find this perfect for head-to-head comparisons, comparing two teams head-to-head or two players. You see one player then you swipe right and see the head-to-head" (Popescu, 2017). Like Twitter, Instagram uses hashtags.

Snapchat

Alexandra Willis sums up the difference between Instagram and Snapchat, with which Wimbledon has a content-sharing deal, as follows: "Instagram is the Wimbledon story as told through us, while Snapchat is the Wimbledon story as told through other people who are here" (Willis, 2017).

Snapchat has three, quite distinct, functions. Snap is a private messaging service – like text messages with pictures or videos. Snapchat Discover is a news aggregator, ie a kind of curation service that sources stories which it thinks will interest users from mainstream media houses. In this sense, it is similar to Apple News or AP mobile – and is widely regarded as one of the best in terms of finding the right kind of content for its users. Finally, Snapchat pioneered Stories, ie the ability to group pictures or videos together to tell a coherent story.

A lot of Snapchat's appeal lies in its design, layout and ease of use. Adding text, filters or emojis to an image is very simple. If, for example, you take a picture at a football match and want to add arrows or symbols to make a point about the team's tactics, this can be done in a matter of seconds without using any other software.

The main reason why a lot of media organisations are keen to get content out on Snapchat is that it is seen as the best way of communicating with under-25s, many of whom associate Facebook and Twitter with their parents' generation. Wimbledon explicitly cited this as one of the main reasons for entering into a deal with the company.

However, some sports organisations have left Snapchat after failing to build an audience. "When Snapchat came about I loved it, I thought it was really good", says cycling marketer Emily Brammeier (2017):

> But now Instagram's got a stories feature, there's less need for Snapchat. I tried to launch it at La Course, the race with the biggest audience for women's cycling in the world, and we had numbers in just the hundreds. We even had the Tour De France Twitter feed trying to push it to get more friends but it didn't work so I just don't think there's an audience for Snapchat in cycling.

CASE STUDY: LIONS' TALES

Warren Gatland delivers wedding team talk to remember

British and Irish Lions

Two British and Irish Lions fans got the shock of their lives when head coach Warren Gatland delivered a "team talk" like no other – on their wedding day.
Lionsrugby.com 30 November 2016 (Lions Rugby, 2016)

Lions Tales: Hammersmith and Fulham RFC head Down Under in 2013

British and Irish Lions

. . . the final day of that incredible trip will go down as one of life's great moments . . .

The group were cheered on by a number of former internationals, including the late Ireland great Anthony Foley, before meeting Lions legend Shane Williams at a pre-Test lunch at the Australian club.
Lionsrugby.com 18 January 2017 (Lions Rugby, 2017)

The British and Irish Lions rugby tours take place once every four years so the organisers have to build up interest in each tour before the squad flies out. Livewire Sport came up with an idea called Lions Tales. It's a great example of how social media can be used to find the kind of stories that traditional media outlets probably wouldn't be able to track down. Phil Harlow of Livewire (Harlow, 2017) explains:

> We put out some archive video of the 2013 tour under the heading "On this day". And underneath someone posted a selfie of herself and this bloke at the game. It turned out she met her fiancé at the game. They'd never met before, ended up sitting next to each other and got chatting. At the time she posted the picture, they were three months from getting married. So we did the story for the website but we also got the Lions' coach Warren Gatland to record a message. We used social media to track down the best man and he played the message at their wedding and that got picked up by the local BBC, the local papers, a lot of websites.
>
> So what started out as a selfie on Facebook turned into a much bigger story. But it ended up getting a lot of shares on social media so that's completing the circle really.

The second Lions tale cited here was also poignant – for an entirely different reason. In 2013, Hammersmith and Fulham Rugby Club went out to Australia en masse and arranged a few games against some club sides.

> They randomly bumped into a few professional players who were out on their holidays following the tour and then they met Anthony Foley the Munster coach [and former Ireland star]. He basically bowled up to a rugby club for a few beers and ended up watching the game and giving out the man of the match award afterwards.

By the time Phil Harlow spoke to the players, Foley had died unexpectedly aged just 42 in 2016.

> Just by digging a little bit deeper it turned into a story about Anthony Foley and he turned out to be a really nice guy. A good story's a good story that would work in a paper or a magazine but it was found on social and it works really well on social.

FIGURE 3.1 Munster coach Anthony Foley "bowled up" to one of Hammersmith and Fulham RFC's tour games in Australia and ended up giving out prizes. Image courtesy Andrew Rogan

FIGURE 3.2 Players from Hammersmith and Fulham RFC with Wales and British Lions star Shane Williams (second from right). Image courtesy Andrew Rogan

YOUR TURN

These three exercises are all about using social media to find stories, interviewees and photographs. You can use any social media channel you wish to try to find content.

1   The funny side
    Choose an upcoming sporting event – maybe it's the British Grand Prix at Silverstone, the Grand National or the Winter Olympic Games. It needs to be something fairly high profile – this probably won't work with, say, the Essex Senior Cup final.

    Your editor wants you to do a "quirky" piece finding some human interest angles. Your piece should highlight a story *behind* a sporting event. You need to look for stories like the one above about the couple who met at a Lions game. Or people who missed the event because something unexpected popped up. Or a strange story that took place in the campsite next to the event.

    Write a 250-word story on "the funny side of . . ." for your website. Aim to include plenty of photographs and social media posts.

    TIP: You should send out appeals using social media and search using some of the tactics shown above. When you get in touch with people, don't simply cut and paste their text comments, try to make contact and speak to them. They'll probably tell the story far better over the phone than in 280 characters.

2   Jubilee
    Find a sporting event that took place 20 or 25 years ago. Maybe it's 20 years since a particular football team won the FA Cup or promotion to the Premier League or 25 years since an outsider won the Grand National or a British team collected an unexpected gold medal at the Olympics.

    It's probably best to avoid, for example, Manchester United's 1999 Treble. Any former United player probably gets dozens of interview requests. Better to focus on, say, a non-League side's run in the FA Cup.

    This time, you're going to write a piece which collects participants' recollections of that day. Try to track down as many of the people involved in the event as you can using social media and, politely, ask them if they'd be prepared to be interviewed about what they can remember about the day.

    Once you get hold of one or two participants they may be able to put you in touch with some of the others. Don't forget to ask them for any unusual photographs they may have from the day.

    Aim to write 500 words for this one. It's likely to be more text-based.

3   Different strokes.
    Choose a fairly low-key sporting event where you are likely to get plenty of access. Arrive early so that you can see the competitors warming up or getting ready. Take a series of 6–10 photographs that tell the story of the event. Post your story on Instagram, Snapchat and Twitter.

    Now, try to work out what worked on each of the three media. Which got the most engagement? Did some photographs feel appropriate for one medium and not another? What about captions or emojis – how did they vary across the three platforms?

TOP TIPS: EMILY BRAMMEIER

Emily Brammeier is the social content editor at Sunweb, one of the main cycling teams that competes in the Tour de France and other major races. These are her tips on how to get the most out of social media (Brammeier, 2017).

1   Always look at what you can do to make it better and more exciting. Fresh content is something we are always looking for. We often use other sports to inspire us and give us ideas. We all take ideas from our personal social media feeds. Football utilises social media really well, as does athletics. The England Women's Twitter channel is really cool, especially their GIFs. If we do a GIF, we'll say to our riders "throw your hands in the air like you've just won a race". They did something very different. They did digital ones so, if they'd just scored a goal, it would go "one-nil to us".

2   Update every day; that's really important. In the busy season, it's easy; but in the quiet season, November–December when there's no racing on whatsoever, still post every day to keep them engaged.

3   Use the three main social media channels – Twitter, Instagram and Facebook. Don't try to introduce too many things into it or the quality will drop. So, focus on a few.

4   Build specific interest in your specific team. I like the fact that we only do team-specific updates. If a race is televised, you don't follow a race on Twitter just to see what's going on – you can get that from the TV commentary. If they're following us, they want to know what our riders are doing.

5   Relevant newsworthy content. For example, if the Vuelta (the Tour of Spain) is coming up, it's not a good time to repost videos from the Giro (the Tour of Italy) or the Tour de France. Your content has to be up to date and relevant.

SUMMARY

- The audiences that can be reached through social media far outnumber those who will visit websites, watch television, buy newspapers or magazines or attend sporting events.
- Social media is effective for both finding stories and sending them out to a wide audience.
- Facebook generates the largest followings. Barcelona and Real Madrid have Facebook communities of more than 100 million people. It is particularly effective for sharing video.
- Twitter is the social media channel most suited to breaking news – including, for example, score updates at sports events. Make sure you understand how to use hashtags and lists effectively.
- Both Snapchat and Instagram enable you to create stories but grouping media together – this lends itself effectively to sport. Instagram is also good for combining strong images and data.
- TweetDeck and Hootsuite allow you to monitor different Twitter feeds simultaneously. Hootsuite also allows you to post to several different social media platforms. But you should be aware that content which is suitable for one platform may not work so well on others.

FURTHER READING

Bradshaw, P. (2016) *Snapchat for Journalists*. eBook Victoria (CA): LeanPub
Swasy, A. (2016) *How Journalists Use Twitter*. Lanham: Lexington

REFERENCES

Brammeier, E. (2017) Interview conducted by the author on 16/8/2017
Corcoran, L. (2017) These are the biggest sports sites on Facebook at www.newswhip.com/2015/11/these-are-the-biggest-sports-sites-on-facebook/#jU7R4tlYBxtpOipB.99. Last accessed on 26/11/2017
Coyle, M. (2017) Interview conducted by the author on 18/7/2017
Daily Record (2017) *Celtic coach Kolo Toure embroiled in bizarre Twitter spat with Piers Morgan hours before Betfred Cup Final* at www.dailyrecord.co.uk/sport/football/football-news/celtic-coach-kolo-toure-embroiled-11589991. Last accessed on 03/12/2017
Gibb, S. (2017) Interview conducted by the author on 11/7/2017
Harlow, P. (2017) Interview conducted by the author on 30/6/2017
Hill, S. and Lashmar, P. (2014) *Online Journalism*. London: Sage
James, R. (2017) Interview conducted by the author on 10/7/2017
Lee, D. (2012) *Spoofs, lies and re-tweets: Is it safe to make parodies online?* at www.bbc.co.uk/news/technology-19360332. Last accessed on 03/12/2017
Lions Rugby (2016) *Warren Gatland delivers team talk to remember* at www.lionsrugby.com/2016/11/30/warren-gatland-delivers-wedding-team-talk-to-remember/. Last accessed 29/11/2017
Lions Rugby (2017) *Lions tales: Hammersmith & Fulham RFC head down under in 2013* at www.lionsrugby.com/2017/01/18/lions-tales-hammersmith-fulham-rfc-head-down-under-in-2013/. Last accessed 29/11/2017
Lipschultz, J. (2017) *Social Media Communication* (2nd ed.). New York: Routledge
Newman, N. (2017) *Digital News Report 2017* at www.digitalnewsreport.org/survey/2017/overview-key-findings-2017/. Last accessed 10/11/2017
Parker, S. (2017) Why your business can't ignore Dark Social at https://blog.hootsuite.com/dark-social/. Last accessed on 26/11/2017
Popescu, J. (2017) Interview with the author, 13/10/2017
RESULT Sports (2017) Global digital football benchmarking analysis at http://digitale-sport-medien.com/global-digital-football-benchmarking-analysis-july-2017/. Last accessed 29/11/2017
Saric, M. (2017) The state of Facebook video in the year 2017 at www.business2community.com/facebook/state-facebook-video-year-2017-video-length-time-watched-01834666#vws9xRDmS4MJcT1Z.99. Last accessed on 26/11/2017
Singleton, I. (2017) Interview conducted by the author on 20/10/2017
Willis, A. (2017) Interview conducted by the author on 14/9/2017

MATCH DAY

Reporting a sporting event

CHAPTER 4

Live blogging

The standard advice for writing a report on a sporting event used to be to use a notebook and a laptop. You take notes on paper and then, early in the second half, you start writing your polished report which you aim to file "on the whistle" – or at match point or stumps.

Today reporters are expected to file as the event unfolds. The notes that used to be written in a notepad are now published immediately as a "live blog" or "minute-by-minute" account, either on a blog or on Twitter.

For football or rugby matches, some media companies will expect the same reporter to write both a live blog and a considered report. However, in this book, we are treating them as distinct skills as they require different approaches.

Live blogs may be the work of one person or of a team. A local paper is unlikely to devote more than one reporter to a lower league football match on a Tuesday evening. But the BBC or *Telegraph* may have a team of three or four people working on a big match with one person responsible for the main blog, one for images, one for video etc. In the case of a test match, writers will probably work shifts as it isn't really possible to blog solidly seven hours a day for five days. In fact, even one-day cricket matches are normally covered by more than one person. Athletics events where several contests are taking place simultaneously are also hard to cover without several people. Sometimes, there is a clear handover when a new writer takes over.

The technique has proved so effective that it has been extended to cover sports news that breaks over the course of a day. Several organisations produce day-long live blogs on the last day of European football's transfer windows, the day of the NBA or NFL drafts or during the Olympic or Commonwealth Games.

There is a wide audience for live blogs, from people glancing at their phone during a wedding to those who are watching on television and seeking someone else's perspective on the game. It might even include people in the stadium. Perhaps it's the last day of the football season and goals are going in elsewhere that could keep your team up or send it down.

Some guides to writing blogs say that the key skill is to come across like a mate who's at the game or down the pub with the reader. This is only half true – the secret is to be a well-informed friend. Phil Harlow (see top tips, below) believes that the "old media" format which live blogging most closely resembles is radio commentary. There are certainly similarities: the absence of moving pictures means they are very dependent on the personality of the commentator. They also both depend on the ability to suddenly change gear, switching from trying to fill dull patches of play to dramatic periods of action. A study of live blogging written by a Swedish academic concluded it is "a hybrid of oral commentary and written reports in newspapers" (Burgh, 2011, cited in Hurrey, 2014).

THE BACK STORY: THE EVOLUTION OF THE LIVE BLOG

The *Guardian* claims to have developed the live blog – or minute-by-minute (MBM) as they called it – during the 1998 Football World Cup (Hurrey, 2014). While I can't verify this, I haven't been able to find any earlier examples of the technique being used.

One of the earliest live blogs of a British sporting event was the *Guardian*'s blog of the 1998 FA Cup semi-final between Manchester United and Arsenal (*Guardian*, 1999). It is worth looking this up to see how much the craft has changed. There are no photographs, no videos, no social media posts (this was six years before Facebook launched, eight years before Twitter), no bylines and no comments from experts. To modern readers, it seems to be upside down: new posts are added underneath the previous ones rather than on top of them, as they are today. The writing itself is strictly informative and reads like a set of notes:

> 5 Anelka ambles down the right flank but his advance is easily snuffed out.
> 8 Butt hacked down near Arsenal box. Looks for penalty but referee waves play on.

The *Guardian* suggests you might want to follow the blog "if you can't get to a TV" (ibid). In other words, it saw it as a poor man's alternative to being able to watch on TV. The writer, doubtless, imagined people who were forced to work in office jobs on Saturday afternoon, flicking occasional glances at the blog. No reporter is bylined.

Around the same time, the BBC began a feature called Clockwatch. The 2000 FA Cup final is described as "a minute-by-minute guide" though (BBC, 2000), in fact, some posts are five or more minutes apart. The writing is more colourful but it is still one reporter's perspective.

The 2002 World Cup was held in Japan and South Korea so the time zone proved a boon for live bloggers as games took place while most of the UK population was at work. By this time, publishers had worked out that it made more sense to order posts so that the most recent events appeared at the top of the page. The Guardian continued to innovate with Scott Murray and Rob Smyth becoming recognised masters of the genre. Murray began his account of the 2002 World Cup final with "feel free to email scott.murray@theguardian.com, not that I'm expecting any" (Murray, 2002). In fact, he received plenty – including from Luke Gibbs who couldn't watch the game because "in Springfield, Missouri there isn't enough of an interest in the World Cup for the local [ABC] affiliate to be bothered with carrying the match live". (Contributions from frustrated ex-pats were an almost compulsory feature of early live blogs.) "Isn't Springfield where the Simpsons live?" replied Murray.

To appreciate just how quickly minute-by-minute reporting moved from the pedestrian style of 1999 to being a vehicle for a reporter's personality, read Murray's "over by over" account of the 2003 Cricket World Cup semi-final between

New Zealand and India (Murray, 2003). It begins with a 500-word stream of consciousness rant in capital letters about how unhappy he was to be sitting in front of a boring computer screen writing something his bosses probably wouldn't read.

This was Smyth's reaction to Zinedine Zidane's infamous assault on Marco Materazzi in the 2006 World Cup final (Smyth, 2006):

> it was a disgusting, nasty, blackly comic chestbutt, delivered with a Hitch-cockian suddenness, and it's an unbelievable ending to Zidane's lustrous career. It was a JFK moment and a GBH moment rolled into one oh-my-giddy-aunt moment. And he could still end up lifting the World Cup!

Remember: that was posted within seconds of the incident itself. Leaving aside the hyperbole, Smyth instantly recognises that this incident will overshadow the great Frenchman's legacy.

By now, live blogs were not just being used to cover football but rugby, tennis, cricket and other major sports. Broadcasters set up live blogs to cover each day of the 2004 Olympics. The BBC started running a daily "Sportsday Live" blog. But these blogs were still mainly text-based with the odd picture. Mobile phone data speeds still weren't sufficient to support video and Twitter had yet to take off. So, there was much more opportunity for blog writers to inject their own personality into their work. Murray and Smyth became minor celebrities and published a book of imaginary blogs of famous football matches from the pre-internet era, such as the 1966 and 1970 World Cup finals.

The *Guardian* continues to publish this sort of minute-by-minute report where the writer is the star; it remains a distinctive feature of the organisation's sports coverage. But editors were beginning to think about media convergence. If, say, the BBC had the services of a former England star as an expert analyst on Radio Five Live's coverage of a big football international, then it made sense to repeat his observations on the BBC's live blog of the match. Other organisations started using blogs to promote their own writers, as in this example from Bleacher Report's Dylan MacNamara covering the 2010 NFL draft (MacNamara, 2010):

> 8:44 EST: And the 49ers take Anthony Davis. Described by B/R's Aron Glatzer as a mental wildcard. No one handles those guys better than Mike Singletary. This definitely fills a need for the Niners . . . should be a day one starter at RT.

The same blog also used polls, encouraging readers to choose between the different options open to the sides competing in the draft:

> 8:36 EST: Second poll of the evening is closed. You guys think Earl Thomas will be a better pro than Joe Haden, 65% or 35%. Interesting. Maybe will pan out that way, but Haden will definitely be richer.

At this time, most blogs would have still been read on computer screens, like Scott Murray's gloomy account of the 2003 India–New Zealand game. If you wanted to follow a game live on your phone, then the best option was to look at Twitter – most professional football games had someone in the pressbox live tweeting. Not many media organisations had specialist sports apps; BBC Sport launched its app, for example, early in 2013, responding to a changing audience:

"There is something different about sport", Ian Singleton (2017), head of BBC Sport Online, believes:

> You've got that passion for your team, your clubs and you want to know those live updates, those scores, which make you keep in touch more when you are out and about on your phone. Maybe other people [ie people who aren't sports fans] don't have that need to keep in touch at three o'clock in a supermarket on a Saturday.
>
> People always have their phones with them all the time. I always keep an eye on how people are using their phones in the different places they can do it. It's not a desktop era, it's not 2011 where you sit and your whole focus is on that screen in front of you, that's not how people are consuming media in the main today.

Once media organisations started embedding views of their own expert analysts, it was a small step to embedding the views of other former players and fans, even if they weren't actually officially working for you.

Today, reporters are under pressure to include expert comment from a variety of sources plus photos and videos. One major employer gives reporters a list of requirements which includes "at least 15 tweets" in every live blog. Others expect writers to include links to other stories on their site.

Also, remember that, for a significant section of your audience, your blog will be on a second screen. In other words, they'll be watching the event itself on a television – or even in the ground itself – while occasionally glancing at your blog to see what other people are saying about the game.

For a really good, modern live blog, I'd suggest looking at the way the BBC covers cricket. The Beeb seems to have captured the richness of *Test Match Special*, its long-running radio programme, while eliminating some of its overly whimsical elements. For example, in September 2017, England were on their way to a comfortable victory over the West Indies in a one-day international at Bristol. As the tension ebbed out of the game in front of them, the BBC's expert analysts' thoughts turned to the upcoming tour of Australia. Graeme Swann says he thinks England need to rethink their test batting order and move Joe Root up to number three. Michael Vaughan disagrees – he thinks the Australians will be wanting Root to move up so they can target him sooner with the new ball. Soon texts and tweets are coming in from the audience siding with one or other of the two retired players. So, the blog contains elements of a match report, an opinion piece and a phone-in or message board all in one.

Clearly the BBC benefits from better resources than most of its rivals and is able to draw on expertise from across its platforms. You may not be in such a strong position; but it is worth looking at some of the techniques BBC reporters use.

HOW TO DO IT

Live blogs can be written at the sporting venue, in a media company's office or by a reporter sitting in the comfort of his or her living room watching a television. If a local newspaper reporter is expected to interview players and coaches after the event, then it makes sense to be at the ground. But the big set-piece live blogs that you see on the BBC, for example, are typically done from an office – partly because they need more space than they would get in the average press box.

As you may have to write on your own or as part of a team, it's worth practising both.

You *could* create a live blog by simply creating a new post on your website each time you have something to say. In practice, this approach is likely to prove slow and cumbersome, and the end-result won't look very elegant.

So, you'll need a tool to help you blog. There are plenty of live blogging tools around, including several which are quite expensive. But you don't need to pay for blogging software. There are many free plug-ins that will work with paid-for and some free websites. In my experience, students tend to find 24liveblog quite easy to use – and it claims to work with any type of website.

Most free websites, such as wordpress.com or Blogger, don't allow you to add plug-ins to your website. But you can still set up an account with 24liveblog. This will enable you to produce a minute-by-minute report on *their* site and then embed it on your own site. So, the blog won't actually be on your site, but visitors will be able to view it.

I'd recommend a bit of experimentation with the software before you do your first blog.

TIP: Every sport has its own conventions. Before you try to blog live, make sure you look at how that particular sport is covered by live reporters.

First steps

As with any match report, you'll have done some prior research. You'll know who all the players are and whether there are any important milestones coming up (Carney is on 19 goals so far this season; Broad has taken 349 test wickets etc), whether any players are up against their former clubs, what was said in the pre-match press conference, whether the international coach is here to keep an eye on particular players etc.

It's also worth opening a few webpages. Make sure you have a source of statistics close to hand, particularly if you're covering a data-heavy sport like cricket or baseball. In football, it might be useful to have open the player profile pages of the two competing teams. It's also a good idea to have your *own* website (or your employer's) open so that you can post links to previous pieces you've written about the competitors.

This is where TweetDeck (Chapter 3) really comes into its own as you can follow multiple feeds at the same time. TweetDeck allows you to follow individuals, topics and lists.

The following example shows my TweetDeck on the morning of the final test between the British and Irish Lions and New Zealand. I'm following former player and pundit Matt Dawson and the All Blacks official feed, and I'm doing a search using #NZLvBIL. Lists can be really useful here; you can't really have more than ten columns open at the same time, but you can include 20+ people in a single list. In this case, I didn't actually need to create my own list, I've simply subscribed to a list already created by the Lions' supporters site.

FIGURE 4.1 Screenshot showing TweetDeck account

I actually had a few more columns set up to the right of this screengrab. I followed the Lions' official feed, and I'm interested in what the Kiwis are saying about the game, so I decided to follow a leading New Zealand sports journalist, Marc Hinton. Finally, I made my own private list including the main UK rugby correspondents so I could make sure I didn't miss anything that they spot.

Don't forget other social media outlets. The BBC had been employing former Lions Gareth Edwards and Ugo Monye to provide analysis on Facebook during the tour, while you may find some great pictures taken by fans on Instagram.

You may be able to draw on a supply of pictures. Most sports photographers now have wi-fi-enabled cameras, so they will be constantly transmitting pictures back to their, or their company's, website. If you are working for a big company like the BBC or a national newspaper, you may find they have an arrangement with a picture agency like Getty so that they can use their pictures. If you are working for a club, they'll probably employ someone to file pictures.

Video is more complicated. If you are working in a team, you may be able to delegate someone to turn around important bits of the action. Of course, you can only use this if your company owns the rights to the footage.

There are likely to be more pithy comments on radio than on TV, so if you are part of a team covering the game, you may wish to delegate one person to monitor radio commentary. If you're on your own, you might opt to listen to radio commentary – in headphones if you are at the ground.

OK, now – and this is important – take a comfort break. Make sure you have a full water bottle to hand. You are not going to get many chances to take a break for the next couple of hours.

The sticky

Very few people are likely to follow your blog throughout the whole 90 minutes. They may be at work, or a family wedding, where they can only sneak occasional glances at their phones. So, it is really important to make sure that they can see the score and the key incidents straightaway. This information goes in a short headlines section at the top of the blog. When you add new posts, this section, known as the "sticky" (because it sticks to its place on the page), remains at the top.

In a game like football, where goals are relatively scarce, it is easy to keep the sticky updated:

Arsenal 1 – Chelsea 1
Costa (76') cancels out Sanchez' opener (4')
Chelsea down to 10 men after Moses' sending-off (68')

Other sports require more regular updating – but there are ways of simplifying the task. For example:

Heather Watson v Victoria Azarenka
Watson wins first set 6–3 but Azarenka bounces back to win the second 6–1 and has a break of serve in the third.

This requires less updating than saying ". . . and is leading 2–1 in the third" – as you'd have to change it after every game.

On some live blogs, particularly those written by one person, there is no sticky. In these situations, you need to make sure you begin each post with the score even if it hasn't changed.

Frequency

Most bloggers begin their coverage well before the event starts. In football, for example, it's rare to see a blog that begins after the team sheets have been distributed (normally 45 minutes before kick-off). This gives you an opportunity to set the scene, build in some colour and generally whet your audience's appetite. For a big game, fans may be dipping in and out of different blogs at this point in time before settling on one to follow during the event itself; so it's a good chance to set out your stall.

Despite the name "minute by minute" it is very hard indeed to post an update every minute of sporting event. You might be able to do it, but the quality will undoubtedly suffer.

On the other hand, if you leave five-minute gaps between updates then you'll soon lose your audience. Why would they want to follow a blog that never updates?

Some sports have natural breaks when it makes sense to post – the ends of a game in tennis, for example. Of course, you'll also need to let readers know if a game repeatedly returns to deuce, if there's a long rally or if a player has a set or match point.

Similarly, in cricket, there's an obvious break at the end of each over. But you should also report wickets, appeals and boundaries. ESPN provides ball-by-ball updates, but they are fairly dry. It's hard to find something really interesting to say about each of 600 deliveries.

In golf, update your audience whenever one of the leaders, or players you are following, finishes a hole but, of course, if someone lands the ball on the green with his tee-shot on a par five, that's also probably worth mentioning. Speedway lends itself to a post at the end of each heat.

Free-flowing sports like football, hockey or rugby are more complex. If nothing's happening there's no point in reporting something. On the other hand, if you don't post anything for five minutes, you're going to lose your audience. So, you may need to include references to people in the crowd or the coaches' facial expresses to make sure people know that you are still blogging. *Daily Mail* chief sportswriter Martin Samuel once said that he and his fellow football journalists should be judged on how well they write up 0–0 draws; in the same way, live bloggers often do their best work when nothing very much is happening on the field of play.

In some sports, you can use lulls in activity to promote something that's coming up later. For example, during a quiet phase at the 2017 Paralympics World Championships, the *Daily Telegraph*'s live feed alerted readers to action later on: "In about 20 minutes . . . Hannah Cockroft, Kare Adenegan, and Carly Tait will be on the track" (Davies and Stone, 2017). This was followed by a short preview of the T34 800m final in which the three British athletes were competing.

Don't feel that you always have to post at regular intervals. Fans of a sport like cycling will expect the blog to get busier towards the end of a day as there are more breakaways;

in cricket, wickets will tend to fall more often at the end of an innings when numbers eight to 11 are at the crease than when the openers are batting.

Some live blogs will end on the final whistle, when the reporter will switch to writing a "considered" report (see Chapter 5). Others, particularly of major events, will continue with post-match reaction from expert analysts and interviews with the participants. You may find you are still blogging an hour after the end of the match.

Writing the blog

The speed needed to deliver a minute-by-minute account means there will never be any sub-editors – those wonderful individuals who can pick up mistakes and save reporters from embarrassing errors – for this form of writing. So, you need to make sure that your spelling, punctuation and grammar are all correct. Equally, you need to make sure you have your facts right. So, it's worth taking an extra ten seconds to check and double-check your writing before publishing.

You can use notes or initials, but only if you think your audience would understand them. Most football fans would recognise RB and LB as right back and left back but probably wouldn't immediately realise that HM means holding midfielder. There's no harm in very short posts but it makes sense to mix these up with longer ones. For example, if you said "Stupendous Federer backhand winner" at the end of a particularly good point, you might wish to write a longer description at the next break between games.

Good bloggers learn tricks to develop interaction. If they are writing a blog about football transfers, for example, they'll know that suggesting a particular club are out of their league if they pay £20 million for a new striker or implying that a central defender is not worth £30 million will prompt comeback from readers.

Use bold formatting and capitals to draw attention to the most important facts, eg "**GOAL – Jodie Taylor makes it 2–0 to England**. The Arsenal forward bends a 25-yard freekick round the wall to score her 41st goal for the Lionesses." You may find that the company you are working for has a particular policy on the use of different formats.

Many blogs begin each post with a category heading. For example, you could start each post with "update", "reaction" or "analysis" to signpost what kind of content is being provided. During multi-sport events like the Olympics, bloggers use headings like "result", "confirmed times", "preview" and "field report" to flag up the type of content that follows.

Finally, use hyperlinks to provide more detail about the participants. If you're covering a transfer deadline day or a draft, you could have some pre-prepared stories on your website about some of the players likely to be involved. If you are working for a big company, it may expect you to link to other stories or recent games on its website.

What if you make a mistake? Inevitably there are going to be occasions when you wrongly identify a player in a penalty box melee. If you spot the error quickly, you may be able to delete the post and repost with the correct information. But your audience is likely to appreciate that you are working under pressure. So, another option is to send out another post, correcting your error – ideally with a touch of humour, eg "Jones is 6'7" and Hughes is probably the last man on the pitch to know that it's raining so I won't be making that mistake again."

TIP: When you finish take a look at how other journalists blogged the same game. What did you get that they missed and vice versa?

TOP TIPS: PHIL HARLOW

Phil Harlow has been writing live blogs for 15 years, initially for the BBC and now for the agency Livewire Sports. His credits include a Rugby World Cup final, Premier League clashes and top games at Wimbledon (Harlow, P., 2017).

1 Preparation

This is within your control. Anything you can do beforehand, whether that's researching history or stats, will help you. If you begin your blog armed with a bit of knowledge, then you're going to be able to tell the story much better than if you pitch up blind. For Livewire Sport, the Premier League is an important client and we dedicate some resource on a Friday for someone to come in to go through the Opta Stats and pick out some landmarks that might happen. For rugby, I'll spend an hour before the match getting some quotes and finding some nice social media stuff that the players have done during the week – that sort of stuff.

Anything you can do beforehand will be time well spent because, when you are working under pressure, you don't have time to google "how many goals has Harry Kane scored against Arsenal".

2 Personality

Tone of voice or style is what distinguishes a blog that I'd go out of my way to read. Some sound a bit dull or worthy or corporate; I think that's a danger for blogs by teams themselves or governing bodies. We are conscious of that and try to inject some personality into it so it doesn't sound like the voice of the Premier League press officer.

A lot of my former colleagues at the BBC, like Tom Fordyce and Ben Durrs, really carved out a name for themselves by finding a niche. In the same way as some people have a favourite radio commentator, people will stick with a blog a bit longer if it's written by one of those guys.

So, try to inject a bit of personality, a bit of tone of voice.

3 Speed

Speed is crucial. It's a live blog, so you have to get that information out there. When a goal goes in, before you've written your description, it'll just be a news flash "Arsenal 1, Man United nil" and the goalscorer and the number of minutes and that will be published because that's the key information. Everything else comes after it: your description, the photo of it and any reaction from pundits.

The reason ultimately someone is reading your live blog is to keep up to date with a live sports event. You need to understand when to pick up the pace and when to slacken off slightly.

4 Think beyond the text

Remember photos, videos and other voices, tweets, Instagram posts and so on. You want to try to find as many ways as you can to get it away from being a monologue and very text heavy. Photos and tweets are the most straightforward way of breaking up the text. Every five minutes or so, take a deep breath and ask yourself how many entries there have been since the last photo or tweet.

5 Put the audience first

Put yourself in the place of the reader. Where's the bulk of my audience reading this? Probably on a phone. So that means shorter paragraphs, keep it short and snappy and up to date. Try to make it a one-stop shop; don't make your audience search for information. The first information they'll want is "what's the state of the game?" or "who's won the medals?" so make that information easy to find. If you don't, they'll move on to someone else who does.

YOUR TURN

Practising live blogs at home is relatively easy. You'll need to identify a match that is being shown on television. (I'd strongly advise you not to watch a match on the same laptop that you are going to use to write your blog – that's going to get messy.)

Find a plug-in that you can use a few days in advance and get a feel for how it works. Do your research and get your TweetDeck set up well before the event starts.

At first, concentrate on getting the basics right. Make sure the sticky is regularly updated or, if you aren't using one, that each post begins with a score update. Aim to report each goal within 30 seconds of it going in and to post something at least once every five minutes.

I get my students to practise by creating a blog based around the Premier League transfer deadline day at the end of January. There's normally so much activity going on that you'll need a team of people to cover all the action. You might delegate one person to focus on finding video, another on creating polls, another chasing pundits or former players on the phone etc.

SUMMARY

- Sports fans demand regular updates on games so live blogs, or minute-by-minute accounts, are likely to get more attention than finished match reports.
- Read live blogs to get a feel for different styles you can adopt. Good examples include the BBC, Bleacher Report, the Guardian and Eurosport.
- Get set up well in advance. Have plenty of statistics at your fingertips and make sure you're following relevant people on TweetDeck.
- Aim to post updates at least every five minutes. Even if nothing's happening, people want to know you are still there.
- Try to include a mix of content including pictures, video, social media posts and comments from expert analysts.

FURTHER READING

Bleacher Report Blog (2011) *Live blogging: What It Is and How to Do It* at http://blog.bleacherreport.com/2011/09/27/live-blogging-what-it-is-and-how-to-do-it/
Smyth, R. and Murray, S. (2014) *And Gazza Misses the Final.* London: Constable

REFERENCES

BBC (2000) *Wembley clockwatch* at http://news.bbc.co.uk/1/hi/sport/football/fa_cup/756783.stm
Davies, G. and Stone, S. *Richard Whitehead slams IPC as Sophie Kamlish lays Rio ghost to rest at World Para athletics championships* at www.telegraph.co.uk/world-paraathletics-championships/2017/07/17/london-2017-world-para-athletics-championships-day-4-live/amp/. Last accessed 27/11/2017
Guardian (1999) *Arsenal 1 Man Utd 2* at www.theguardian.com/football/1999/apr/14/newsstory.sport3. Last accessed 27/11/2017
Harlow, P. (2017) Interview conducted by the author on 30/6/2017
Hurrey, A. (2014) *The minute by minute – as it happened* at www.theguardian.com/sport/football-cliches/2014/may/01/-minute-by-minute-as-it-happened-mbm-live. Last accessed 27/11/2017
MacNamara, D. (2010) *NFL draft 2010 live blog* at http://bleacherreport.com/articles/382808-nfl-draft-2010-live-blog-results-pick-by-pick-analysis-and-reaction. Last accessed 27/11/2017
Murray, S. (2002) *Brazil 2 Germany 0* at www.theguardian.com/football/2002/jun/30/minutebyminute.worldcupfootball2002. Last accessed 27/11/2017
Murray, S. (2003) at www.theguardian.com/sport/2003/mar/14/cricketworldcup2003.overbyoverreports. Last accessed 27/11/2017
Singleton, I. (2017) Interview conducted by the author on 20/10/2017
Smyth, R. (2006) *Italy 1–1 France (5–3 pens)* at www.theguardian.com/football/worldcup2006/minbymin/0,,1788448,00.html. Last accessed 27/11/2017

CHAPTER 5

Match reporting

In the last chapter, we looked at the practice of a sports journalist during the 70, 80 or 90 minutes of a match. In this chapter we're going to look at what happens in the 90 minutes following the final whistle.

Live blogs are often written by reporters who are not at the event; this is particularly true if the game is being screened live on television. This chapter is mainly concerned with journalists who are at the game – it would be hard to conduct post-match interviews without being present.

Wiser people than me have been predicting the demise of the match report for some time now. If fans can see video highlights of a game, why would they want to read a report? Young sports fans have short attention spans; they won't read a 600-word report. It's all about "five things we learned" or player ratings nowadays.

This, it seems to me, misses one of the key points of online journalism, namely the freedom it allows journalists to create all sorts of different types of report from the broadly conventional (which we'll be looking at in this chapter) through to illustrated or animated pieces (which we'll encounter in Chapter 7). For example, when non-league Kingstonian FC played Leatherhead who, at the time, were managed by former the former Wigan, Fulham and Hull player-turned reality TV star, match reporter Jamie Cutteridge decided to get creative. His report took the form of a conversation supposedly overheard in a pub; one of the participants has just gotten back from the game:

> "I wasn't there for Ks, mate. That legend Jimmy Bullard is Leatherhead's manager. I just went for a taste of that sweet Bullard banter."

> "Bullard? LEGEND! Remember that time he jumped on those guys? Or the time he pointed at those people like Phil Brown? LEGEND. How was it?" (Cutteridge, 2017).

The entire report continues in the same vein. I'm not proposing every report should take this form, but it's an example of how even a club website can allow a writer a bit of freedom.

CAST STUDY: REPORTING THE CHAMPIONSHIP

Is the traditional match report dead? A little bit of research suggests not. The table below shows how all the games in English football's second tier, the Championship,

TABLE 5.1 Coverage of Championship football, 5 August 2017

	Local press coverage during game	Official club website coverage during game	Local press coverage with 30 minutes of final whistle	Official club website coverage with 30 minutes of final whistle
Bristol City v Barnsley	Bristol Post – live blog	Bristol City website – live text, audio and Twitter; Barnsley website – live text	Bristol Post – 700-word match report; Sheffield Star 350 words	Bristol City 800-word match report; Barnsley 700 words
Burton v Cardiff	Wales Online – live blog; Burton Mail – live blog	Burton website – live text and audio; Cardiff website – live text and audio	Wales Online – 350 words; Burton Mail – 600 words	Burton 750 words; Cardiff 500 words
Fulham v Norwich	Eastern Daily Press – Twitter commentary	Fulham website – live text and audio; Norwich club website – live text and audio	Get West London 300 words; Eastern Daily Press – 900 words; Paddy's Pointers	Norwich City – 600 words; Fulham website 1,000 words
Ipswich v Birmingham	Birmingham Mail – live blog; East Anglian Daily Times – live text	Ipswich website – live text and audio; Birmingham website – live text and audio	Birmingham Mail – match report, East Anglian Daily Times – 450 words	Ipswich website – 550 words; Bristol City 700 words
Preston v Sheffield Wednesday	Lancashire Post – live blog; Sheffield Star – live blog	Preston website – live text and audio; Wednesday website – live text and audio	Lancashire Post – 600 words; Sheffield Star – 600 words.	Preston North End – 600 words; Wednesday – 300 words
QPR v Reading	Get West London – live blog; Get Reading – live blog	QPR website – live blog and audio; Reading website – live text and audio	Get West London – 400 words; Get Reading – 550 words	QPR – 700 word match report; Reading 500-word match report
Sheffield United v Brentford	Sheffield Star – live blog; Get West London – live blog	Sheffield United – live audio and text; Brentford – live audio and text	Sheffield Star – 450 words; Get West London – Player ratings only	Sheffield United 400 words; Brentford 600 words
Wolves v Middlesbrough	Express & Star – Twitter commentary; The Gazette – live blog	Wolves website – live audio (subscribers only)	Express & Star – 750 words; The Gazette – 650 words	Wolves – 350 words; Boro 500 words

that kicked off at 3pm on the first day of the 2017–18 season were covered by the main local papers and by the clubs' websites.

A few explanations:

The table is based on what appeared on the news organisations' and clubs' websites. It may be that some of these organisations tweeted throughout the game, but this not listed unless the tweets appeared on the website.

The table only lists games that kicked off at 3pm on Saturday, 5 August.

A distinction is drawn between a live blog, which conveys just basic information, and live text, which simply reports key developments in the game. Some clubs produced only very basic text updates, but these have still been listed in the table.

The table records what appeared at 5.30pm on 5 August. At that point, only the Eastern Daily Press *had filed a "Five Things" type report (Paddy's Pointers) though several other publications did so soon afterwards.*

Several teams are covered by more than one paper. For example, the Birmingham Mail *and the* Express and Star *cover Wolves. In these cases, I generally monitored the first organisation to appear on a Google search.*

We should be careful about reading too much into this data. Local papers are, inevitably, among the most conservative of media organisations; other sites, such as goal.com, were producing other sorts of content during the games. Nonetheless, there are some important points to note:

- Almost every organisation surveyed produced some kind of live blog, text or Twitter updates during the game. It is clear that this is now an essential skill for would-be sports journalists.
- Equally, almost every organisation also produced a "traditional" match report on the whistle, or soon afterwards. It's interesting to note that many of these are actually longer than the 500–600 words that were typical for local papers during the 20th century. One of the defining characteristics of the internet is that writers are not limited by the amount of space available in the paper. So, reports of 700 words upwards are possible – particularly on club websites where the official record of a match might be expected.
- There is still an expectation that a comprehensive account of every match should be produced and recorded for posterity. Both clubs and local papers feel it's their responsibility to do this.

So, for a typical reporter covering football, rugby or hockey, the hour or so after a game looks something like this:

Match report: Aim to file on, or soon after, the final whistle. (You may be expected to file on Facebook as well, though many content management systems do this automatically.)

Player ratings: Typically, file within five minutes of the match report.

Post-match interviews: These will normally be filed within an hour of the whistle.

Analytical or "considered" report – which often takes the form of "Five Thing we Learned . . .": This generally comes out within an hour of the final whistle.

We'll now look at each of those pieces of writing in turn.

THE MATCH REPORT

Let's take a moment to consider the structure of a match report.

When news reporters tell a story, they don't start at the beginning of a story – "a fire began when a fridge freezer developed a fault" – but rather with the most important facts – "three people died in a fire". The next paragraph contains what the reporter considers the second most important fact – "a neighbour ran into the burning house and managed to rescue two children from the blaze" – and so on. This style of writing is known as the inverted pyramid.

Most important or interesting facts

Less important facts

A match report begins as though it is written in the inverted pyramid style:

Chelsea beat London rivals
Tottenham 2–1.

Marcus Alonso got both goals. He opened
the scoring midway through the first half then,
after Spurs equalised through an own goal,
got the winner two minutes from time.

It was Spurs' seventh defeat in 10 games while playing at
their temporary home of Wembley.

When you're writing your report, think about the questions that a friend, who was not at the game, would ask you:

What was the score in today's game?
Chelsea beat London rivals Tottenham 2–1.
Who scored?
Marcus Alonso scored both goals. He opened the scoring midway through the first half then, after Spurs equalised through an own goal, got the winner two minutes from time.

This move to Wembley isn't going well for Spurs is it?
It was Spurs' seventh defeat in ten games while playing at their temporary home of Wembley.
Why did they lose?
Hazard and Pedro controlled the midfield making it hard for Tottenham to play their normal passing game.

We could carry on like this for another 450 words, but it would soon become very complicated. You'd find yourself referring to a save in stoppage time at the end of the game, then jump backwards to a yellow card handed out in the first half, then forward to a shot that went wide just after the interval. A report that moved around like this would be confusing for readers. So, at some point, we're going to have to switch to reporting the game in the order things happened.

So, a classic 400-word match report is a hybrid. It begins in the style of the inverted pyramid but then settles down to a more traditional blow-by-blow account of game.

Introduction, inverted pyramid (100 words, approx)

Main body of the story, chronological order (300 words, approx)

Most match reports that you read online follow this structure, although on national websites such as the BBC's there tends to be more analysis before the report switches to a chronological approach, while less attention is paid to the precise details of the game. This is particularly true if the game was shown on television as the writer may suspect that much of the audience will have already seen the game.

What needs to go into your introductory section?

There is no definitive list but one might normally expect to see:

- the result,
- the score,
- the impact on each of the teams (extends Saracens' lead at the top of the table, leaves Newcastle four points from safety),
- the scorers (and the order in which the goals came),
- sendings-off,
- suspensions and injuries,
- landmarks (100th goal, 100th catch, 20th try of the season),
- some attempt to explain how team A won or why team B lost (though this will be addressed in more detail later in the "considered" report).

You should, in passing, refer to *where* the game is being played – "United's poor run of home form continued" – and the *competition* – "Munster have reached the quarter finals of the European Cup for the third year running". You wouldn't normally refer to when the game is because it's assumed that the report is being filed on the final whistle.

It may also include some comments from players or coaches. The trick is to remember to ask yourself: "what would someone who didn't see the game want to know?"

When you switch from your introduction into the main body of the report (ie when you go from the triangle at the top into the rectangle), this should normally be clearly indicated. Reporters tend to use a very obvious phrase to show that they are moving into an account of the game:

> "From the kick-off, Spurs looked the more likely to score"
> "West Indies won the toss and chose to bat"
> "Surbiton came close to scoring in the first minute".

This sort of phrase lets the reader know that the game is now being reported in the order in which things happened.

Similarly, you should also clearly indicate half time:

> "Harlequins' dominance increased leading up to half-time and they ran in two more tries before the interval"
> "With the final kick of the first half, Austin fired narrowly wide".

If you have been writing a live blog or been live tweeting the game, then it is a relatively straightforward process to transfer the most significant incidents from your blog and paste them into your match report, though you may need to flesh them out a bit so you can go into more detail about each move. As a general rule of thumb, aim to include at least four incidents from each half – though, clearly, if the game ends 5–4 with two sendings-off and all the goals coming in the second half, you'll need to include more.

Organisations like the *Mail*, the *Telegraph* or the *Guardian* don't expect their big-name reporters to file minute-by-minute accounts. This gives them time to write more creative reports of the game itself. An effective approach is to focus on two or three players. Maybe, one particular player caught your eye? Or there's a youngster who is being considered for international selection? Perhaps an established player is under fire with pundits questioning his places in the side?

The more information you can include, the richer your writing is likely to be. A few years ago, I was covering a fairly average game in the Championship between Colchester United and Coventry City which ended in a 2–1 win for the home side. The second half was fairly uneventful so, with ten minutes to go, I looked over my report. It was fairly straightforward: a list of the goals and some of the near misses. I decided to rework it, focusing on the four strikers: Freddie Sears and Clinton Morrison of Colchester and Callum Wilson and Chuba Akpom of Coventry. Sears scored the first goal and created the second. Having described both of these, the report changes tack and provides a bit of background on some of the key players:

> Three years ago, Sears left West Ham for the Ricoh Arena in an attempt to reignite his Premier League career. Currently, Chuba Akpom is hoping that a loan spell at Coventry could launch his; the 18-year-old's form for Arsenal's under 21 side has led to England under 19 honours.
>
> Akpom's first significant contribution nearly pulled a goal back – a measured low shot that Sam Walker saw late and did well to parry. But for much of the first half, he gave the impression of not being quite sure what he was doing in League One. At one point, he attempted an exaggerated step-over,

dragging the ball through 270 degrees behind his back – and promptly lost control.

Akpom was just two and a half years old when his opposite number Clinton Morrison made his Premier League debut. Morrison's game these days seems to consist mainly of wildly over-dramatic gestures, directed at either the referee or his team-mates. A career on stage awaits when the 35-year-old finally hangs up his well-worn boots.

It may seem odd to focus on what players are thinking – after all you're not a mind reader. But, if you read a lot of match reports, you'll notice it's quite a common technique:

> Lingard perhaps broke forward with only thoughts of relieving territorial pressure in his mind. But as he entered Watford's defensive zone and players started to back away from him, it was obvious that Lingard realised the opportunity to do so much more beckoned.
>
> – Ian Ladyman (2017) for MailOnline

> He's been patient, occasionally aggressive, and – Warner being Warner – he will be enjoying the thought that he has landed some psychological blows on top of the more obvious.
>
> – Alan Tyers (2017) for *Telegraph* Sport

In attempting to enter the players' minds, these reports go beyond what even television pictures can achieve.

Some general tips for writing match reports:

- Stick to the past tense. Don't be tempted into writing as though you're commentating on the radio: "Twenty-three minutes in, Vardy is tripped just outside the area." (When you're blogging, this is less important.)
- Use the active voice. "Ireland won a penalty . . ." not "a penalty was won by the Irish".
- Sport is about players – describe what they do, not what the game does. "Two players were sent off . . ." not "the game saw two sendings-off" (a former colleague of mine used to say "the game can't see – it's got no eyes").
- Try to ensure your report flows. Don't give your reader an excuse to break away from your report. Note, in the example above how the first three paragraphs link to each other.
- Vary your pace and style. A simple list of one event after the other soon becomes very repetitive. Try to mix in a bit of background information and include long and short sentences.
- Try to include details that the audience watching on television are not privy to. Refer to the atmosphere in the ground, fans' chants and reactions to particular players or the referee or even comments from fellow journalists. This is taken from a famous report written by Hugh McIlvanney. George Best had just beaten "three or four challengers" before scoring, seemingly effortlessly from the tightest of angles:

"What was the time of that goal?" asked a young reporter in the Manchester United press box. "Never mind the time, son," said an older voice beside him. "Just write down the date."

(McIlvanney, cited in Giller, 2011)

PLAYER RATINGS

I first came across player ratings when reading an Italian newspaper. They have been a normal part of Italian sports journalism for 40 years and have, more recently, crossed to other countries. Many reporters admit to not liking them. "National reporters can throw in whatever marks they like," sighs Andy Naylor (2017) of the Brighton Argus:

> I've got to see these guys week-in, week-out. It is one of the things you'll get called on by players. You could say anything in the report but if you give them a five you'll get a little mention. They'll ask you why you only gave them a six and I'll say "a six? I put nine – they must have published it upside down."

Inevitably, you won't be paying attention to all 22 players on the pitch, or 28 including substitutes. The quietly efficient defender probably won't catch your eye in the way creative players will. Even if you have to assess your side's performances only it can still be challenging. And how much weight should you give to the quality of the opposition? The difficulty is compounded by the short amount of time you'll have to file your ratings – typically ten minutes at most. So, it's important not to over-think your assessments or to assume that they are the definitive judgement on each player's performance.

The quickest way to write player ratings is to choose an "average" score that, initially, you assign to *all* the players. Then you can decide whether or not to move the mark up or down for individuals who have had notably good or bad games:

> "You start off with some kind of benchmark. I use six – that means he's had an alright game", explains Andy Naylor. You start off from that point and you either work up or down depending on how you think that individual has done. Inevitably key moments will stick in your mind. For a striker, for example, if he's scored or missed a chance. Some things you'll never know – was a player assigned to pick someone up at a corner? You'll never know that.

(ibid)

If you look at marks on local paper websites, you'll see that most reporters stick to 5–7, with, perhaps, the star player being awarded an eight. "The lowest mark I can ever recall giving is a four", Naylor admits (ibid). This reflects a degree of conservatism but it's also pragmatic. If you regularly award nines, then you'll soon come across a better performance that warrants a ten and then you'll have no room left to go higher.

You'll also need to include a sentence or two explaining why you assigned that particular mark. It's useful to have a sheet of paper on which you write all the players' names down the left-hand side. Whenever they do something notable make a short note so that you have something to refer to when you are writing your ratings.

THE "CONSIDERED" OR "FIVE THINGS WE LEARNED"

Radio reporters are long accustomed to having to file a *considered* report, typically about an hour after the end of the game. While the match report was mainly focused on answering the question *what happened*, the considered addressed *how* the match was won, *why* a side is struggling and *what* is likely to happen next.

The *considered* is still used in radio and has crossed into online writing. But the most common way of analysing a match is a piece titled *Five Things We Learned From* . . . This encourages the writer to identify several features of the game rather than becoming overly embroiled in just one. It's also a good way of encouraging comments (fans are bound to disagree with at least one of the five things) and shares.

The Independent's Five Things report of Liverpool's Champions League win over Hoffenheim in August 2017, written by Jack Austin (2017) is very typical:

- Liverpool still have defensive frailties and seem to be opting for a philosophy that relies on outscoring their opponents.
- Given their strength up front and weakness at the back, it might be good business to allow Barcelona to buy their star forward Philippe Coutinho to free up funds to reinforce the defence.
- Emre Can is the best goalscoring midfielder Liverpool have had since Steven Gerrard's retirement.
- There is a still an amazing atmosphere at Anfield for European matches.
- Liverpool could face a big name like Real Madrid or Bayern Munich in the group stages (the draw was due to take place shortly).

The first point is a general observation about the game; the second follows on from this and reflects the fact that the transfer window is due to shut in a few weeks' time; the third singles out an individual player's contribution (with a reference to one of the club's past greats); the fourth praises the fans' contribution; the fifth throws forward to upcoming hurdles in the competition.

Common characteristics of Five Things reports include:

- analysis of the performance of a new signing or a youngster recently promoted from the club's academy;
- analysis of the manager's tactics and how he has approached the game differently to the way his predecessor would have;
- *they really miss* . . . a player who is currently injured or recently sold and not adequately replaced; a variant on this is the post that says the team can cope perfectly well without the recently departed star player;
- *they could really do with* . . . a player who might be available to buy (this is particularly popular if the transfer window is open, or is about to be);
- . . . *is not really a centre half* – a comment on a player who is being tried in a new position;
- *the unsung hero* – praise for a reliable, unshowy player;
- *the even less-sung hero* – praise for a member of the coaching staff because defending at set pieces has improved;

- *x always plays well against United* – especially if x is a former United player;
- *this referee never gives United many decisions* – or some other comment on the officials;
- *the defence did well today, but are they good enough to deal with City next week?* – a look forward to upcoming fixtures.

If you are stuck for ideas, it's always helpful to return to this list of common themes. Writing analysis can be slightly formulaic; fans choose to read these pieces because they are interested in your views of the new signing's performance and want to know if they reflects their own views. It makes sense to decide *before* the game what the five things you plan to talk about are going to be. If the game proves to be eventful, you can always change them but, at least you'll have something to fall back on.

Nonetheless, when you cover the same team week in, week out, it can be hard to find new things to say. The team you cover has defensive shortcomings; there are only so many times you can say that. And besides, you won't be telling your readers anything they don't know already as the team's conceded 20 goals in the first five games of the season.

One way to address this is to identify key moments or turning points:

> the angry way Marcel Franke reacted to Jamie Mackie's high boot towards the end of the first half was a significant sign. The verbals that followed from the German, after emergency action to hard clear was the first real sign of aggression from [the] centre back.
>> – Paddy Davitt (2017) of the Eastern Daily Press identifies the moment Norwich's Marcel Franke comes to life in their draw against Fulham

> It was [Kirby's] superb dummy that took two defenders out, setting Taylor free to score her first, before winning the free-kick wide on the left that led to England's second.
>> – FourFourTwo.com's Kieran Theivam discusses the decision to select Fran Kirby, who was returning from injury, for England's Euro 2017 clash with Scotland

Another is to make use of statistics:

> Palace had ten corners . . . and failed to score from any of them. Indeed Palace were average from dead-ball situations and were not ranked inside the top five last season.
>> – Nick Kituno (2017), News Shopper

> In his first test in New Zealand, the 23-year-old [Sean McMahon] had 13 carries for 31 metres, made 11 tackles and won a turnover as well.
>> – Beth Newman (2017), rugby.com.au

Try to identify aspects of the game that may not be immediately obvious to your audience:

The fact that [Sam Warburton] sticks his body in places that few others are prepared to means that most of what he achieves on the field remains unseen . . . To appreciate what Warburton does, don't look at him, rather look at effect on players around him.

– Paul Williams (2017), Rugby World

YOUR TURN

Choose a different game and repeat the exercise described in Chapter 4. This time, however, bear in mind that you are going to have to write a 350-word match report at the end of the game.

As you blog about the game, copy and paste the most important posts into a separate word document. Early in the second half, start thinking about what your top line is going to be and which incidents need to be mentioned in the opening – inverted pyramid – section of your report. Remember you still need to keep blogging about the actual game as well.

Initially, allow yourself 20 minutes after the final whistle to produce your report. Make sure it is factually accurate and grammatically correct. You can start reducing this time as you become more confident.

If you are following a game on television and the managers or players are interviewed straight afterwards, try to incorporate one or two quotes in your opening section.

Aim to post player ratings within ten minutes of filing your match report and an analytical report 30 minutes after that.

SUMMARY

- There's still a demand for traditional 400-word match reports.
- In the hour after the final whistle, reporters will tend to file a match report, player ratings and a "five things we learned from . . ." piece.
- A match report begins with a selection of headline facts about a game – the score, the scorers, the effect the result will have etc – and then moves into a chronological account of a game.
- Imagine someone is watching a TV feed of this game. Aim to provide something that they can't simply see with their eyes – eg background, statistics or an insight into the players' mindsets.
- For a "five things we learned" feature, prepare a list of topics that you know you can always come back to if you're stuck. These might include performance of debutants, performance by former players returning to previous clubs and how each team will perform in their next fixtures.

REFERENCES

Austin, J. (2017) *Five things we learned as Liverpool forgo defending in favour of attack to reach the Champions League Group Stage* at www.independent.co.uk/sport/football/european/liverpool-vs-hoffenheim-emre-can-mohamed-salah-goal-highlights-five-things-we-learned-a7909381.html. Last accessed 29/11/2017

Cutteridge, J. (2017) *Leatherhead Match Report* at www.kingstonian.com/news/leatherhead-match-report-1742477.html. Last accessed 30/3/2018

Davitt, P. (2017) *Paddy's pointers: Five observations from Norwich City's 2–0 championship win against QPR* at www.pinkun.com/norwich-city/paddy-s-pointers-five-observations-from-norwich-city-s-2-0-championship-win-against-qpr-1–5152125. Last accessed 29/11/2017

Giller, N. (2011) *Hugh McIlvanney remains the matchless master* at www.sportsjournalists.co.uk/the-giller-memorandum/hugh-mcilvanney-remains-the-matchless-master/. Last accessed 29/11/2017

Kituno, N. (2017) *Five things we learned from Crystal Palace 2 Ipswich 1* at www.newsshopper.co.uk/sport/palace/15490112.Five_things_we_learned_from_Crystal_Palace_2_Ipswich_1/. Last accessed 29/11/2017

Ladyman, I. (2017) *Watford 2–4 Manchester United* at www.dailymail.co.uk/sport/football/article-5126527/Watford-2-4-Manchester-United-Jesse-Lingard-settles-it.html#ixzz4zpfB5ORs. Last accessed 29/11/2017

Naylor, A. (2017) Interview conducted by the author on 16/8/2017

Newman, B. (2017) *All Blacks v Wallabies; Five things we learned* at www.rugby.com.au/news/2017/08/26/10/25/all-blacks-wallabies-dunedin-bledisloe-five-things. Last accessed 29/11/2017

Theivam, K. (2017) Women's Euro 2017: 5 things we learned from England 6–0 Scotland at www.fourfourtwo.com/features/womens-euro-2017-5-things-we-learned-england-6-0-scotland#Vg2WQJJpSsOJLMGv.99. Last accessed 29/11/2017

Tyers, A. (2017) *Ashes 2017: England out for 195, David Warner and Cameron Bancroft glide to brink of Brisbane victory* at www.telegraph.co.uk/cricket/2017/11/25/ashes-2017-australia-vs-england-first-test-day-four-live-score/. Last accessed 29/11/2017

Williams, P. (2017) *Lions second test: Five things we learnt* at www.rugbyworld.com/countries/england-countries/79252-79252. Last accessed 29/11/2017

NEW TECHNIQUES

CHAPTER 6

Attracting an audience

If you set up your own website in Chapter 2 and have populated it with interesting content, you may now be wondering how to get people to actually see it. If you're writing for someone else's site, they'll certainly want you to demonstrate some understanding of how to boost its popularity. This chapter looks at some of the devices that media organisations and individuals can use to attract and keep an audience.

SEARCH ENGINE OPTIMISATION AND STICKINESS

Journalistic websites need visitors to survive. So, two of the key aims of the site are to lure audiences to the site and to keep them there once they arrive.

You have probably heard of the term "search engine optimisation" or SEO. Essentially it means ways of getting your story to appear high up on the page when people search using Google. Most people stumble on a website through searching on Google or via social media. Very few people now type in a web address.

In the 1990s, several companies had their own search engines, such as Yahoo!, AOL, Dogpile and Ask Jeeves. Most of these still exist today, but Google is by far and away the market leader with Microsoft's Bing a distant second.

The reason why Google came out on top was that it was better at:

- finding relevant content that addressed the searcher's needs. If I typed in "Gilchrist centuries" some search engines might have taken me to a genealogy site telling me a about the Gilchrist family who lived in western Scotland in the 17th and 18th centuries. The more intuitive Google seemed to know that I was interested in the Australian cricketer Adam Gilchrist.
- finding more trustworthy and up-to-date information. There'd be no point finding a site that said Adam Gilchrist had scored five fewer centuries than he actually scored.
- finding the information presented in a clear and easily accessible format. No one wants to spend ten minutes reading through dense text to find out how many centuries Adam Gilchrist scored.

In order to remain on top, Google continues to refine its search engine, regularly changing the algorithms that determine what a particular search will generate and to keep one step ahead of web managers who are trying to trick Google into over-promoting their sites. Since 2000 it's launched three significant updates: Panda, which is designed to identify good quality content; Penguin, which penalises sites that try to manipulate the rankings; and Hummingbird, which is designed to better understand more "conversational" searches (as opposed to those which are simply a list of search terms).

Major media houses employ large teams to try to understand Google's algorithms. It's very hard for individuals to compete with them. But there are a few basic principles:

1   Make sure you include the terms people are likely to search for in your headline and opening paragraphs. This is part of reason for the effectiveness of Mail Online's summary paragraphs that we looked at in Chapter 1. The bullet point style enables them to cram in a lot of possible search terms.
2   The more visits a site receives, the higher it'll tend to rank on Google.
3   The more links there are to a site, the higher it'll tend to rank. This is where Panda comes in: if, say, the BBC includes a link to a particular site, that may lead to it being regarded as good quality and push it up the rankings. But Penguin's job is to weed out sites that have managed to build a network of links from spurious sources.
4   Google penalises sites that duplicate a lot of content that can be found elsewhere. Avoid copying and pasting large chunks of content from other sites.
5   Google penalises sites that suffer malware attacks. If a site becomes infected, Google will remove it altogether from search lists and it can be very hard to rebuild your ranking.
6   Google rewards regular posting.

More sophisticated websites, such as wordpress.org sites, will allow you to add a Search Engine Optimisation tool, such as Yoast or AllInOneSEO. These will give you tips on refining your headlines and opening paragraphs to make them more SEO-friendly. But they should not be blindly followed. For example, they may tell you to reduce the number of links you set up to other sites. That's probably good advice if you run a site designed to sell jeans, but, in journalism, linking to your sources is good practice (see below).

Most employers will expect staff to be aware of SEO and to have a basic understanding of it. I would advise young writers to concentrate on producing the best possible content and not being overly obsessed with SEO. There is a concern that too much focus on SEO has led some publications to concentrate overly on stories about big names, even when the stories themselves are fairly trivial.

"What can compromise journalism is when you have a situation such as we have in England where Manchester City are clear at the top of the table but they don't get that many hits," explains freelance football writer Jonathan Wilson.

> The sports editor of a national paper said to me "Manchester City are kryptonite [the drug that drained the strength from Superman]; they don't get eyeballs". So papers are more likely to run a story about Manchester United than Manchester City even if City are playing the better football.
>
> (Wilson, 2017)

Perversely, while big organisations try to pack their stories with key words like Arsenal, Chelsea, Messi or Barcelona, for the novice setting up their own website it is unlikely to help. If you write a story about Arsenal, you are really going to struggle to push it up the rankings, ahead of the club's official content, stories on mainstream media sites and well-established fan sites. On the other hand, if you write about Badshot Lea Football Club, you face much less competition and it could be possible to get your site on the first page of Google rankings.

Once they have lured readers to their websites, how do journalists encourage them to stay there?

"There are all sorts of ways and means of trying to keep people interested and then clicking on other stories," says Jim Mansell (2017) of Mail Online Sport. For example, most websites have a block of stories in a column, known as a "side bar", on the right-hand side of the web page. As the reader begins to tire of the story that actually led them to the site in the first place, he or she will, hopefully, be tempted to click on something else. There may be links to other stories elsewhere on the page, on the left, for example, or at the bottom.

Another tactic websites use is to include hyperlinks within a story. Hyperlinks are words which, when clicked, will take you to another web page; they are normally blue and underlined so they are obvious to the reader. So, for example, in a *Guardian* story about tennis star Maria Sharapova, the word "Sharapova" itself is blue (*Guardian*, 2017). If you click, it'll take you to an index of all the *Guardian*'s stories about the five-time grand slam champion.

A website that encourages readers to hang around to read more than one story is referred to as "sticky". You'll find a lot of articles online that advise you how to make your site more sticky. Most of these focus on the design of the site: a cleanly laid out site with a clear navigational structure which makes content easy to find should pay benefits. Good use of pictures will also help.

You should be able to find data about how many visitors you have and how long they stick around by using your site's dashboard. It's good practice to be aware of these numbers and to be thinking about how you can improve them.

MORE ABOUT HYPERLINKS

As we've seen, one purpose of hyperlinks is to keep readers on your site. If you use an SEO plugin it will probably advise you not to link to *external* sites. However, this advice is only partly true for journalism.

Good journalists should be as transparent as they can about their sources. So, if you have taken your figures for Joe Root's batting average from CricInfo, then it's good practice to include a link to that source. Collaboration between journalists is healthy and helps generate a conversation. So, don't feel you should only include hyperlinks to other parts of your own site.

Be careful, however, about overuse of hyperlinks for two reasons:

- You do want readers to stay on your site. So, hyperlinks should be used judiciously.
- Some organisations are putting up paywalls. It's very frustrating to follow a link to what appears to be an interesting story, only to find you can't read it without taking out a subscription to that publication.
- Your text will start looking messy if every third word is underlined.

YOUR TURN

Perhaps the best way to understand SEO is to look at which outlets tend to get their stories to the top of a Google search.

For this exercise, it's probably best to disable, or at least ignore, auto-complete.

Choose three leading sports stories: perhaps a match that took place yesterday evening, a big race meeting that's coming up in the next few days and, maybe, a transfer rumour that's doing the rounds. Now, search for these stories using Google News (it's best to select news because otherwise you're likely to be taken to official club sites).

For each story, print out the top three search results and then pick two more from much lower down the rankings. Study the headlines and the first two paragraphs.

Questions:

- What have the writers of the "successful" posts done to push their versions of these stories up the rankings?
- Can you spot any mistakes that those lower down are making? Are they missing any opportunities?
- Why do some companies come higher on one story but lower on another? Is the *Sun* ahead of the *Mail* on a racing story but behind it on a rugby one? Why?

OK. Now, look for the stories again but this time change your search terms. So, if, first time round, you searched for "Messi leave Barcelona", this time try "Messi transfer rumour". How does it alter the search results?

Finally, compare your findings with a friend or classmate. Did you get the same results? Google remembers your search history, so you may find you generate different lists.

INTERACTIVITY: QUIZZES, GAMES AND POLLS

Remember, many, perhaps a majority, of your readers are going to be using their phones to visit your site. Smartphones are designed to encourage interactivity; they are – to use a quasi-academic phrase – "lean forward media". So, if you want to keep people on your site, you need to give them things to do.

WordPress – and many of the other platforms we looked at in Chapter 2 – make it quite simple to set up a poll on your site. While answering a question won't hold your visitors' attention for very long, they might return, later in the day, to see what results the poll is generating.

If you work for a company that employs people with sophisticated coding and design skills, you may be able to come up with an idea for an interactive graphic. We'll be looking at these in more detail in Chapter 8.

One of the most popular devices for holding onto readers is a quiz. I was part of the first generation of British school children to be taught computing and still remember how, aged 12, I created a quiz on the ZX81, a very early form of personal computer, for a school open day. The reason why I mention that is to make the point that quizzes, particularly multiple-choice ones, are quite easy to create. The content, however, needs a bit of careful thought.

TOP TIPS: WHAT MAKES A GOOD QUIZ?

Ben Milne is an online journalist who used to write the BBC's weekly news quiz.

1   What's the theme? Is it the news of the past seven days, or is it about a specific subject? Just as you need a top line for an article, you need a top line for the quiz.

2   Think of it as a short feature with facts, and small rewards (getting the answer right) for the reader. Go a little bit further than simply asking the questions. "When was the Battle of Hastings?" is a perfectly good question but a bit boring. (The answer's boring too.) Have a conversation with the person doing the quiz: "1066 is one of the most famous dates in English history – but how did King Harold supposedly meet his end?" is more interesting.

3   With a few exceptions, most online quizzes are multiple-choice affairs. So, think about how you're going to present this. Don't give one obviously correct answer and two obviously false ones, eg a) He was beheaded by a Jedi lightsaber; b) he was gored to death by a crocodile; c) he was shot in the eye by an arrow. Make the false ones as plausible as possible eg a) He fell upon his own sword rather than surrender; b) he was trampled to death by his own horse; c) he was shot in the eye by an arrow.

4   Be sure you know the correct answer. This sounds obvious but isn't. Note that I wrote "how did King Harold supposedly meet his end?". This is in case your quiz is read by a keen scholar of Norman history who points out that we don't actually know how King Harold died. Always couch your terms in case there's a doubt and have a source you can refer back to in case of dispute (the same goes if you're setting a pub quiz). In this case you can reply, "Ah yes, but the story of the arrow in the eye is a tradition dating back at least to the 12th century Italian historian Amato di Montecassino."

5   Go the extra mile when giving the answer. So maybe add some extra value in there. Instead of "Correct – he died with an arrow in his eye" add a little more detail. "Correct – although there's little evidence that it actually occurred, the story of the arrow in Harold's eye became one of the most famous things about the doomed Saxon king. The story is thought to have originated among historians in the century after his death." An answer usually begs another question and it's quite good to be able to answer that as well (Milne, 2017).

Let's apply Milne's advice to the world of sport.

In September 2016, there was a vacancy for the role of head coach for the England football team. (Isn't there always?) Some pundits were proposing Arsenal boss Arsene Wenger for the role. BBC Sport ran a poll entitled "Can you name these Wenger signings?" (BBC, 2016).

Quizzes which require you to identify players from previous eras are particularly popular – particularly on local newspaper and even fan-run websites. Let's look at how this quiz meets the criteria outlined above.

1   The theme here is Wenger's ability to spot talent. This is an important talking point because, if he were to become England boss, he'd need to seek out new stars for the national side.

2   This piece could have been conceived as an opinion piece: Is Wenger a good talent spotter? It makes the point that Wenger has actually signed a lot of players who fell by the wayside and, a few years later, are barely recognisable. So, yes, this works a bit like a feature.

3   As with the example of King Harold, the answers were all reasonably realistic. For example, the player pictured in question six is wearing large gloves and a yellow shirt and, so, is clearly a goalkeeper (Rami Shaaban). So the other two alternative answers are both goalkeepers – the quiz-setter hasn't thrown a centre forward in.

4   Probably less of an issue for sports quizzes than news ones, but it is pretty embarrassing if you incorrectly identify a player.

5   Each answer tells readers not simply *who* the player is but also provides a bit of added information. For example: "After joining the club as a teenager, [Philippe] Senderos played more than 100 times but was rarely a nailed-on starter. Since leaving, he's become a bit of a journeyman – most recently getting sent off on his Rangers debut in the Old Firm derby." Having said that – the added value for Rami Shaaban is slightly less informative: "He signed in 2002, two years after Ricky Martin's She Bangs hit the charts. We assume there was a chant . . ."

APPS AND EMAIL NEWSLETTERS

Using a web browser like Safari or Chrome on a mobile phone is not always easy. How many people can be bothered to use their thumbs to type in "Manchester United v Borussia Dortmund Telegraph report"? And, even if they can, will the content be presented in a phone-friendly way when you get to it?

As a result, leading media organisations have developed "apps", which are special programmes designed to enable you to quickly access content from a specific site without going through a browser. The word app is short for both application and Apple, the company that coined the phrase.

Like websites, apps need to be developed and managed. Most apps require updates several times a year to adapt to new types of phone or tablet. For this reason, they are probably, for now, not a realistic proposition for individuals or small companies. This may change.

One alternative to developing an app is to send out an email newsletter. Most people who work in an office-based job will check their emails several times a day, so this is a good way of capturing their attention. Email newsletters are normally free. You become a subscriber simply by signing up online and, of course, providing an email address. By law, they also have to be easy to unsubscribe from – normally just a single click at the bottom of the letter.

Research published in 2017 (Pew, 2017) suggests that a newsletter may be more valuable than an app. The respected Pew Research centre studied 36 new media companies (ie ones that originated online and not through an existing newspaper or broadcaster) and found that while fewer than two-thirds of them had apps, all but one sent out newsletters. The list included sports specialists such as Bleacher Report, 247 Sport, Deadspin and SB Nation, as well as mainstream news providers which also cover sport as part of a wider mix.

Most of these organisations enable you to sign up for different newsletters for different sports. That makes sense. If you're a big baseball fan, you don't want your inbox clogged up with content about the NFL during the World Series. One of the risks associated with email newsletters is that you actually damage your brand by sending out spam that readers don't want. Because people have to actively opt *in* to your emails, you know you are addressing a knowledgeable audience who are interested in the same sport that you are; you're not shooting in the dark.

Sports newsletters (can we call them sportsletters?) tend to focus on stories generated by the company that writes the email – or those produced by its sister companies. Deadspin's effort, for example, tends to consist of four stories from its own site, followed by a sponsored story (ie one that's paid for by an external company), then four from other sites within the Gizmodo Media Group, which owns Deadspin. The purpose of the email is clearly to encourage subscribers to visit the site.

Bleacher Report is an exception to this. While most of the stories in their emails link back to Bleacher itself, some don't. For example, their baseball newsletter sometimes includes links to the sport's official site, MLB.com, or to ESPN or FanRag Sports. Its soccer one links to the *Guardian* and, again, to ESPN. This may seem irrational – why send readers to your rivals? Because linking to a variety of sources adds to Bleacher Report's credibility. "We don't have all the best stories," it seems to be saying, "just most of them".

People tend to skim their emails; so, the writers of this mailshot only have a sentence or two to pitch their stories. So, there's real skill involved in both writing the story summaries and choosing the accompanying pictures.

CASE STUDY: THE *FIVER*

The *Guardian* makes extensive use of newsletters covering areas such as fashion, music, books and travel. Its sports department produces the *Breakdown* (rugby) and the *Spin* (cricket) as well as what is probably its best-known mail-out, the *Fiver*.

The *Guardian*'s former editor Alan Rusbridger visited Silicon Valley in the mid-1990s. The trip made him realise that news*papers*' days may be numbered and to begin a process of digital transformation at his organisation. The *Fiver* was one of the first innovations during this period of change and, as a result, it has now evolved a highly distinctive outlook and language.

It's written by a different writer each week day, drawn from a small team, which includes Scott Murray who we've already encountered in the chapter on live blogging. Some, such as Barry Glendenning, the deputy sports editor, have been involved for more than a decade.

The purpose of the *Fiver* seems to be not simply to drive readers to the "Big Website" but to build an empathy with the *Guardian* as a brand. If someone only reads the *Fiver* each day and does not then progress to other *Guardian* content, they're still likely to feel that they are a *Guardian* Sport reader or part of its community. The *Fiver* always includes a link encouraging readers to make a contribution to support *Guardian* journalism.

That sense of community is fostered by the *Fiver*'s extraordinary language which takes a while to decipher. By understanding the language, you become part of the community. Taxpayers United? West Ham (a reference to deal the club secured to use the former Olympic stadium); Bernard Cribbins? Steve Bruce (the former Manchester United captain supposedly resembles the actor). The *Fiver* appears to be a person, one whose life revolves around supplies of "purple tin" and has a bizarre extended family which includes "Weird Uncle Fiver" and "stereotypical French cousin Street Miming Embarrassing Rap Music Haw-Hee-Haw-Hee-Haw Fiver". It includes a letters section in which many of the same correspondents seem to appear regularly, most notably Noble Francis, who rarely goes a week without having a letter published. A Letter of the Day is awarded (and fiercely competed for) which sometimes wins a prize.

Perhaps the most surprising feature of the *Fiver* is the use it makes of the delayed drop. This was a journalistic technique, beloved by mid-market papers such as the *Daily Express* in the mid-20th century, in which the writer, instead of getting straight to the point of a story (the "drop"), would deliberately tease the reader. The best exponents of the technique could string out a story for several paragraphs before revealing what a story was actually about. By the 1990s, delayed drops were out of fashion, and the emergence of the web seemed to consign them to history: no search engine would pick up on a post if the meat of the story was buried in the fifth paragraph.

An excellent example of the *Fiver*'s use of delayed drops was provided by Simon Burnton in November 2017. It starts with a synopsis of John Wyndham's novel *The Day of the Triffids*. In the book, Burnton explains, people everywhere are captivated by green shooting stars and then blinded – all except the narrator Masen whose eyes were bandaged up at the time of the shooting stars. In the fifth paragraph, we finally begin to get a hint of where Burnton is going with this story:

> At top-flight football training grounds across the country this morning a handful of miraculously able-bodied footballers experienced their own Masen moments (Burnton, 2017) as six leading Premier League stars all suddenly report injuries.

Burnton continues in the same tone until the end of the seventh paragraph when he finally reaches the drop:

> This may well be, The Fiver is sad to report, the end of the world. Either that or England are playing some friendlies.
>
> (ibid)

After its main introductory story, the *Fiver* moves onto Quote of the Day, Letters, snippets of football news and, finally, a series of links to some of the main football posts on the *Guardian* website. Unlike the examples we looked at above, the *Fiver* doesn't promote match reports or the latest football news, because it assumes readers will already be aware of them. Instead it directs readers to substantial features or opinion pieces from the likes of Jonathan Wilson or Suzanne Wrack.

Most of the links lead to the *Guardian*'s own content but it sometimes features external material – particularly YouTube clips of brilliant goals, calamitous defending or memorable own goals.

As an email, the *Fiver* is not dependent on search engines. As it is sent out just as people are leaving work (around 5 pm – hence the name), it assumes readers will be prepared to devote a bit of time to a story, which is why writers can indulge in leisurely delayed drops.

The *Fiver* is now such an established part of the *Guardian*'s culture that, when the current editor-in-chief Kathryn Viner was appointed to the role in 2015, she referenced it in her hustings statement: "We have a reputation for playful intelligence, from G2 to the Fiver; a witty voice and a distinctive tone" (*Press Gazette*, 2015).

YOUR TURN

It's useful to write a regular newsletter covering your specialist area in sport – I suggest you try it once a week. But, if you're starting out, you probably won't have enough content on your own website to produce a very substantial mailshot. So, I'm going to recommend that you deliberately draw on a wide range of media. This will encourage you to visit a variety of different sites and experience diverse writing styles as you build up your expertise. You can, of course, include your own stories (and your friends'), but try to also feature a mix of material from new and legacy sports sites.

Aim to link to around eight stories each week – that's broadly typical for an email newsletter. It's up to you what style you use. You could follow companies like Bleacher Report or Deadspin and go for a single sentence to promote each story in as quick and concise a fashion as possible. Or you could adopt the *Fiver*'s more quirky approach. You might also try the style adopted by news company Vox whose *Sentences* email is worth a read; it tells stories in a series of paragraphs, each of which links to a different news provider, such as Buzzfeed, BBC, *New York Times* etc.

Once you've built up a bit of confidence, you may want to start sending out your newsletters for real. This is easy to do using free sites such as MailChimp. In 2017, a newsletter tool was launched called Opt In which not only sends out mail to a subscriber list but also advises you on how to write your newsletter.

SUMMARY

- Most people are led to websites by searching using Google or via social media; they tend not to type in urls.
- Employers will expect writers to have some understanding of how to push their stories up Google's rankings.
- Don't become obsessed with search engine optimisation. Just because more people search for "Manchester United" that's not a reason to ignore Manchester City.
- While it may be hard to get people to visit your site, there's much more you can do to get them to stick around once they do drop in. Tactics include hyperlinks, placing

interesting, related stories on side-bars and incorporating quizzes, polls and interactive activities.

- Treat a quiz like any other kind of journalistic content; there should be a reason for it and a compelling introduction.
- Consider using email newsletters to build an audience of people who share your sporting interests.

FURTHER READING

All the email newsletters referred to in this chapter can be found at the relevant companies' websites.

REFERENCES

BBC (2016) *Quiz: Can you name these Wenger signings?* at www.bbc.co.uk/sport/football/37496279. Last accessed on 25/11/2017

Burnton (2017) *A bizarre Wyndhamesque overnight knack* at www.theguardian.com/football/2017/nov/07/a-bizarre-wyndhamesque-overnight-knack. Last accessed on 25/11/2017

Guardian (2017) *Maria Sharapova under investigation for real estate conspiracy in India* at www.theguardian.com/sport/2017/nov/22/maria-sharapova-housing-fraud-india. Last accessed on 25/11/2017

Mansell, J. (2017) Interview with the author, 14/08/2017

Milne, B. (2017) Email exchange with the author, 16/11/2017

Pew Research Centre (2017) *Digital news fact sheet* at www.journalism.org/fact-sheet/digital-news/. Last accessed on 25/11/2017

Press Gazette (2015) *Guardian editor candidates face journalists in election hustings* at www.pressgazette.co.uk/guardian-editor-candidates-face-journalists-election-hustings/. Last accessed on 25/11/2017

Wilson, J. (2017) Interview with the author, 14/11/2017

CHAPTER 7

Video-making

While writing this book, I attended several conferences and workshops about digital journalism. A common theme was the growth of video. There seems to be an assumption that people under 30 do not want to read text on their phones or tablets and would prefer to watch short clips. Video is the future.

Speakers also discussed advertising. Ad blockers may be able to stop pop-ups appearing in a story on a browser or on an app, but it's much harder to remove preroll (ie a short advertisement at the start of a clip) from video clips – or references to products within the film itself.

Sometimes, I'd try to button-hole one or two of the speakers after their presentations. I'd explain that I was writing about sport and their faces would drop. Sport is difficult, they'd explain, it's all about the rights.

In one sense, they were right. What people really want to see is the goals from that Champions League tie, Simone Biles' Olympic routine, Chris Froome powering to the front of the peloton etc. Sport is about competition and rights to most competitions are owned by Sky, BTSport, the BBC etc. As we saw in Chapter 2, even if you don't own the rights to these events, you can still embed links to them in your online content.

But there are some very creative and enjoyable programmes being made by people who are not rights holders. One of the best-known examples of this is probably Spencer Owen, whose Hashtag United has now become a massive brand generating "old media" products such as books and DVDs. Hashtag United falls outside the scope of this book as it's not exactly journalism but it's a great example of a project that depends not on rights but on the creative ideas of its makers.

There seems to be a general consensus from people who run YouTube-based channels and other online-only programmes that the best content should complement mainstream coverage – not compete with it. Generally, for example, the new media video-makers covered here do not chase player interviews, recognising these are done better by the BBC or Sky. They are adding an additional perspective, not a competing one.

Simon Wear founded the Global Cycling Network having been chief operating officer at the magazine group Future Publishing. There's a clear similarity between the audiences for sports magazines and sports video channels; they're both groups who want more than simply coverage of an event – they want to know more about their preferred sport. "My focus was always going to be 'how are modern generation of consumers going to get their specialist information?' and I was always of the view that it was always likely to be video", says Wear (2017).

> [When we started] I was making something that I wanted to make and I didn't want to play in a rights game around people who had much deeper pockets than me and greater amount of strength so I didn't really give it a second thought. I thought 'let's do something we can control and not have our business beaten by outside influences'.

BACKSTORY: THE DEVELOPMENT OF ONLINE VIDEO

In the 1990s, it was unusual to see online video. Internet connections were not powerful enough to enable audiences to stream video and uploading and downloading videos was time-consuming. In the early noughties, big media companies began to host video, but they had the advantage of owning enough server space to manage sizeable video libraries.

Another limitation was the cost of cameras. The camera operators who I worked with in the 1990s put the cost of a full electronic newsgathering kit (ie a camera, alternative lenses, microphones, tripod and lights) at around £70,000, which was a serious obstacle to young people wishing to become freelance video makers.

The big game changer was the launch of YouTube in 2005 by three employees of the online payments company PayPal, working out of a garage in California. The company's growth was extraordinary. At the end of 2006 it was bought for $1.65 billion by Google and the channel was named Person of the Year by Time magazine. (Technically, it was YouTube's content creators and audience that won the accolade as the magazine cover showed a YouTube screen with a large mirror.) At this time, I was teaching music journalism, and I realised that YouTube had already become the main vehicle through which my students were discovering new music.

It was now possible for ordinary people with no interest in owning or designing a website to upload their videos. Meanwhile, laptop computers fitted with cameras were now selling for around £500. So, people could create "programmes" from the comfort of their own living room and upload them in two or three clicks.

Not surprisingly, sport formed a large proportion of YouTube content in its early days. The site was a treasure trove of archive clips as fans uploaded episodes of *Star Soccer* or the *Big Match* from the 1970s. Technically this was illegal, but it was impossible for rights holders to keep control of the amount of content that was being posted. This was also the era when fans all over the world began to share comical own goals or goalkeeping mistakes, dogs interrupting tennis matches and ice hockey fixtures descending into full-on brawls.

Part of the appeal of early YouTube videos is their amateurishness – in stark contrast to the sleek professionalism of, say, Sky's sports channels. One early video that went "viral" showed a boy sitting in front of his computer lip-syncing to a dance number, known as the Numa Numa song. Jump cuts were a common feature of videos. Some argue that part of the appeal of "viral" video is the poor production – it makes it feel more "real' and gives it a slightly clandestine feel. If you are going to post a lot of video though, audiences will expect higher production standards – perhaps not as high as broadcast television, but a basic understanding of film-making grammar is needed and this is addressed below.

YouTube started paying contributors a proportion of the advertising revenue generated by their uploads, and so it became possible for a few content creators to earn a living. Many professional broadcasters set up YouTube channels but, at the same time, they were developing their own On Demand or Catch Up services where their programmes could be watched online. Broadcasters would prefer audiences came to their own websites where they receive a greater proportion of advertising. For instance, Sky Sports Football currently has a relatively meagre 88,000 subscribers on YouTube as most viewers will go to the Sky website or app.

In charting the development of digital sports video, the period between 2010 and 2013 is crucial, with some of the most successful content creators emerging in this period and taking advantage of better wi-fi connectivity, the new 4G mobile network, Google's willingness to support start-ups and cheaper digital SLR cameras:

2009 – Satellite TV station Setanta collapsed, bringing about the closure of Arsenal, Celtic, Rangers and Liverpool's in-house TV stations. What seemed a setback led to the first three all setting up internet channels which proved successful and paved the way for most top-flight clubs to set up some kind of TV station.

2010 – Fremantle Media (makers of *Pop Idol*, the *X-Factor* and *The Apprentice*) launched the Football Republic, a network of fan channels and fan-driven online football shows.

2012 – Another football channel Copa90 launched, managed by Neil Smythe who also worked on the Football Republic channel FullTimeDEVILS.

2012 – Simon Wear secured funding from Google to launch the Global Cycling Network.

2012 – The BBC transmits coverage of up to 26 sports simultaneously through its London 2012 Olympics website.

These companies have all been among the pace-setters in terms of sports video.

Another interesting date in our story is June 2017. This is when Fox – one of America's largest sports broadcasters – announced its "pivot to video" (Putterman, 2017). It scrapped much of the news and comment on its website, replacing it with video. Twenty writer and editor posts were replaced with video specialists. The result? By September, traffic to the site had, apparently, dropped 88%, down from over 143 million views in a monthly period to just under 17 million.

These figures are disputed and – as several commentators have noted – the decline in views doesn't necessarily equate to a drop in income because Fox has saved money by reducing staff and can make more from video preroll than it could from page advertising. Nonetheless, it appears to confirm a phenomenon seen elsewhere, including at Vice Sports; namely, if a company attempts to switch to 100% video, it will lose audience. Sports fans seem to want a mix of video and text, with the latter providing essential context for the film clips.

Since 2005, we've definitely seen an improvement in the quality of online video, both in terms of higher definition pictures and a greater conformity to the traditional grammar of film-making. There is now a debate about how "clean" online footage should look. BBC Trending, for example, deliberately tries to break some of those traditional rules in order to make their video look a bit more subversive. The thinking is that someone is more likely to share something if it looks unofficial. On the other hand, there seems to be something fake about pretending you are worse at making films than you actually are – if you can shoot something well, why make it look amateurish?

But, typically, digital video-makers are producing a lot of content with smaller crews than in mainstream television. "The thing about the internet is that it's quite forgiving", says Simon Wear whose three YouTube-based cycling channels make more than 1,500 films a year. "The challenge with what we do is how do you produce a significant volume of content at decent quality. It doesn't have to be broadcast standard but it needs to be a decent standard" (Wear, 2017).

WIDE OR SQUARE? TEXT? EMOJIS? ANYTHING ELSE?

I've been encouraging students to film with their mobile phones for years and one of the things I've gone on about most is trying to get them to hold their phones "horizontal" to shoot in landscape, not portrait. For some reason, we tend, instinctively, to hold our phones upright and tend to shoot that way as well. This means that, when amateur footage is used on television or YouTube, the broadcaster has to stick black bars either side of the picture.

But, in fact, pictures don't always have to be landscape. The first ever television, John Logie Baird's "televisor", had a portrait-shaped screen. Logie Baird envisaged television programmes as mainly consisting of public service information being delivered by talking heads (most of them, presumably, wearing black ties and dinner jackets). Later television manufacturers realised that drama, documentary, game shows and sport all tended to look better in landscape as you could see more people or objects in relation to each other. In the late 1990s, there was a move away from 4:3 televisions (ie sets on which the picture was four units wide to three units high) to widescreen, or 16:9, which was much closer to the letterbox shape of film. This change is credited with encouraging the more cinematic style of television programmes such as *Breaking Bad* or *Game of Thrones*.

Today, many companies are going back to Logie Baird's approach and experimenting with portrait or square video. For example, ` 4 News has started producing square video to go out on Facebook, recognising that that's the way people look at Facebook on their phones.

So, some basic principles:

1   Think about what you are showing. Most sports won't look good in portrait – particularly field sports like football or rugby where you need some idea of where all the participants are positioned.
2   Think about how people will be viewing your content. If they are approaching it via Facebook (and, as we saw in Chapter 3, Facebook dwarfs all other social media), then there is a case for square or portrait images. Twitter and Instagram are also well-suited to portrait video. But YouTube and Vimeo are still designed for landscape.

3   It's generally easier to go from landscape to portrait than the other way round. If you've shot an interview in widescreen, it's a simple process to cut off the edges to make it square. But, if you've shot it in portrait, then cutting off the top and bottom of your picture is likely to leave you with a close-up of your interviewee's mouth and nose.

4   Don't mess with aspect ratios. Your interviewees won't thank you if you stretch your pictures so they look fatter. They probably won't appreciate being squished either. It's much more professional to add strips to the edge of your picture than to distort the shape. If you suspect that the footage you are using might have been meddled with, look out for objects that you know ought to be round, eg clock faces or wheels. If you see a car with weirdly elongated wheels, that's a sure sign that someone has messed around with the aspect ratio.

5   Where possible, stick with what you have. The beauty of online video is that, unlike with old-style television, you are not tied to any one particular shape. So, for example, ClickOn wrote a piece about Fay Crocker, the first non-American to win the US Women's Open. Most of the footage they had of her was shot in 4:3, because that was the conventional shape of television pictures in the 1950s. So, they sensibly kept these pictures in 4:3.

Next question: to emoji or not to emoji? My sense is that this is a trend that will pass. I also notice that people often fail to find the right emoji – the one that accurately conveys what they are trying to say, possibly because human emotions are a bit too complex to be reduced to a little yellow face. Designer Jean Popescu is certainly not a fan:

> It's a trend that's about to die. I don't think they are going to survive. I work with social media, with design, with websites, with apps. I see lots of companies using emoji messages but they never get any results back. I stick to the idea that less is more.
>
> (Popescu, 2017)

Finally, how long should your piece be? One of the downsides of television is that everything has to fit a given timeslot: typically, half an hour or an hour (less in the case of commercial television because of adverts). Even a news report is constrained: an editor might initially allocate one minute, 45 seconds to all the reports in the programme and then, reluctantly, allow a story a bit more time. Television sports reporters might be given a minute to tell the story of a match regardless of whether it was a nil–nil draw or a 4–3 win with two sendings-off.

On the web, these constraints do not apply – but there are still plenty of people suggesting optimum lengths. BBC regional reporters are told to aim to produce 45 seconds to a minute, for example. I don't doubt that this is based on solid research; but my advice would simply be – and this is true of almost all journalism: *make it as short as you possibly can.*

This doesn't mean everything has to be 30 seconds or less: we can all probably think of 700-page books or three-hour films that don't need to be cut down at all. It does mean you have to be ruthless and ask "is this bit really necessary?". An ITN programme producer once told me about a journalist whose reports tended to go over their allocated time. The reporter would phone from the edit suite and say he couldn't tell his story in less than two minutes.

"I need 1'45"", the producer would say.
"That's impossible." came the reply.
"Well how long is your piece-to-camera?"
"Fifteen seconds."
"Cut it out!"

The producer smiled and said that the reporter always managed to cut his piece down to the required length with the piece to camera (the bit where the reporter him or herself appears in shot) left *in*. It took the threat of not appearing in vision to force him to be sufficiently ruthless.

UNDERSTANDING HOW YOUR VIDEO IS BEING WATCHED

YouTube provides really helpful data on the videos that you upload – though it's not particularly easy to find.

Login to your YouTube account and, in the top left-hand corner of the screen, you'll see a symbol made up of three horizontal lines. Click on this and it brings up a menu. From that, select "Settings", then choose "Additional Features" (at the bottom of the box titled "Overview"). You will then be able to open your dashboard.

The dashboard will bring up all the videos you've uploaded. If you click on an individual video, it'll show you the data for that video. This includes how many people have watched it and if anyone has liked or disliked it. It also shows the average amount of time people devote to watching the clip and at what point in the video they tend to switch off.

Learn from this information. If you regularly post three-minute videos and people only seem to watch for a minute, maybe your films are too long? Do people stop watching midway through an interview (quite a common phenomenon)? Perhaps the clip you've chosen could be shorter? Or maybe you could have chosen a more interesting interviewee? Perhaps the piece doesn't need an interviewee at all.

CASE STUDY: COPA90

If any organisation proves that you don't need access to rights to make engaging short films about football, it's Copa90. Launched in 2012, Copa was not an overnight sensation. It largely grew through word of mouth until 2015 when it had crept up to having a million subscribers (*Guardian*, 2015). At this point, Google decided to throw its backing behind the channel, with a billboard advertising campaign in London, similar to ones the tech giant had previously mounted for Zoella and Vice News. It's also part of the *Guardian* Sport Network, which means that selected films are embedded on the *Guardian*'s website.

Copa90 makes a range of programming: documentaries (which can run for up to 15 minutes), explainers (eg to explain tactics; these are typically animated and rarely last more than five minutes), challenges, goal animations and shows. The longest-running show, *Comments Below*, has 1.4 million subscribers and has run to more than 300 editions.

Despite this range – Copa90 seems to have a strong brand identity. There's something about all their content that feels Copa-ish. Perhaps the most obvious feature is that the content is all about fans. The documentaries invariably include shots of packed terraces with waving flags and interviews with fans. Films are often presented by a fan of the club that's being featured. If players or officials do appear, they are not treated as any more important than the fans. For example, in 2014, Copa made a series of films called *Derby Days*. One of these looked at the rivalry between Arsenal and Tottenham Hotspur (Copa90, 2014) and opens with a sequence in which various fans and celebrities talk about how much the derby means to them. In the middle of this sequence there are contributions from two Spurs players, Jan Vertonghen and Michael Dawson, but they are simply two talking heads among many.

There is also an arty quality to Copa films. They tend to be well-shot and well-edited. Films set in stadia often include creative shots of staircases and corridors from quirky angles. A lot of use is made of music – from hard rock to ambient and classical. There are jump-cuts, but these tend to be used intelligently to speed the pace rather than as a clumsy editing device.

The presenters don't look like anyone you'd see on the BBC, ITV, BT or Sky. For example, their best-known presenters are two fans called Poet and Vuj. Poet is beanpole thin with long dreads; Vuj is from Serbia with stern-looking eyes and a beard which, at one time, was neatly trimmed into a triangle. They look about as different from Dan Walker or Jake Humphreys as it's possible to get.

In many ways, Poet and Vuj offer a clue to the success of Copa90. They appear to be ordinary football fans, casually chatting about the game or – in the case of one show, *FIFA and Chill* – playing *FIFA* while chatting to guests. But they are very good indeed at what they do; Copa works hard to find its talent – some of whom were chosen by viewers following competitions – and their success is not an accident. Like Copa's films, they appear "YouTubeish" but they are actually very slick. In *FIFA and Chill*, guests appear to enjoy relaxing but Poet and Vuj get them to open up in a way that many professional journalists would struggle to do.

Copa is justifiably proud of its international character. The *Derby Days* strand included several films about eastern European derbies which audiences in the UK would be unlikely to know much about and other films have been made in locations as far apart as New Zealand and the United States. A feature on the Escuela de Tablones (Copa90, 2017a), a terrace choir in the Argentinian town of San Lorenzo that has a reputation for converting chart hits into crowd chants, is typical Copa90.

The Escuela de Tablones feature is a great journalistic story which would work well on any medium in any era. But Copa90 doesn't rigidly follow journalistic rules. For example, in a feature on Leyton Orient's relegation from the Football League (Copa 2017b), fans repeatedly condemn then-owner Francesco Becchetti. He is portrayed as living in a mansion while failing to pay staff wages. Journalistically, one would expect Becchetti to be afforded the right of reply. If he decides not to take part, fair enough, but the film could have said "we approached Mr Becchetti for a comment, but he has not replied". Like most Copa films, this one is unashamedly partisan – on the side of the fans.

The Orient film is worth viewing. At 15 minutes long, it is longform by YouTube standards. Graphics are deployed with a sense of humour and the viewer is taken on a journey: Orient unexpectedly win a game that could have ended in their relegation, so presenter Eli Mengem then travels to Crewe where the Londoners' demotion is confirmed. A more journalistic style creeps in when, in the course of the journey, Mengem meets a fan on the train to Crewe who shows him evidence which purports to show that some wages are not being paid. Finally, he is present at their last home game of the season when the match is suspended for two hours due to a pitch invasion.

YOUR TURN

In this exercise, you are going to have a go at making a Copa90-style film. Choose a local non-league football club and try to create a sense of what makes it special. Aim for around five minutes.

What will you need?

The quality of pictures that can be captured on a mobile phone is improving year on year and is increasingly popping up on mainstream television news programmes. The picture below shows Sky reporter Joe Tidy's backpack. In a small rucksack, he can fit everything he needs to film short "packages" that can be broadcast on Sky News and to conduct live interviews with Sky's presenters from the scene of a breaking news story.

Joe's rucksack contains two phones (he can broadcast on one, while listening to the studio director via the other), a back-up power supply, two microphones (one a clip-on), a selfie stick, a gorilla-pod (a mini tripod which can also be used to secure his phone to a solid object such as a bench or lamp-post), a small but powerful lamp and two earpieces. Note – even though he's using a phone, it's still really important to capture good sound and to have a stable picture.

Even though the cameras on phones have improved steadily, the same can't always be said for microphones. And, if you are trying to film an interview, the best position for the camera – about six feet away at head height – is not a good position for the microphone, which should be no more than a foot away from the speaker, ideally at chest height. So, a microphone is a good investment. Your audience might forgive a few duff shots but, if they can't hear what someone is saying, they aren't going to carry on watching.

Having a stable shot is probably the single factor that most clearly distinguishes the professional from the amateur. As discussed above, there is something charming about the lack of professionalism of early YouTube videos – the wobbly shots somehow making the footage more "real". But, if you want to regularly post videos, your audience will soon tire of wobble-vision, so clamps or mini-tripods are also useful.

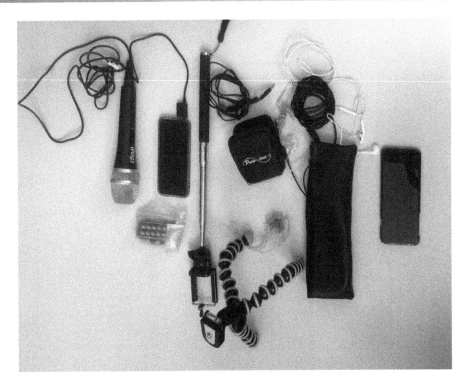

FIGURE 7.1 Photograph showing the contents of Joe Tidy's backpack, courtesy of Joe Tidy

One advantage of filming on a phone is that it is now easy to send your pictures back to a colleague who can edit them or even to edit them yourself on your phone to upload to social media. I have a Google Drive on my phone and simply drag pictures into it; I would only recommend doing this if you can find a wi-fi connection as it will eat up a lot of data if you're on 4G.

If you use an iPhone, then you can edit with Apple's iMovie. Adobe have also produced a phone-based version of their Premiere software, called Clip. Qik, which is free, and Lumix have both been around for a while and are easy to use. But new mobile editing programs are released every day and it's worth playing around with several to find out which is best for you.

If you're filming a lot of pieces, however, you will eventually want to move up to a more professional camera. Certainly, most Copa90 content seems to be shot on good quality equipment.

There was a time when, if you wanted to take still images, you used an SLR (single lens reflex – now succeeded by digital SLR (DSLR)) camera and, if you wanted to shot moving pictures, you used a camcorder. (Camcorder is a contraction of the words camera and recorder, ie it both shot the pictures and stored them in the camera. For around 25 years from the early 1980s onwards, the pictures were stored on bulky cassette tapes which sat at the back of the camera – hence the long, thin shape of camcorders.) Today, both can take stills and videos – but there are still advantages and disadvantages to each.

DSLR camera – the pros

- easy to carry, just sling it round your neck;
- will tend to perform better without extra lights;
- has a greater depth of field;
- will take better stills.

Camcorder – the pros

- rests on your shoulder. So, if you are filming a long sequence without a tripod, you can get a steadier shot than if you're holding a camera in your hands;
- tends to be able to store more footage – either on the camera's own memory or an SD card;
- looks more like a professional TV camera (not to be underrated if you're trying to persuade an important sports person to give you an interview).

Whichever you opt for, make sure there is an external microphone socket – that's absolutely essential. An optional consideration is whether you want your camera to be wi-fi-enabled. This means that, as you shoot, your pictures can be streamed onto a website. Most matchday photographers at Premier League or Championship games are expected to be able to offer a live stream of images.

If you're looking at camcorders, Canon's Legria range starts at around £800; for twice that money, you might consider Sony's x70. In both cases, you can expect to spend another £500 on a good quality camera bag, a microphone, tripod and replacement batteries. For DSLRs, Canon have a similarly priced range called EOS; its main rivals include Panasonic's Lumix and the Nikon D5300. A new development – the mirrorless camera – is also worth considering.

If you can, try to borrow a few cameras – perhaps from a university equipment store – to a get a feel for what suits you before you make a major investment.

TOP TIPS: FILMING AND EDITING – SOME BASICS

Put simply, in video news or sports reports, there are two ways of telling stories:

- interviews with people who explain something or express and opinion, and
- pictures which show something.

For example, if you are making a short film about an up-and-coming hockey star, you might interview the player herself and, perhaps, her coach, who will explain why he thinks she has a bright future in the sport. Then you might film her dribbling or shooting or taking part in a practice game. The pictures of the player in action support the coach's claims that she's one to watch.

The interviews are known as A roll; the other pictures as B roll. When you come to edit your report, you will probably record a voice-over or commentary to go *under* the B roll.

The word "editing" suggests that you are cutting some down; you're trimming your footage a bit. In fact, this is misleading as the act of editing is more about deciding what you want to put *in* to your two-minute finished report from maybe half an hour of raw material.

This is a very concise list of basic filming tips based on 25 years of making videos about sport for a variety of publishers. I've recommended some more in-depth texts at the end of this chapter.

They are based on the assumption you know a little bit about filming and editing; I've really tried to focus on some of the special characteristics of sport.

A Roll

- Aim to frame your interviewee so that his or her chest is at the bottom of your picture; make sure you get all of their head in. This is called a mid-shot. It means you can hold a microphone just out of shot, about a foot away from the interviewee's mouth.
- The interviewee should not be in the centre of the screen, nor should he or she be looking at the camera. Ideally, they should be a third of the way into the picture on either the left- or right-hand side of the screen and looking across the frame. Imagine you could draw a speech bubble coming out of their mouth.
- If you are shooting more than one interviewee, vary the backgrounds if possible, and get them to stand on different sides. So, if we film our hockey player on the left of the frame, we'll want to film the coach on the right-hand side.
- While interviewing, wear headphones to check you're capturing clear sound. Listen back to the interview afterwards.

This is Paul Doswell, the manager of Sutton United, interviewed ahead of the non-league side's 2017 FA Cup tie against Arsenal. There are at least three things that the camera operator should have done differently here – can you spot them?

This is a well-framed interview shot on a mobile phone. Jesse Craig, captain of the Guildford Flames Ice Hockey team, is looking into the shot with his eyes roughly a third of the way from the left and a third down from the top. The club logo on the door behind him

FIGURE 7.2 Photograph of Paul Doswell

FIGURE 7.3 Photograph of Jesse Craig by Alex Antzara

helps make the right-hand side of the picture more interesting. It's shot in a dark corridor, so the camera operator has done well to make use of what light is available. In an ideal world, you'd have a small lamp (as in Joe Tidy's rucksack, above) to throw more light onto Craig's face.

FIGURE 7.4 Photograph of Paul Tanner by Thomas Cann

Once again, light was a problem during this interview with Farnham Town manager Paul Tanner. But the camera operator has made good use of the floodlights, so he's well lit. Note, also the small personal microphone on his lapel – which really helps ensure the sound is clear even in a noisy environment.

B Roll

- Shoot much more than you think you need. There was a time when film was a scarce and expensive resource, so camera crews tried to film no more than four times what would be needed in the final report (so, if their film was expected to be two minutes long, they'd shoot eight). Today SD cards are inexpensive and can store hours of footage so there's no reason why you shouldn't shoot ten times the length of the final report.
- Try to resist the temptation (I know it can be hard) to move the camera around a lot. Avoid pans (moving the camera left to right and vice versa), tilts (moving it up and down) and, especially, zooms (going in tight). Ideally the camera should be still and all the movement should be taking place *within* the frame. Early in my career, I went to shoot a profile of the Olympic Silver Medal-winning yachtsmen John Merricks and Ian Walker. We were filming from an inflatable motorboat and I was keen to travel alongside the pair's yacht. A more experienced colleague said: "No, we've got to stay still – we want to be able to show how fast these guys are."
- Think about where the action is taking place. For example, in football, if a player is taking a corner, you know the ball is likely to be delivered into the penalty area. In cricket, most of the action will happen close to the wicket (batter hits the ball, batter is bowled, batter is caught by the wicket keeper or slips). So, an understanding of the sport you are covering will help.
- As a general rule, with all filming, try to ensure you have the strongest source of light *behind* you.

Editing

- When editing a *news* story, I normally advise students to write their script first and create a framework for their report made up of their voice track and interview clips. They can then add pictures to this. For sport, I recommend the reverse. A shot of a cricket ball flying towards a boundary or a golf ball on its way down the fairway will last a set amount of time; sports shots tend to be difficult either to cut down or extend. It makes more sense to cut the pictures first and tailor your script to fit the pictures.
- *Natural sound* is important. This is the sound you record on location, in our case the sound of our hockey player hitting the ball, the ball hitting the back of the goal and maybe the coach shouting advice. If you leave this out, then your pictures may sound eerily silent. If you leave these sounds in, then it doesn't matter so much if you've only written eight seconds to cover a ten-second shot – you're allowing the pictures to breathe.
- I tend to start by selecting the best clips – or soundbites – from the interviews I've conducted. These should be short and punchy – ideally 10–20 seconds long – any more and your viewer will switch off.

- Next, we need to consider the best opening images. In television newsrooms, journalists were often advised to start with "an establisher": something that clearly indicates where we are and what's going on, such as a sign saying "White Cliffs Canoe Club", two football teams coming out onto the pitch or a golfer addressing the ball at a tee. But, if someone is scrolling down their Facebook timeline and only gets to see the first two seconds of my film, they are not going to be impressed by a shot of a sign saying "Hockey Club". Instead, I'm going to start with something more dramatic, like the young player hammering a ball into the goal.
- A variety of voices helps make a piece more interesting, so I always try to get one of my interviewees to pop up early on in the report. Just as in Chapter 1 we saw the value of embedding a tweet or an image after two or three paragraphs of text, so it's good to get a new voice in within the first 20 seconds of a video piece.
- If your first clip was of the hockey player, then you could cut straight to the coach immediately after hearing from her. Generally, though, I think it helps to have a bit of a gap so you can prepare the viewer for the new interviewee. So, we could put a sequence of her dribbling in there.
- Don't end on a clip unless it's really strong ("by this time next year, I think she'll be an England international"). The "pay-off" is your chance to add some kind of reflection on what you've seen.

Finally, a word about jump-cuts. A jump-cut occurs when two images that don't go together are joined up. For example, if you have an interview and you cut a chunk out of it, then you will probably notice that the interviewee appears to "jump" slightly where you've made the edit. If you film a piece to camera outside a stadium and then join that to another piece to camera in which you are standing on the touchline, then you are "jumping" from one location to another.

Traditional television news rooms hated jump-cuts; they were an immediate giveaway indicating poor craftsmanship. By contrast, early YouTubers made extensive use of them; they captured some of the quirky, experimental personality of the era. My advice would be to use them with caution; a 15-second soundbite with three jump-cuts will look just awful. On the other hand, a jump-cut often looks better than that rather tired concept, the noddy (a reverse shot of the reporter pretending to nod in response to what the interviewee has just said). In the example of our hockey star, you might be able to create a quirky sequence using jump-cuts.

IF YOU CAN'T USE PHOTOGRAPHS, MAYBE YOU CAN DRAW THE ACTION

It sounds ridiculous: if you don't have the rights to the action, could you draw it. But that's exactly what Copa90 did for football's 2016 European Championships.

Copa couldn't show the goals because they didn't have the rights; so they approached an animation company called Grizzle who put together a team of four to recreate more than 100 goals (Copa90, 2016), using a rotoscope, a device that enabled the team to trace over the still frames that made up the footage of each goal.

"On average it took us about an hour and a half to recreate each goal," estimates one of animators Stewart Power (2017).

> Our best was probably an hour with four people working on one goal lasting five or six seconds. One person would be drawing goalposts, one the ball, one the goalscorer, one the defender – a massive team effort. We're not using the footage – the final product is not the footage. But we do use the footage to help us do our work.
>
> (ibid)

Of course, by the time each animated goal was ready, the original video footage would have been viewed millions of time, on television, on the BBC or ITV websites and on social media. Grizzle's interpretations of the goals weren't competing with the real thing – they were offering another perspective.

> It's an alternative look at something you've already seen which is key for social media; if they've already seen something they won't be interested. If they see something animated or illustrated, it just varies up their feed which is what I do is all about. It's giving an alternative look at something they've already seen.
>
> (ibid)

Stewart went on to work for Livewire sport who applied the same technique to rugby.

> The England rugby team went unbeaten for a whole year and the RFU wanted a video to showcase such a massive achievement. It was pretty much the same process as the Euro goals and we put out the video on social media and it did really really well.
>
> (England Rugby, 2016)

SUMMARY

- The rights to footage of sports events are highly prized but you can still make engaging sports films by focussing on the stories behind the big games.
- Sport generally works in landscape rather than portrait. But always consider how your work will be received by audiences. Square videos work well on Facebook, less well on YouTube.
- Don't feel you have to make all your films a certain duration. Your videos should be as short as they possibly can.
- Do your research into cameras and make sure you understand the pros and cons of DLSRs and camcorders before you spend a lot of money.
- You don't have to be a film production graduate to make short films for YouTube but some understanding of the grammar of pictures is helpful; don't assume that, just because someone else has used a wonky shot or a crude edit, that it's now standard practice.

REFERENCES

Copa90 (2014) *"I Hate Everything About Them" – North London Derby* at www.youtube.com/watch?v=nbHK9Z8tFYw&t=119s. Last accessed on 29/11/17

Copa90 (2016) *Every goal of Euro 2016* at https://copa90.com/animations/every-goal-euro-2016-animated. Last accessed on 1/12/17

Copa90 (2017a) *Despacito | From the charts to the football terraces* at www.youtube.com/watch?v=OP018YHl3SM. Last accessed on 29/11/17

Copa90 (2017b) *Riots and relegation: What the f*** happened to Leyton Orient* at www.youtube.com/watch?v=lvYSJomCp08. Last accessed on 29/11/17

England Rugby (2016) *England in 2016 – an unbeaten year in animation* at www.englandrugby.com/ertv/video/england-2016-unbeaten-year-animation/. Last accessed on 1/12/17

Guardian (2015) *YouTube football channel Copa90 takes on big broadcasters with new ads* at www.theguardian.com/technology/2015/sep/29/youtube-channel-copa90-marketing-campaign. Last accessed on 29/11/17

Popescu, J. (2017) Interview conducted by the author on 13/10/2017

Power, S. (2017) Interview conducted by the author on 21/7/2017

Putterman, A. (2017) *Fox sports just one of several notable sites to lose millions of page views after pivoting to video* at http://awfulannouncing.com/fox/fox-sports-among-several-notable-sites-lose-thousands-page-views-pivoting-video.html. Last accessed on 29/11/17

Wear, S. (2017) Interview conducted by the author on 7/9/2017

CHAPTER 8

Sports journalism and data

After the invention of the world wide web and the development of smartphones, the technological change which has had most impact on journalism is our ability to collect, manipulate, interpret and present data.

Greater use of data isn't limited to online journalism – most newspapers carry many more charts or graphs than they would have ten years ago.

"We believe, at Mail Online, this is a key element in keeping younger readers attracted to what we are doing", the consultant sports editor Jim Mansell (2017) says.

> Maybe it's down to the influence of American sports which have crept into how we report on British Sports, but I do find younger people are much more attuned to look out for any type of stat to go with any type of sport. Sometimes we do our own research and sometimes we use a company called Opta who supply a lot of statistical information to media outlets. For example, we did a panel on how Jurgen Klopp fared in his first 100 games as Liverpool manager. And he's only halfway down a list of 12 managers who've done 100 games for Liverpool; he's not been that successful basically. In that instance, we could approach Opta and say we want some stats on Liverpool managers and 100 games and they can supply it.
>
> (ibid)

This has been a two-edged sword. New data streams have helped us understand sports in ways we couldn't in the past but, at times, they have allowed sports journalists to wallow in data and to tell stories that are unlikely to be of interest to anyone beyond a handful of geeks.

Go a stage further: if you story is just about data then do you need a journalist? Researchers at the Northwestern University have designed a computer program called Stats Monkey, which can write baseball reports (NPR, 2010). Because the sport is very data-heavy, the reports are fairly readable and are regarded as a good way of covering Little Leagues – the leagues that parents and grandparents love to hear about but to which it is not judged cost-effective to assign human reporters.

WHAT DO NUMBERS TELL US ABOUT PEOPLE?

Strong data journalism focuses on the human dimension. What do numbers tell us about the sports person in question?

Take for example the figure of unforced errors in tennis which is, in part, a measure of risk-taking. Alex Willis, who runs Wimbledon's digital channels, explains what she wants audiences to get out of that sort of statistic.

> I would hope that a 19 year old sitting in Indonesia would find Wimbledon more approachable if, within his WhatsApp message group, he's able to tell his friends "oh isn't this Dominic Thiem amazing because he takes so many risks and that's how I want to be in my life and I'm going to look up to him for that reason" rather than "Dominic Thiem won by hitting 95 per cent more or 95 per cent less errors than another player". These platforms play an amazing role but it's up to us to put the right content on the platforms.
>
> (Willis, 2017)

"It's all about personalising, making it relevant to someone, making it interactive", believes Ian Singleton, assistant editor at BBC Sport (Singleton, 2017).

In this chapter we'll be looking at various ways that data visualisation has been used to tell sports stories but – according to a recent study – sports journalists could do better. The researchers looked at 225 projects that had been shortlisted for data journalism awards and said "Culture, sports, and education attract little coverage (2.7% to 5.4%)" (Loosen, Reimer, and de Silva-Schmidt 2017, cited in Hazard Owen, 2017). By contrast, politics accounted for nearly 50% of projects. This is surprising given the enormous amount of data that sport generates and suggests that this is an area where we might see considerable growth over the next few years.

YOUR TURN: DATA VISUALISATION

Without any knowledge of graphic design or coding, you can still produce simple charts to visualise data. Most word-processing software like Microsoft Word or Apple's Pages allow you to create simple graphs; spreadsheets like Excel and Numbers have more powerful tools, such as pivot tables, that allow you to analyse data in different ways. Given how important statistics are to sports fans, there is really no reason not to experiment with some of these. An employer would undoubtedly be impressed by an applicant who has started thinking about graphic content, even if they don't have the most sophisticated tools to work with.

On the eve of golf's Open Championship in 2015, the *Daily Telegraph* profiled the game's new wunderkind Jordan Spieth who, at the age of just 21, had already won that year's first two majors (*Telegraph*, 2015). The article compared Spieth to the man who held the record for major wins, Jack Nicklaus, and the most successful current player, Tiger Woods, and used a chart to compare the three players.

I've recreated the chart using Pages, which has an option to insert a chart. Down the left-hand side I've listed the three players while the line at the top (the x axis) indicates the players' ages when they won a major.

My chart certainly isn't as elegant as the *Telegraph*'s, which would have been the work of a professional designer. But it is an effective way of conveying information; it's certainly a much more concise way of doing so than if I were to try to put this information into words.

TABLE 8.1 Chart showing championship wins by three top players in golf, based on a table published by telegraph.co.uk, July 2015

		21	22	23	24	25	26	27	28	29	30	31	32	33	34	35	36	37	38	39	40	41	42	43	44	45	46
Spieth	**Masters**																										
	US Open																										
	Open																										
	PGA																										
Woods	**Masters**																										
	US Open																										
	Open																										
	PGA																										
Nicklaus	**Masters**																										
	US Open																										
	Open																										
	PGA																										

At first glance, the chart tells a simple story. At 21, Spieth is currently outperforming the two greatest players of the modern era – but there's a long way to go, as Nicklaus won his titles over a 20-year period.

A good chart should save the reader time. It should be instantly easy to understand. But, if the reader does have a bit of time of time to spare, charts, and other forms of data visualisation, give him or her the chance to find their own stories. Closer study of the chart reveals that the Open proved to be the hardest major title for Nicklaus and Woods, both in terms of how long it took them to win it and how many times they were champion. (Interestingly, Spieth went on to win the Open aged 23 – the same age Woods was when he first lifted the Claret Jug.) It highlights the importance of the years between 25 and 32 in terms of clocking up major titles. It shows the dramatic way that Woods' dominance of the sport came to an end.

OK – over to you. Try to replicate the chart above, but this time show either the three male or female *tennis* players who have won the most grand slams – and the ages at which they won each of the slams.

(Note – as with golf, tennis has four grand slams each year: the Australian Open, the French Open, Wimbledon and the US Open. Tennis historians will sometimes refer to the "open era", ie the professional era which began in 1968, and disregard Grand Slam wins from earlier. Margaret Court won 24 grand slams but only ten of these were in the open era, so it's up to you whether you include her in your chart.)

Now, see if you can design charts or graphs for other sports. Perhaps you could take the highest run scorers and wicket takers in cricket and show how successful they were at different ages?

DATA VISUALISATION FOR SOCIAL MEDIA

While the charts we've created may be effective ways of telling a story, their appearance leaves quite a bit to be desired. And all we can really do with them is put them on a website.

In the next section we're going to look at two data projects which have been designed to be shared on Instagram.

When I worked in television news, there was a bit of client-and-tradesman relationship between journalists and graphic designers. We'd fill out a form describing what we wanted a graphic to look like and listing the text it needed to display, and then take it down to a darkened room where the graphics team lurked. Nowadays, at places like the *Guardian*, BBC or *New York Times*, journalists and graphic designers sit alongside each other and swap ideas. The relationship works best when the designer is free to make editorial suggestions and the journalist to be creative.

Ian Singleton says BBC Sport has "a slick templated graphics tool that takes care of 95% of our graphics needs" (Singleton, 2017). This means that sports journalists themselves can design most of the graphics – they don't have to explain sport to someone who isn't particularly interested in it. For the 5% of jobs when creative specialists are needed, they are fully integrated in the team.

CASE STUDY: VELON

Vincenzo Nibali won the 2017 Giro di Lombardia, a one-day road race that takes in several punishing climbs. When the peloton started the steepest part of penultimate climb, the Civiglio, two riders broke away, but Nibali stayed with the pack. 500 metres before the summit the gradient becomes a little less steep. At this point, he made his decision to chase down the riders in front of him. The first, he overtook just before the summit; the second at the start of his descent.

When he was in the peloton, Nibali was travelling at 16 kilometres per hour and using 418 watts of power. These figures jumped to 21.9 Km/h and 462 watts when he launched his attack (Velon media team, 2017).

FIGURE 8.1 Image showing data collated by Velon on Vincenzo Nibali, courtesy of Velon

For the cycling fan, this is very revealing. Even after six hours in the saddle including numerous climbs, he was still able to increase his speed by more than a third on top of what he was already doing and dig deep to find an extra 10% of energy. More importantly, the statistics reveal the tactical acumen of the Sicilian and his Bahrain Merida team, choosing to break away from the peloton just as the two leaders were tiring but before they had established an unchallengeable lead.

But there's another story behind those statistics and Nibali's achievement. Velon, which was covering the race, puts a device on all the riders' bikes to measure their speed and power. In order to get the data, Velon has had to enter into complex arrangements with the main cycling teams. What data can and cannot be made public? What data can they display during the race as opposed to after it? And how long data can be displayed on screen?

The result is data which is far more precise than could have been gathered in the past. A few years ago, fans would have been impressed to discover a rider's average speed over a climb – now we can break down the rider's performance over different sections of the ascent.

The next stage of the story concerns what Velon went on to do with the data. A team of four people were involved in deciphering the data, turning it into a story and presenting it in an easily accessible way – initially on Instagram and, later, on Velon's website. The image on the previous page is the culmination of experts crunching thousands of pieces of data and designers finding the most effective way to communicate the results.

The result is very Instagram-friendly – a big, square attention-grabbing image. The text is big enough to be easy to read on a phone while still conveying interesting information.

CASE STUDY: CHAMPIONS LEAGUE

Jean Octavian Popescu is a designer with a love of football. Ahead of big matches, he posts info-graphics that combine striking images with easy-to-grasp data. "The images I create are like a trailer for something bigger that's still to come – like a film trailer", Popescu (2017) says.

The Danish-based designer's starting point was a block of text on the UEFA website. "It contained all-time historical records of the event itself, records that, probably, nobody is going to read: too much information and no graphics".

Popescu has a background in web design and has taken these ideas into his sports graphics.

> Showing the faces of people will get much more traction, more interaction with users than anything else. Every text book on web design says "use faces". As long as you can see a face, I'm going to use it. A lot of people prefer to use action – dribbling, running or shooting – I think you can identify more with players if you can see their faces and see their emotions. You can see Buffon's fighting spirit or Ronaldo's proud face.
>
> (ibid)

He also uses the term "information architecture". This is a term that web designers use to understand what visitors to a site want. In this case, Popescu believes his audience want strong images roughly twice as much as they want statistics. So, his finished product is 70% image to 30% text.

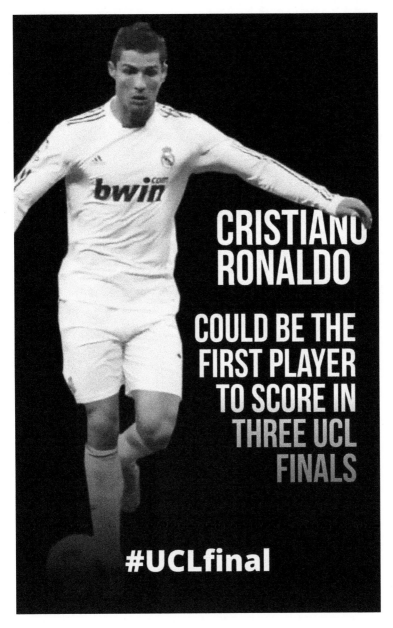

FIGURE 8.2 Graphic by Jean Octavian Popescu showing Cristiano Ronaldo statistic, incorporating image by Jan Solo

GIANLUIGI BUFFON

CAN BECOME THE OLDEST EUROPEAN CHAMPION

#UCLfinal

FIGURE 8.3 Graphic by Jean Octavian Popescu showing Gianluigi Buffon statistic, incorporating image by Muhammad Ashiq

YOUR TURN: PRESENTING STATISTICS

Below is a set of facts about the Arsenal and England Lionesses' defender Alex Scott, who retired from international football in 2017. As Jean Octavian Popescu would say "too much information and no graphics".

> Alex Scott made her England debut in 2004 and went on to represent her country 140 times, making her England's second most capped player. She has scored 12 goals for the Lionesses. Over the course of three separate tournaments, she made 12 appearances in the World Cup Finals, including playing in the side that recorded England's best-ever finish: third place in Canada 2015. Scott featured in four European Championships, including the 2009 tournament when England won silver.

Find a strong image of Scott on Creative Commons (there are quite a few out there) and pick out a few key facts that will fit easily on to your graphic.

Popescu used Figma, which is free online software, to put his image together. If you have access to the Adobe suite then you could use Illustrator to complete your project.

REALLY BIG DATA

For really big data projects, you need to look to the legacy organisations like the BBC, the *Guardian* or the *New York Times*. These boast big enough staffs to take people off normal duties to spend time compiling and analysing data.

Soon after football's transfer window closed in 2016, the *Guardian* produced a series of graphics showing when each of the Premier League clubs did their main business (*Guardian*, 2016). Each transfer was represented by a circle: the bigger the circle, the more money the club spent on that particular player. The positioning of each circle indicated when the transfer took place: on the left, May or June; on the right, August or September.

The data suggests that, during the three years covered by this graphic, Liverpool tended to do most of their buying and selling in June and July while Everton tended to leave their shopping to the last minute. The size of the circles also indicates that Liverpool spend significantly more on personnel.

Of course, not all clubs had such distinctive spending patterns; some spent heavily one summer and then proved more frugal the next. But, the chart showed that at least half of Premier League clubs do have distinctive spending behaviours. My students spent ages poring over this chart, trying to work out who were the biggest spenders, whether there was a link between well-planned purchasing and success or trying to guess which player each blog represented.

The *Guardian* considers this an interactive graphic – and it is, in the sense that you can select which club you want to look at and you can hover over each circle to identify which player's transfer it represents.

BBC Sport, however, has gone a stage further and produced several projects which require you to enter information about yourself to see how you measure up against top sports men and women. These include:

- The footballers' wages calculator (BBC, 2015) – you can enter *your* salary and it will tell you how long it would take Wayne Rooney, Cristiano Ronaldo or other well-remunerated stars to earn what you earn in a year. Or you can use it the other way round – how long would it take you to earn what Rooney earns in a day? Originally published in 2015, the BBC updated this one two years later.
- Olympic Body Match (BBC, 2016) – the BBC loaded up the height and physique of all the competitors at the 2016 Olympics. You could then enter your own statistics and find out which Olympic sport you were best suited to, based on your body type.
- Psycho-metric tests – similar to the above, except that, this time, the program asked you questions designed to find out about your personality and aptitude. Based on your answers, it tried to map you to a sport you might like to try.

Ian Singleton (2017), the editor of BBC Sport online, says these projects are "commissioned with a wry smile on your face. You've got to be a little bit playful to get that sharable quality."

CASE STUDY: THE COST OF FOOTBALL

One of the biggest sport-related data projects is called the Price of Football. The BBC has been running this since 2011 (BBC, 2011). Initially, it was a catalogue of prices – the cost of tickets, of match day programmes, pies and so on – which enabled fans to compare how much one club was charging compared to others. Over the years, it's become more interactive so that now, for example, you can work out what proportion of a player's wages you are contributing when you buy a season ticket and a replica shirt (BBC, 2017).

Ian Singleton's department oversees it:

We gather the data from all of the clubs in the English, Scottish, Welsh and Irish Leagues and some of the top teams from around Europe as well. We get their cheapest match day ticket, most expensive match day ticket, cheapest season ticket, most expensive season ticket, pie, programme and tea. We now do junior and adult shirt and away travel and the mean price that people pay for a ticket.

It's something ridiculous like 2,200 data sets that we gather so we take two of our journalists off diary, a couple of months before. We email and speak to all the clubs and talk them through it. It takes about six weeks to get all the data in. You need really clear processes for how you log the data, where you log the data and how you check the data that's really important when you've got multiple staff working on it.

The personalisation of the projects is key. So when you go on the Price of Football calculator tool, you put in your team and we ask for some data relevant to you and your habits and it personalises it for you. It will take every bit of data like "you support Manchester United, this is how Manchester United rank, this is the highest, this is the lowest, this is how much Man United have gone up by, this is how much a ticket costs in relation to a Man United player's weekly wage". If someone personalises it and we give them something more shareable – like "my matchday ticket pays for 0.00002% of Wayne Rooney's wages", it's quite a sharable thing.

The PFA has given us data for average wages in each league and then there are some players where we've got their wage on record.

(Singleton, 2017)

This isn't a project that can be undertaken by a computer. As Singleton warns, "data can mislead you" – it needs human beings to add context or explanation.

When I did the Price of Football, the two things that stood out in the Premier League data was that the average price of the cheapest ticket had gone above £30 for the first time and the average price rise in the division was more than five per cent, well above inflation. On the face of it that's a strong news line, something that's happened in the League. But, I didn't feel completely comfortable with it. And, as we looked into the data more, 13 of the clubs in the Premier League had either frozen or reduced prices. When you looked into it, the price rise was caused in part by the teams that were relegated charging less than the ones that were coming up and then, I think, one other club that was just skewing it. But, for the majority of clubs, ticket prices were either frozen or reduced.

So, we changed the way we interpreted it: we still kept the percentages but we also looked at the amount of clubs that increased, froze or reduced their prices and it gave a completely different way of looking at the data. I think that when you're doing a piece of data journalism, you want to be robust and fair and if you go off on data without thinking it through you risk misleading people and they're going to feel the BBC has not been fair and balanced.

(ibid)

SUMMARY

- The use of data is growing in all forms of sports journalism, not just online. Younger sports fans appear to have a greater appetite for data.
- The basic office tools you can find on any computer will allow you to create charts that use data.

- Clear presentation of data works well on social media – particularly Instagram.
- Interactive, or personalised, data projects are growing in popularity because they are very sharable. People like to show their friends how they scored on this sort of test.
- Data is incredibly powerful, but it needs to be handled with care. It needs ethical journalists to put it in context.

REFERENCES

BBC (2011) *The price of football – premier league clubs* at www.bbc.co.uk/sport/football/14367608. Last accessed 30/11/2017

BBC (2015) *How long would it take you to earn a top footballer's salary?* at www.bbc.co.uk/news/world-31110113. Last accessed 30/11/2017

BBC (2016) *Who is your Olympic body match?* at www.bbc.co.uk/sport/olympics/36984887. Last accessed 30/11/2017

BBC (2017) *Price of football: Full results 2017* at www.bbc.co.uk/sport/football/41482931. Last accessed 30/11/2017

Guardian (2016) *Premier league: Transfer window summer 2016 – interactive* at www.theguardian.com/football/ng-interactive/2016/aug/23/premier-league-transfer-window-summer-2016-interactive. Last accessed 30/11/2017

Hazard Owen, L. (2017) *Not a revolution (yet): Data journalism hasn't changed that much in 4 years, a new paper finds* at www.niemanlab.org/2017/10/not-a-revolution-yet-data-journalism-hasnt-changed-that-much-in-4-years-a-new-paper-finds/. Last accessed 30/11/2017

Mansell, J. (2017) Interview with the author, 14/08/2017

NPR (2010) *Program creates computer-generated sports stories* at www.npr.org/templates/story/story.php?storyId=122424166. Last accessed 30/11/2017

Popescu, J. (2017) Interview conducted by the author on 13/10/2017

Singleton, I. (2017) Interview conducted by the author on 20/10/2017

Telegraph.co.uk (2015) *How golf's new wonderboy compares to the game's legends* at www.telegraph.co.uk/sport/golf/theopen/11742616/The-Open-2015-Jordan-Spieth-says-ghosts-of-St-Andrews-past-intimidate-him-more-than-his-rivals.html. Last accessed 30/11/2017

Velon media team (2017) *Vincenzo Nibali's Il Lombardia data: How the Bahrain Merida rider won* at www.velon.cc/en/news/2017/10/vincenzo-nibali-il-lombardia-data-how-the-bahrain-merida-rider-won. Last accessed 30/11/2017

Willis, A. (2017) Interview conducted by the author on 15/9/2017

ONE-CLUB JOURNALISM

CHAPTER 9

The club journalist

A few years ago, I was sitting in a press box at a struggling Championship football club and got into a conversation with my neighbour. She was a recent graduate from one of the country's most highly regarded sports journalism courses and was aiming to become, she said, a "club journalist". Our hosts were her local club and, although they didn't currently have any vacancies, they allowed her to attend games to build experience and contacts.

This was the first time I'd heard the term "club journalist" and it wasn't one that I liked. You can't be a journalist, I reasoned, if you are working for a club – or, indeed, a sports governing body or tournament organiser. As George Orwell may have said (there's some debate about it) "Journalism is printing what someone else does not want printed; everything else is public relations". A "club journalist", I assumed, was really just a new term for press officer.

But, on further reflection, I recognise that there are good reasons to use the phrase. The modern-day club journalist is far removed from a traditional press officer who might have been mainly concerned with responding to requests for interviews and press passes, dealing with bad news stories and putting out press releases about new sponsors or progress on the club's west stand redevelopment. Today, big football clubs employ large teams whose job is to work as a newsroom providing 24/7 coverage of goings on at the club across a wide range of platforms. Like newsrooms, they aim to break new stories before any rivals, they aim to come up with amusing ideas to attract readers and, perhaps surprisingly, they often struggle to get access to the players and manager. A large part of their job involves trying to connect with fans using social media.

Speaking at a conference organised by Leeds Trinity University in 2016, a speaker from Everton Football Club revealed they employed eight club journalists, ranging from staff assigned traditional duties such as producing a match day programme through to camera operators and editors. It's probably safe to say that the likes of Manchester United and Chelsea employ double that number while, even when they were in League One, Wolves had a press team of six.

As we saw in the introduction, there was a time when there was a hard and fast wall between journalism and promotional work. Today, there is much more crossover and there are grey areas between the two. Many leading journalists do both. So, working for a club doesn't prevent you working for a newspaper or broadcaster at the same time or at a later date.

> I think it is journalism. Not even a form of journalism – it is journalism. Journalism for me is about storytelling in whatever form that comes in. As the economics of journalism have changed there have been fewer and fewer reporters who have been able to spend the time finding the stories that now-adays might be being provided by club journalism.
>
> – Mark Coyle, head of Media at Velon (Coyle, 2017)

Positive or negative, club media teams are here to stay and represent a significant source of employment for sports journalism graduates, so it would be irresponsible for a book of this kind to ignore them.

THE BACK STORY: FROM HANDING OUT PRESS RELEASES TO RUNNING A 24/7 NEWS CHANNEL

The growth of these roles has been dramatic. As recently as the 1990s, when Alan (now Lord) Sugar was running Tottenham Hotspur, there was no press team to deal with the criticism his management style generated. He brought in PR specialist Nick Hewer, who dealt with the business tycoon's other companies, to help out. I interviewed him in 2011 and he told me that it was "sheer hell":

> The phone started ringing at 6am and it didn't stop until after midnight . . . I sat in the executive box and all around me were people screaming obscenities. Behind me there was a high court judge and a senior partner at a big accountancy firm. And they just spent 90 minutes screaming obscenities. All because some people were chasing a ball around. And then on Monday morning they'd go back to court as though nothing had happened.
>
> (Hewer, 2011)

At the end of the last century, relatively few football clubs outside the Premier League had a media team. Requests for interviews or match passes and news about the signing or release of players were all conducted through the club secretaries or by a direct phone call to the manager if they'd given reporters their phone numbers (which they usually did).

This began to change. By 2005, most league clubs had at least one employee to deal with the press. Looking back on the period 2000–05, when I worked on a regional television sports desk, I can see other changes that took place. At the start of this period, the clubs tended to phone us to say they were holding a press conference to make an announcement, which they then expected us to relay to fans. On Friday afternoons, we'd collect the team news by calling someone at the club.

Within a few years, this changed. We started taking most of our stories from the club website. It was quicker than calling the manager, who, of course, was very busy.

But, of course, if we could get the news from the club website, so could fans. We were adding very little to what was already publicly available.

Of course, we could still make interesting reports. Club websites at that time weren't showing very much video or interviews. But that was to come soon, as sports journalist Paul Hassall relates:

> I worked at Trinity Mirror's Sport Media (magazine and book publishing arm of the company) where we had extensive access to Liverpool FC players through our contract with the club. The focus on [Trinity's] LFC Weekly magazine, souvenir specials and the match day programme meant we generally conducted more interviews than the official website. By the end of 2007 and the launch of LFC TV, this began to shift with the demands of the online and visual medium taking priority.
>
> (Hassall, 2017)

Clubs wanted to take control of how they were represented in the wider world. A club like Liverpool boasts as many fans in America or south-east Asia as in the United Kingdom, so why allow journalists based in the north-west of England to remain as its principal channel of communication? The development of the world wide web and the club's own television station meant it could reach out to its fans without depending on traditional media channels.

Other sports didn't change as quickly. There was probably a much smaller core of people who regularly checked out cricket club or boxing gym websites, so they still relied on the media like us to publicise their events. But, with the advent of social media, that began to change. Now a niche group like boxing fans living in Kent could be targeted very precisely. But football remains a bit of a special case, as Mark Coyle, head of media at cycling group Velon, explains:

> So, if it's a football club's star signing, the general sports media are not being given the opportunity to interview that person but the club will provide one interview. You might rightly feel aggrieved because you've not got a God-given right to speak to that person but conventionally you would have had access to that person. But there is a difference between what happens in football and what happens elsewhere. I have not come across one instance in a year working in professional cycling where access has been denied to a rider.
>
> (Coyle, 2017)

You might expect a club journalist to enjoy outstanding access to the club's players and coaches – after all, they all work for the same employer. In practice, as in any large organisation, relationships are not always harmonious. For example, in February 2017, Arsenal's media team was caught on the hop when Ian Wright, a former Arsenal player now working for the BBC, said he'd spoken on the phone to the club's manager Arsene Wenger. Wright said Wenger had told him this might be his last season at the north London club.

POACHERS TURNED GAMEKEEPERS

Traditionally, some journalists have moved into public relations because it often pays better and offers more predictable, family-friendly hours. Increasingly, though, I've noticed students want to go directly into club journalism, which perhaps reflects the lack of career security in conventional journalism.

For some, the limitations feel too restrictive. For example, in the summer of 2017, all the media outlets that covered Liverpool Football Club were buzzing with rumours that star player Philippe Coutinho was set to leave the club to join Barcelona. The one outlet that barely mentioned the story was Liverpool's own club media channels. Clearly, they didn't want to add fuel to a fire that they were struggling to control.

You'll also need to focus on your own club to the exclusion of everything else. Within a newsroom, even a specialist reporter normally has some scope to go off-topic; press officers don't. "Every tweet we post will always say where Team Sunweb is", explains the cycling team's social content editor Emily Brammeier. "We won't post general race updates. We'll never post the winner of the race. It's always where *we* finish" (Brammeier, 2017).

If you're the sort of person who finds these sorts of constraints irksome, then club journalism probably isn't for you.

> Our race organiser came to me with a specific request, a perfectly reasonable request – could a reporter have access to a rider for a newspaper interview ahead of a race? And the short answer from the team was yes but we would rather – and here they were being polite – you don't ask questions about another team because every time this rider is interviewed he gets asked about this other team because he used to ride for them. So I guess I've gone from poacher to gamekeeper. If I had a problem with that then I'd be in the wrong job.
>
> – Mark Coyle (Coyle, 2017)

THE SCHEDULE: ALDERSHOT FC

To get an idea of what working as a club journalist entails, it might be useful to look at the working routine of one. Steve Gibbs is a lifelong Aldershot fan. For many years, he combined working as a music and arts journalist and PR with running a fan-based website and talking about the 'Shots on local radio. He became the club's full-time press officer in 2013.

Below, he takes us through what he does on a match-day.

12.15 Arrive at the ground. I like to try to get to a game as early as possible. For a 3pm kick-off that means about 12.15 which, if the game is in the north-west, means leaving home around 8. The earliest I left home last year was 6.30 to get to Gateshead.

I like to get a few photographs of the ground, get set up and just try to create the atmosphere for people who are on their way or not making the trip, through Twitter, through Facebook, through the club website and, increasingly, through Instagram and Snapchat as well. We try not to reproduce the same image or video across all of them – that defeats the object of having all the different platforms.

14.00 Teams announced. Our manager normally lets me know the team a little beforehand. So, I'll have a tweet and a Facebook post prepared in advance with headline team news – these two players in, these two out. If it's a home game, I have to pick up the team sheets from the referee's office, run down to my office to type them in, wait for the archaic photocopier to churn out 200 copies, then run back to the press room to hand them out.

At an away game, I know I'll get the team sheet sometime between ten past and half past two. So, I can't be down beside the pitch at that point, in case everyone else gets the news and I don't.

Once I've got the team sheet, I'll photograph it and put it on all the platforms, so it reaches as many people as possible. Instagram's a very visual medium. Sometimes a photo of a team sheet isn't right for it, so I'll try to find something different that conveys the same information, a professionally-taken picture of the player who's come in maybe.

14.30 During the warm-up. I like to stand behind the goal and get the goalkeeper and the striker warming up and put that as a piece of live video on Twitter. Then I might do some quick feet shuttle runs and put that on Snapchat. You sort of get to know what works on what platform. With Snapchat, you can have a bit more fun with it and put little faces or captions on it. Some of the players, they'll see you with the phone and they'll respond so you get that interaction. I suppose the mantra is you take people somewhere they wouldn't otherwise be able to get.

14.55 Teams come out. Clearly the home team will have better access to good content. If I'm away at, say, Tranmere, I'll be in the press box, which is on the third tier, and that means I can't get down to the tunnel to get a close-up video of the teams walking out. So, you know the opposition will have access to that so you re-tweet their tweet.

1500 I do a text commentary, a live blog on Twitter, moment-by-moment. We let people know that from 3 to 5 on matchdays, we'll be on Twitter: you want to follow the game, that's where to go. You try to make it as descriptive as possible for people who aren't there. That can get really good interaction.

You have to self-censor. Sometimes I think, 'this might turn into a good move' so I'll start writing it up – "ball picked up by the left back" – but then it doesn't develop into anything.

15.45 At half-time, I do a summary on Facebook.

16.05 Second half and back to Twitter commentary. After about seven minutes, even if it's a dull game with no chances, people will think I've fallen off the edge of the Earth or they've lost their wi-fi connection, so

I might tweet "little happening here, few chances, still nil–nil" or "you're not missing much – there's an injury".

You see more and more, even at our level, a photograph immediately gets delivered to the folder on the press officer's laptop. He can drag and drop that photo into Twitter as an in-action shot. So, if there's a goal, then two minutes after it's gone in you can have a photo of the player celebrating on your Twitter feed. We don't have that yet but it's standard in the Championship.

16.50 Final whistle. You hope the manager's got quite a lot to say to the team and isn't out of the dressing room straight away. You want a bit of a gap between the end of the game and you having to do an interview because you need time to reflect the result as quickly as possible across five or six different platforms.

On the other hand, if he's very late coming out that makes the half hour from 5.30 to 6pm more pressing because I've got to write 500 words for the Non-League Paper by 6pm. I need quotes from him to go into the report, so I can't finish it until I've got his view on some of the incidents. But, at the same time, I've got to relay what the manager has just said on Twitter and other outlets.

You're trying to do three or four things at once. Sometimes, your plans go out of the window and you just have to wing it. You are juggling and you are beholden to the manager's schedule – there's nothing you can do about this. There have been times when it can be quite a while – the latest a manager ever came out was quarter past six; he locked himself in his own office so he had some calm time to gather his thoughts – and everyone else in the press box is saying "what are you doing Steve, we've got homes to go to?".

6pm I upload the interviews. I do the manager and then, depending on the result, up to three or four player interviews as well. In the same way that you don't post 30 Facebook posts during the two hours of the game, you don't put four interviews out at five past six. You keep them and you give them each their own time, and they get more hits. Facebook allows you to schedule posts even up to six months in advance, so, within the 24 hours after a game, you can schedule. I tend to post them at three-hour differences. So, I put the manager out as soon as possible at 6pm, then a player at 9pm. You don't post at midnight, you save the next one until 9am on Sunday morning, then one at midday and another at 3pm.

6.20pm Editing match footage. Whether you are home or away, you should get the raw footage within an hour to 90 minutes of the final whistle. You've sometimes got over two hours of footage that you've got to distil into ten minutes of highlights. Because the demand is there and it's such a live medium, if I leave the highlights edit until a Monday morning, it feels like I've missed the boat a bit. When Barrow played us, their video guy had a six-hour journey home on the coach. So, what else was he going to do but edit the game? He had a full 10-minute highlights package with graphics and all on YouTube by the time he'd got to Stoke.

> That sort of thing is going to get you so much more engagement than, say, a gallery of still photos.
>
> **8pm Trailer.** If I'm not driving home from the game, I'm either on the team bus or the train, then I sometimes put short highlights out as a Facebook post or a tweet as a trailer. If I put that out at 8, 9pm, the way Facebook prioritises video, that little clip could have had 50,000 views by Sunday lunchtime.
>
> **And finally**: If there's a game on Tuesday, I'm already posting, looking ahead to that.
>
> (Gibbs, 2017)

Gibbs doesn't talk very much about the club website. He doesn't expect fans to come to him; he knows he has to reach out to them, using whichever platform they prefer. He can't say "everything you need is on the website": some fans want updates on Facebook, some on Twitter, some on Snapchat etc.

Despite this, he *does* focus on just Twitter during the 90 minutes of the match itself. Realistically, he knows he can't "juggle" five balls when a fast-paced match is unfolding in front of him.

He understands how each platform works. Facebook is good for video; Twitter for regular updates; Instagram for pictures.

Preparation is key. He prepares team announcements in advance; he plans when he'll release interviews; he looks ahead to the next game.

He collaborates with his opposite number from the other team – and also makes use of volunteers and students to get more done.

YOUR TURN

The best way to practise being a club journalist is to actually do the job. The great thing here is that there are lots of sports clubs out there who would really like help from digitally literate people.

- Make contact with a local amateur or semi-pro sports club which doesn't seem to be publicising itself very well. Look for one that only posts rarely on social media or rarely updates its website; one that perhaps doesn't make much use of video or photographs. Try non-league football clubs, cricket, hockey or rugby clubs.
- Ask them if you can take over their media channels for three months.

This probably sounds a very big undertaking – but I've seen several students make a real difference to a club by looking after their communications. Most of these clubs are run by amateurs – often retired people who find social media complicated. If you then go for a job at a big club, they'll be hugely impressed by someone who has already managed an organisation's digital streams.

A BIGGER CLUB OR ORGANISATION

Steve Gibbs' job is principally about providing a commentary on what's going on at Aldershot Football Club. Fans want to know when tickets go on sale, when players come and go, injury news and, of course, updates on matches they can't attend themselves. He also has relatively few external media outlets to think about – three or four newspapers, a couple of radio stations, BT Sport (who hold the rights to the Vanarama National League) and, perhaps once a season, he'll get a visit from the regional television station.

When we move to a bigger club, there are more media outlets to satisfy and, sometimes, different parts of the club to promote. For example, a lot of Premier League clubs have their own TV channels. Arsenal, Chelsea, Manchester City and Liverpool are all currently working hard to push up attendances at their games in the Women's Super League. Your club may have links to a foundation or other sporting charity that it wants to promote.

Whatever your feelings about club journalism, it is worth looking at how some big clubs go about promoting themselves and their players. "Arsenal are doing really great stuff with their player interviews," says Neil Smythe, formerly of Copa90 and the Football Republic. "Man City have done something recently where they've got players to commentate over their own action. The FA have got players to interview themselves" (Smythe, 2017).

In the meantime, your club will always be in the news whether you want it to be or not. For example, international breaks are a constant headache for big clubs. Players are apt to return to their home country and give interviews in which they say something that suggests they don't think much of the club manager or that they'd be interested in a move to Barcelona, Real Madrid or Bayern Munich. There are only so many times you can say that their quotes were mistranslated.

YOUR TURN

Each of the following scenarios is based loosely on something that did actually happen. In groups, discuss how you might handle the situation. In each case, there is no particular right answer. I've given you a few ideas to help you discuss the first question – after that you're on your own.

1   The unexpected answer
    You're part of the media team at an English county cricket club. The county has just signed a new South African batsman as its overseas player. He's an experienced player, now retired from the international game but still capable of scoring a quick-fire half century. To drum up interest in the forthcoming T20 matches, you are putting out a short video of highlights from his career along with an interview that's been conducted for you by a freelance journalist in South Africa.
    The interview is just 90 seconds long and is made up of a series of short questions and answers. Question three is "Who's your cricketing hero?" The player replied "Hansie Cronje".

(Cronje was a very successful captain of South Africa between 1994 and 2000. He was later banned from the sport after it emerged he'd taken part in match-fixing. He died in a plane crash in 2002.)

The simple approach here is simply to edit the interview, removing the answer about Hansie Cronje. Your job is to promote your club not get into a debate about an event that's now a piece of history. Why bring negative publicity to the county, suggesting it condones match-fixing?

But there are other issues to consider. Was the interview conducted exclusively for you? Could it get out by other channels? In which case, it might be better for you to release it so that you have some control over the story.

You might also want to consider the player himself. Do you think he gave that answer because he wants to provoke public debate about rehabilitating Cronje? The video might lead to requests from journalists asking for interviews. Do you think your player could handle himself well in that situation and give intelligent answers? He's an experienced player so he's probably been interviewed hundreds of times and probably knows what he's doing. Those interviews will all help generate extra publicity for the county. On the other hand, if he were younger, then that answer could really dog him throughout his career.

Finally, you need to consider the fact that this is an official voice. If you are putting the interview out on the county's Facebook Live or YouTube channels, you could be seen to be condoning his admiration for Cronje. If you do want to provoke a debate, it might be better to arrange an interview with a trusted journalist and speak to the player in advance to make sure he's happy to talk about the match-fixing controversy.

2   Working with children

You work for a leading rugby union club. One of your star players has agreed to lead a training session for the under eights at a local amateur club. He sets up some simple passing drills for the youngsters and then notices that one of them is a girl. As a joke he says "hey, girls can't play rugby". Although the comment is meant ironically, the seven-year-old doesn't understand that and bursts into tears. The scene is spotted by a local paper reporter; she interviews the girl's family who say they are "bitterly disappointed".

HINT: Try to come up with creative solutions to this one.

3   Striker's strop

You run the media team at a lower division football club. Your number nine, signed a few years ago for a big fee, has been out of form the first two months of the new season. At one game, a section of the crowd is constantly booing him and this, in turn, leads to him missing two good chances. Soon after half-time, the manager decides to replace him. As the player walks off, he receives more abuse.

That evening, one particular fan continues to slate the player on Twitter, sending a message saying "you're not fit to wear the shirt". The player responds: "Screw you. I hope you die of cancer."

HINT: You may have some sympathy for either the player or the fan but don't forget your main interest is to promote a positive image of the club.

4   Striker's strop, part two

Re-read 3. This time, however, consider whether you would handle the situation differently if:

- the tweet sent by the fan included a racially offensive term;
- you knew that the player in question was suffering mental health problems.

TOP TIPS: MEDIA STRATEGY

Another form of club journalism is when you are working for a governing body or promoting a particular competition. This presents a new problem because, as well as satisfying audiences on social media and the professional media, you also have to think about the competing teams or individuals who may complain that you're favouring some of their rivals. In the next section, Alexandra Wills talks about some of the challenges of managing communications for one of the biggest sports tournaments in the world.

Alexandra Willis wrote for a tennis magazine and then the *Daily Telegraph* before joining Wimbledon, where she's head of Communications, Content and Digital. Under her leadership, the comms team at the All England Lawn Tennis Club has won numerous awards, including Best Digital Platform and Best Use of Social Media at the BT Sport Industry Awards, 2016. She also writes a tennis blog.

1 Understand what the purpose is. It doesn't matter if you don't understand tennis when you come and work here – though, of course, it helps – but what's more important is understanding the purpose of the content you're creating.

   I wouldn't give someone who applied to work here a quiz on tennis players and who tennis players are. I would be more likely to give them a challenge about how would you handle a specific situation, how would you work as part of a team, who would you ask if you didn't know something?

2 You need an aptitude for multi-platform. So not just thinking about things in a very linear fashion but actually thinking "well Roger Federer is doing a balcony walk. So, let's take a video of that, then we can take the first 30 seconds and put it on one platform and take the long form and put it in another platform and then that last bit we can use to tease something else." So, thinking about the spread of a moment or a content opportunity.

3 Creativity – no idea is a bad idea in social media. Don't be afraid to push the boundaries because the industry is such that everyone is looking at what everyone else is doing so someone will come up with an idea and everyone will copy it. So, you need to change and refresh your ideas.

4 A passion. Some people who come and work here are passionate about Roger Federer or they are passionate about video or about animation or illustration. It may seem contradictory because we want people to be multi-functional but I still think having a passion is a good thing.

5 There's no substitute for accuracy.

(Willis, 2017)

SUMMARY

- In a little over 20 years, most leading football clubs have gone from having just one or two press officers to having a full newsroom dedicated to just that single club.
- Whether you are covering a small club like Aldershot or managing a major international event like Wimbledon, social media is likely to be central to everything you do. Effective club journalists can repurpose content from one platform to use on another.
- As a communications officer or club journalist, you may enjoy greater access to the players or athletes themselves; think about how you can exploit that access creatively.
- As you're covering one club or organisation exclusively, you need to be passionate – either about the club itself or about a particular aspect of your job.

REFERENCES

Brammeier, E. (2017) Interview conducted by the author on 16/8/2017

Coyle, M. (2017) Interview conducted by the author on 18/7/2017

Gibbs, S. (2017) Interview conducted by the author on 11/7/2017

Hassall, P. (2017) Email exchange with the author on 1 & 2/12/2017

Hewer, N. (2011) Interview conducted by the author on 9/2/2011

Smythe, N. (2017) Email exchange with author on 23–26/7/2017

Willis, A. (2017) Interview conducted by the author on 14/9/2017

CHAPTER 10

The fan journalist

At the opposite end of the spectrum to club journalists, who have to bear in mind that their priority is to consider the interests of the club or organisation that they represent, sit fan journalists, who are answerable to no one but their audience.

Like club journalists, fan journalists may have a narrow perspective on the world of sport, concentrating on just one club, but, unlike club journalists, they can call for the sacking of the manager, rip into the star centre back or tell the board they should put the club up for sale.

The downside of this is that very few fan journalists actually make a living out of what they do. A few do. For others it's a spin-off from their other journalism which helps them build a social media following. But, for the most part, it's a labour of love. You could start a Halifax Town podcast because you've noticed there's a gap in the market. But, for it to work, you need to be a dyed-in-the-wool Halifax fan who goes to all the games and knows the club's history.

However, for a young person wanting to break through as a sports journalist, it's hard to think of a better way of establishing yourself than running a podcast or Fan TV channel. It demonstrates that you can build a following if you're well-organised and you're persistent – particularly if you can produce something several times a week for a couple of years.

> If you're an Oxford fan and you want to create a fan channel, there's not going to be money in it; you're going to want to do it for the love of it. I'm not going to do it because I'm 46, I've got a family and I live in Surrey. But there must be a 21 year old out there who is out of uni, or wants to get in the media who can pick up a camera and do it and I'd be really happy.
> — Neil Smythe who set up a group of fan channels for Freemantle Media and supports Oxford United

Before we go on, a word of apology. This chapter focuses almost exclusively on content produced by fans of football clubs. It seems that the idea of media produced essentially for the fans of a single club hasn't really caught on in other sports, even though there have been some great fanzines and podcasts looking more generally at the sports of cricket, both codes of rugby, boxing, mixed martial arts and many others. These are covered in the chapter on podcasting. Another parallel from other sports is the tradition of producing videos (initially on tape and now on DVD) for fans of speedway and mixed martial arts.

THE BACK STORY: FROM FANZINE TO FAN CHANNEL

The story begins with fanzines – fan-produced magazines. Fanzines have covered a wide range of topics such as science fiction, horror and music. *Foul*, which was published between 1972 and 1976, is regarded as the first football fanzine (Barber and Williams, 2002). The topics it covered included poor media coverage of football and the lack of creativity in British football – both of which are still regularly debated by fan media today.

But the big boom in football fanzines came in the 1980s. There are several reasons for this:

- Music fanzines, particularly those produced by punks and new wave aficionados, had shown how effective fan-driven publications could be. Just as music fans had gigs as an obvious location to sell fanzines, so football fans had matches.
- A big, but largely overlooked, technological innovation, the photocopier, had become commonplace in offices by the late 1970s. At the same time, fewer people were working in manufacturing and more were now in offices. Access to the office photocopier meant fanzines could be printed quickly and inexpensively.
- The mainstream media wasn't covering football in the ways fans wanted. Matchday programmes were expensive and often dull, while newspaper coverage tended to be earnest and humourless – there was a space that wasn't being covered.
- Intelligent football fans increasingly started to demand a say in how their clubs, and the game more generally, was being run. This came to a head when Margaret Thatcher, the British Prime Minister in the 1980s, attempted to introduce a membership card scheme for anyone wanting to attend a football match, which provoked widespread opposition.

Every club in the top four divisions probably had at least one fanzine with the top teams generating half a dozen or more. These often reflected different sections of the club's support. For example, one Manchester United fanzine, *Red Issue*, which, on several occasions, published offensive content about Liverpool, claimed to be the authentic voice of United's working class Mancunian support.

The content of fanzines varied but typically included:

- comment on the team's recent performances, including praise and criticism of individual players;
- match previews including advice on the best pubs near to away grounds;
- comment on the wider management of the club such as ticket prices, replica shirts, ownership etc;
- articles attacking rival clubs;
- elevens made up of great players from the club's past;
- cartoons.

It is worth noting that these continue to be part of fan websites, podcasts and video channels today.

When controversies arose at clubs, for example if the owners became unpopular, fanzines, inevitably, tended to head the protest movement. For example, the Brighton fanzine *Gulls Eye* was at the forefront of attempts to remove the club's chairman Bill Archer, who agreed the sale of the Goldstone Ground. (*Gulls Eye*'s editors were also sued by another group of Brighton directors and had to pay £6,000 in legal costs.) Charlton fanzine *The Voice of the Valley* was launched in 1988 when the Addicks were not in fact playing at their traditional home but ground-sharing with Crystal Palace; as the fanzine's name suggests, part of its purpose was to raise awareness of the homeless club's plight.

If journalists wanted a comment from fans, they would tend to approach the fanzine's editor; the magazine *When Saturday Comes* printed a handy directory at the back of each issue so it was easy to get hold of contact details. Today, there is a still a temptation to seek comments from podcasters or fans who run websites, but it is important to remember that they are not always typical of the average fan. They tend to be younger and to hold stronger opinions.

In the 1990s, many fanzines developed websites; this meant fans could still share their views without having to stand outside the ground for two hours before kick-off trying to sell fanzines and spend time and money photocopying.

The same era saw the emergence of message boards where fans could instantly exchange opinions and information about their clubs. Sometimes message boards formed part of the fanzine website – at other clubs, the local newspaper site became the focal point of communication. Frequently fans of rival clubs would hijack each other's message boards to post abuse. Working on a regional TV sports desk at this time, I would occasionally post on the message boards of the clubs we covered to explain why we had taken a particular approach to a story. I sometimes found myself getting sucked into arguments, but I think there was a silent majority that appreciated my doing this.

By this time several fanzine writers had moved into mainstream journalism, and television companies were trying to work out ways of capturing the spirit of fanzines on the small screen. BBC2's *Fantasy Football* and Sky's *Soccer AM* were examples of where this transition was successful – at least for a short time.

Paper fanzines are still around today at most clubs – though there are far fewer than in the 1980s and 1990s heyday. At some, the print versions have outlasted the fan websites which attempted to succeed them. Rather than websites, today it's the podcast which is probably the most lively area of fan media.

Podcasts really took off between 2005 and 2010. Early efforts, unsurprisingly, sounded like audio fanzines: young men grumbling about their club's lack of investment or the manager's poor team selection. Within a few years, however, there were some genuinely insightful or creative podcasts.

An interesting, and unusual, example is *Hornet Heaven*, which celebrates Watford FC (Wicken, 2017). Each episode takes the form of a short story, written by Ollie Wicken and narrated by Colin Mace. It transpires that, when good Watford fans die, they go to a place called Hornet Heaven. There they find a giant programme store. By selecting a match programme, they are whisked back to the game in question. This simple idea has now generated five seasons of podcasts.

Hornet Heaven sounds as though it could be the work of one person. In fact, there's quite a big credits list, including the writer, narrator, musicians and website artist, plus it draws on the work of two club historians. In short, good fan media is normally a team effort.

The next stage, inevitably, was for fans to start producing fan TV channels or video-casts (terminology is a source of debate – some fans dislike the term "TV" arguing that their approach is very different to that of traditional television), using YouTube as their distribution channel. Most of the leading clubs' fan channels were set up between 2012 and 2014. In 2013, FremantleMedia, makers of programmes as diverse as the *X-Factor*, *American Gods* and Jamie Oliver cookery programmes, decided to enter the market, launching a string of fan TV channels including Full-TimeDEVILS and Spurred On. There has been some dispute about whether these were authentic fan channels as they had big media backing, but Neil Smythe, the company's former head of sport, insists the presenters and most of the staff on these channels were die-hard fans of their clubs.

Today, most Premier League clubs and a smattering of lower league teams have fan channels. With a few, high-profile, exceptions, they haven't achieved the same level of popularity as podcasts. For example, even though Burnley are enjoying a rare extended spell in the Premier League, broadcasts on Burnley Fan TV channel struggle to attract five figures (McInnes, 2017). Bradford City's Bantams Banter (a frequent award winner) has started trying to crossover to "videocasts" but the editors admit it's been difficult. In a 2017 podcast, they reflect: "YouTube is like the holy grail. It's the toughest nut for us to crack. It's making us feel that we only have voices for radio. As soon as they see our faces they're like 'ugh, oh no!' " (Bantams Banter, 2017).

HOW DO CLUBS – AND PLAYERS – TREAT FAN-BASED MEDIA?

Back in the 1980s, clubs reacted with almost universal hostility to fanzines as, rather simplistically, they saw them as a threat to sales of the matchday programme. Of course, in some instances, fanzines *were* actively hostile to the club's ownership or management.

Ironically, several of the fanzine editors of the 1980s and 1990s went on to become press officers at their clubs. Perhaps this explains why, when podcasts and fan channels started popping up, clubs were a little bit more sympathetic and, for the most part, realised that it was a good thing for people to be exchanging news and views online.

They also perhaps realised that it would be a mistake to give fan-based media too much oxygen of publicity. When some contributors on Arsenal Fan TV called for manager Arsene Wenger to be sacked, Sky Sports pundit Gary Neville labelled them "embarrassing". He generated more exposure for the channel than a 100-grand advertising campaign would have done. To his credit, Neville invited the channel to interview him at Sky's HQ (Arsenal Fan TV, 2017); that episode attracted more than one and a half million views. So, clubs and mainstream media seem to treat new fan media with cautious warmth.

"Our relationship with the club has gone through ups and downs", says Liverpool podcaster Neil Atkinson (2017):

> Broadly speaking, they could make our lives more difficult than they do but they could help us more than they do. We're not persona non grata but the

club's media is moving more towards the club, full stop. The club wants the club to cover things, to release things; they want people to subscribe to LFC TV. We're not allowed to go to club press conferences. We sometimes get invited to press conferences for European games sometimes by UEFA. We go but they are of limited value really because we're supporters and our customers don't want to hear media polished interviews; they want to hear supporters.

Neil Smythe, who worked for Manchester United fan channel FullTime Devils, agrees that audiences don't want conventional "polished" interviews on fan media.

Strong shows, whether broadcast or digital, set a specific tone for their content. As a result the audience has an expectation. And if that expectation in terms of content or tone isn't met, the audience doesn't respond well. This is particularly prevalent on YouTube where audiences generally subscribe for one particular tone, face or format. So if you build a channel on independent, edgy, opinion and you then have a dry interview with a player, then naturally the audience won't respond. They can find better player features with better access elsewhere, so they don't come to unofficial channels for that.

(Smythe, 2017b)

If the opportunity does arise to speak to players, don't be too overawed. Remember you're a journalist looking for insights, not a fan looking for selfies. "My whole approach to doing these sorts of interviews is just to have a few outlying questions but really just to have a conversation with the person – something which journalists don't seem to have the time or wherewithal to do these days", says cricket podcaster Nishant Joshi (2017). "It's very important to treat these guys as human. You're meeting someone for the first time – how would a normal conversation go?"

Of course, fan channels do, from time to time, get to meet past or present players, either through personal connections, sponsors or, sometimes, through the club. If this opportunity arises, then players seem to respond best to quirky suggestions rather than traditional interviews. A good example of this was Liverpool channel Redmen TV's Dizzy Pens (Redmen TV, 2015). Selected players had to run 15 times round a cone to make themselves dizzy before attempting to taking a penalty against a presenter from the channel. This came about through close cooperation between the channel, the club and sponsors Vauxhall. Crucially, though, you can see on the video that the players themselves really enjoyed it. "When the shackles are off and players are allowed to do something different, their content can fly," says Neil Smythe (2017).

PODCAST OR FAN TV CHANNEL?

In this section, we're going to look at podcasts and videocasts – or Fan TV channels as they are commonly known. Although the latter have been attracting a lot of media attention (particularly Arsenal Fan TV), podcasts are probably the most popular form of fan journalism at the moment. Fans can download a podcast and listen to it on public transport, in the car or around the house. You don't have to sit down and watch it. What's more, most fan channels aren't particularly visually interesting; they don't have match highlights, for example, and often consist of two blokes sitting on a sofa in front of a static camera, which is not enough to persuade audiences to lend them their eyeballs for up to an hour. And, while almost every club in the top five divisions boasts at least one podcast, only a handful of top clubs can pull in sufficient audiences to justify the considerable time and effort that goes into a Fan TV channel.

If you are going to produce a videocast, it's worth asking yourself "Why is this in vision?" "What is my audience going to see that they couldn't get from a podcast?" For example, Chelsea Fans Channel presenter Sophie Rose produced a video in which she asked Manchester United fans to spell "Ibrahimovic" and "Mkhitaryan" (Chelsea Fans Channel, 2016). On-screen graphics showed how many letters the fans were getting right.

Another reason to be in vision is because your audience likes to know what the people whose opinions they are listening to look like. This is particularly true of Arsenal Fan TV and Full Time Devils both of which have a cast of regulars with distinctive points of view.

The most successful fan channels have two income streams. For example, Arsenal Fan TV has a sponsor and receives money from YouTube for the number of views it attracts. Popular broadcasts such as the interview with Gary Neville (see above) don't just have preroll advertisements but ad breaks in the middle of the interview as well. This enabled the man behind the channel, Robbie Lyle, to give up his day job 14 months after starting the channel. Monetising podcasts is not impossible but harder (see Case study, below and Chapter 11).

The leading fan channels produce huge amounts of content; Lyle uploads around 15 films on a match day, each around five minutes long, followed by longer, more analytical content the following day. It's important to get this content out as quickly as possible; fans want to know whether other Arsenal supporters feel the same way about the game they've just wanted as they do. This means producers have to know where to find free wi-fi close to grounds – it often means having a good relationship with local coffee shops or hotels.

CASE STUDY: *THE ANFIELD WRAP*

Liverpool's *The Anfield Wrap* (TAW) is interesting for a number of reasons. It has evolved from a variety of different attempts to produce content for Liverpool fans, it's an interesting example of fan-based media partnering with existing mainstream media and, unusually, it charges for content.

This account of the project's evolution is based mainly on an interview with the podcast's producer Neil Atkinson.

In 2011, Andy Heaton and Gareth Roberts decided to set up a project based around a website, which would have the best football writing about Liverpool and produce a weekly podcast. Gareth had been the editor of a fanzine called *Well Red*.

The website went live with about 60 pieces of writing.

If anything, there was too much writing and anything that was half decent got lost in the noise. But what it did was it made an enormous splash. So, it came through with a properly produced podcast at Parr Street studios [the venue where Coldplay recorded their first three albums]. For the tenth episode, Rafa Benitez, former Liverpool manager, came in for an interview. It immediately grabbed people's attention.

A period of experimentation now began.

In 2012, a decision was made to produce an online magazine; they were quite vogueish at the time, where you read it on your tablet and you had audio and video embedded. So, it was like a magazine with bells and whistles. And that looked like the direction of travel at the time. The problem is that you could have a really good piece of longform writing and no one cared. Three sentences on the website about a player injury got more views.

Sponsorship and advertisers didn't come aboard; the whole sector struggled with this kind of magazine. Meanwhile, we were the biggest one-team sports podcast in the world and a programme on the Monday after Liverpool had won a big game would get 60,000 listeners. We were doing two shows a week and could only put six out of our 25 contributors on air each week. We had all this talent that we couldn't get on air enough.

So, we realised that the product that they wanted was the podcast. The smart move was to go to a subscriber model over the podcast and get rid of the magazine.

Around this time, Atkinson left his job at a shipping company and was able to throw all his efforts into taking the podcast to the next level.

We launched TAW Player (the app which the podcast runs on) in March 2015 and for two months we gave all the shows away for free. We launched at 12 shows a week; we now do 15 a week during the season. We created show formats like a regular history show, a show that looks at players from the past, an immediate post-match show called *The Pink* and so on.

To help produce the magazine, the team sought external funding from an Australian company called Red Touch Media, but Atkinson says the company no longer supports them financially.

Since we've had TAW Player, it's been entirely self-sufficient. The guy who's their CEO is a really helpful person for me in terms of running the business; he's a mentor. And we're sharing office space. But there's not a hard financial exchange from them to us. The player had to be self-sufficient within a month. For them, we're a pretty small company;

the interest they've got is not significant in terms of the percentage of the company.

The Anfield Wrap also has a good relationship with local radio station, Radio City Talk. They present a Friday evening programme for the station and, in return, are able to use their facilities during quiet times.

If you visit their website, you will see plenty of video, but Neil says it's secondary to the podcast.

> The video exists to sell the audio. It's only since 2016 that we've been looking for a way to do consistent video. We do a video a week called the Wrap Up where we shoot in all different ways and try to have fun. It's good for the brand.

Another reason perhaps why *The Anfield Wrap* hasn't expanded into video in a big way is the existence of another Liverpool Fan TV channel called Redmen TV. Typically, there isn't room for too many TV channels covering any one particular club.

Atkinson also sees part of his role as being to bring on new talent.

> Too quickly, I think, a fanzine quickly becomes dominated by the voice of 30something white men: all the obvious bands, all the obvious clothing, all the obvious allusions. So you lose the energy to find new people with new voices and new ideas. I'm on the look-out for people who aren't 30something white men.
>
> A football podcast is sometimes supposed to sound like a post-match chat in a pub. But that skews it towards people who are used to sitting in a pub talking about football. Those people have got the lineage and the history, copying their dad, drinking in a particular type of pub. There is an issue for women, for people of different ages and people of colour who could be saying perfectly interesting things in a slightly different way and, just because that's not what a section of your audience expects, why shouldn't they?

Now it's established, *The Anfield Wrap* can afford to take risks and expose its audience to people and ideas they wouldn't normally listen to. For example, they've interviewed Juliet Jacques, author of the book *Trans* (and Norwich fan) and Vasily Petrenko, conductor of the Liverpool Philharmonic Orchestra.

By the middle of 2017, the company was employing ten full-time staff including a social media specialist, a web designer and a business manager, as well as welcoming nearly 100 contributors each season to their studios. It's tempting to dismiss them as a one-off. Clearly most clubs don't have sufficiently large fan bases – particularly worldwide fan bases – to sustain a team of that size. However, Everton's *The Blue Room* recently launched a similar subscription model for their podcasts and it's possible to see other club podcasts following on a smaller scale.

TIMING AND PREPARATION

It's worth thinking carefully about the type of content that works best at different times of day. For any sort of fan channel, it's important to get something out as soon as possible after the end of a match while feelings are still raw – be that the exhilaration of a win or the frustration of a defeat. At this point in time, fans don't want anything too analytical – they're looking for outpourings of emotion; some of the best-known performances on Fan TV channels have been post-match explosive rants.

"After we beat Everton 3–1 (in April 2017) we had Paco Ayestarán, the former assistant manager, on our post-match show", recalls Neil Atkinson of *The Anfield Wrap* (ibid). "He's a deep thinker about the game and there was a lot of tactical analysis – and we had loads of complaints. what people wanted was to hear us going mental after we'd just beaten Everton 3–1."

After 24 hours, there's likely to be more appetite for more considered, thought-out shows, which perhaps analyse tactics or team selection. By this time, you will of course know how other teams in your division have got on, which provides an opportunity to analyse your team's performance in the context of other results. And, of course, to pour scorn on local rivals. Later in the week you can experiment with more creative ideas.

When it comes to video, you also need to consider what platforms to use. For breaking news, such as the announcement of the teams shortly before kick-off, it makes sense to broadcast on Facebook Live or Twitter's equivalent, Periscope. This is because the news that you are going out live will pop up in fans' Facebook stream or Twitter notifications and, as a result, grab their attention. Later on, it makes more sense to post videos on YouTube, which is much more easily searchable; also Facebook has only recently allowed video-makers a cut of the advertising revenue that is placed around their content – and even that comes with conditions (Wagner, 2017) so that makes YouTube more easy to monetise.

While you can stream live from a mobile phone, the results can be a bit hit and miss. Many fan channels stream via a laptop which means they can add graphics, switch between cameras and, generally, produce a more polished programme. In order to do this, you'll need to download some live-streaming software. The two best known are called Wirecast, which is paid for, and OBS, which is free. The biggest advantage of Wirecast is that it lets you stream to two platforms simultaneously – so you can be live on both Facebook and YouTube at the same time (Filmora, 2017).

THE SCHEDULE: FULLTIMEDEVILS

FulltimeDEVILS is a Manchester United fan channel, owned by Fremantle Media and managed (until 2017) by Neil Smythe. This section looks at how the channel gets content online on match days (Smythe, 2017).

> The single most important factor in the success of matchday content was the speed with which it was posted. Channels like FullTimeDEVILS and Arsenal Fan TV have got their post-production process absolutely nailed. It's not about multi-camera, perfect audio; it's about relevant content at the right time.

The producer has almost a minute-by-minute schedule of what is expected. He needs to be able to react and be agile. But he knows in the morning he might be shooting content to bank for the next week.

An hour before kick-off, we'd go live on YouTube with the team news. Ten minutes later than that, we couldn't do it because the connection would be lost because there'd be too many people there on 4G. We knew exactly where to stand and when. Broadcasters don't need to worry about that.

The presenters go from there to do a Facebook live. Throughout the day, they'll post on Instagram and Twitter. They go into the ground and, if they're able, send clips of fan chants to a producer in a hotel. The moment the game ended, we'd reconvene outside the ground, shoot for approximately an hour and then get that batch load of fan-cams back to the nearest hotel or cafe where you know they've got a strong internet. On some occasions, Arsenal FanTV will have mobile dongle, editing in their car; FullTimeDEVILS have a friendly hotel near the stadium.

Chop, chop, chop. Put the clips into a template where there's already a graphic overlay and export. The producer would edit that while the presenters do a Facebook Live stream. And they're doing a Snapchat story as well.

(ibid)

Smythe believes FulltimeDEVILS was the first media outlet on the scene at Old Trafford on the day former manager Louis Van Gaal was sacked: "We were there outside the ground interviewing fans before anyone else – but it's hard to prove that. It was a semi-pro set-up which went camera into laptop through Wirecast onto Facebook Live."

Smythe left the company in 2017 but still takes a keen interest in new developments:

The content has moved faster than the technology. We dreamed of times when 4G was more prevalent in stadia. There'll be a time in the next couple of years when we can hook up fans live from different parts of the ground and edit them live in the cloud.

TOP TIPS: NEIL SMYTHE

Neil Smythe has worked on a wide range of fan-based media including Sky's *Soccer AM*, Copa90 and Manchester United fancast FullTimeDEVILS. Until 2017, he was head of sport at Shotglass Media, the company behind the Football Republic fan channels.

1   Put your audience first. Think about it – fans can get interviews with players, match highlights and so on elsewhere. What they can't get is a pure reaction from a fan outside the ground. Think about what they want to see.

2   Authenticity is so key to this content. People come to this sort of channel for more authentic, immediate, reactive style content.

3   Think about how the platforms work. You need to know that the platforms prioritise different types of content at different times. It's quite hard finding out that information but, if you're engrained in the content, you'll get to know it. Broadly speaking, right now, YouTube is pushing watch time, so don't post a bunch of 30-second clips on YouTube. Look at what the big YouTubers are doing. They are posting 20-minute clips because it's pushing up their watch time, which pushes them up the algorithm, which gets more views and they get bigger.

4   Be agile/flexible. If you sit on your laurels, if you think you've got it nailed, something will come along to trip you up.

5   Be multi-skilled, because that's the way the industry is going. I'm hiring people who can shoot, who can edit, maybe who can appear on camera, who can do a bit of graphic design, who can work in a team. In some ways, it's easier than ever to get into the industry because there are more outlets. That's great: content is democratised. But in some ways, the expectations are higher. The budgets are lower but the expectations of young staff are higher. Twenty years ago, you could get a job as a runner in telly without having any production experience because you couldn't really get your hands on a camera or an edit suite. Now, I probably wouldn't see a candidate who said they were interested in digital media but had never bothered to shoot or edit because it's practically free nowadays. We can get free edit software, we can shoot on our phones. If someone says they are interested in editing and they've never done it – that's a real sign for me. So, grow your skills and experience from an early age. Go out and shoot some stuff yourself. You don't need to have 100,000 subscribers but go out and shoot some stuff. Show the industry you're keen to learn.

(Smythe, 2017)

YOUR TURN

Before starting any kind of fan-based media, have a look at what's out there already. There's no point in producing, say, a fantastic podcast about your club if someone is already doing one and has built up a following. Fans enjoy developing a relationship with a regular presenter and getting to know a familiar voice. Prising them away from that presenter may be hard – and pointless. Almost anyone who has worked in fan-based media will tell you that they've been trying to address a need that isn't being met through official channels.

Make a list of all the media outlets (excluding national media) that cover your club including local papers or radio stations, the club's own channels, fanzines, Twitter accounts that aim to break news about the club, podcasts and videocasts. What's covered and what's missing? Maybe the coverage of your club is all a bit serious and something more quirky is needed. Maybe there are disputes over the ownership or financial management of your club and some kind of financial expertise would be useful. Could you come up with an off-the-wall idea like *Hornet Heaven*?

If all the bases seem to be covered then perhaps you should approach an existing fanzine, podcast or Fan TV channel. Most of them are always hungry for fresh content and fresh ideas.

SUMMARY

- Fan-based media has evolved from printed magazines, via message boards, websites and podcasts to the full-on Fan TV channels that exist today.
- All these media forms still exist. If you want to produce a fanzine – why not? If you're prepared to put in the hours standing outside the ground on match days, you'll probably get enough customers to make a small profit.
- There's a really wide range of podcasts out there. It's hard for new ones to make a splash but you've a better chance if you can come up with something creative and different.
- Fan TV channels depend on slick organisation and a really good understanding of social media platforms, technology and timing.

REFERENCES

Arsenal Fan TV (2017) *SHOWDOWN: GARY NEVILLE Meets ArsenalFanTV (Ft DT, Troopz, Claude & Moh)* at www.youtube.com/watch?v=VmgVPi_YQ7E&t=659s. Last accessed 1/12/2017

Atkinson, N. (2017) Interview conducted by the author on 2/8/2017

Bantams Banter (2017) *#129 Vs AFC Wimbledon* at www.bantamsbanter.co.uk/podcasts/. Last accessed 1/12/2017

Barber, G. and Williams, J. (2002) *Fact sheet 7: Fan 'Power' and democracy in football* at https://web.archive.org/web/20100821184842/www.le.ac.uk/so/css/resources/factsheets/fs7.html. Last accessed 1/12/2017

Chelsea Fans Channel (2016) *Can man Utd fans spell Ibrahimovic?!* at www.youtube.com/watch?v=laNKW0pntxl&t=10s. Last accessed 1/12/2017

Filmora (2017) *Wirecast Vs OBS: Which is better?* at https://filmora.wondershare.com/live-streaming/wirecast-vs-obs-which-is-better.html. Last accessed 1/12/2017

Joshi, N. (2017) Interview conducted by the author on 12/7/2017

McInnes, P. (2017) *Fan TV: Revolution or just a vehicle for venting attention-grabbing fury?* at www.theguardian.com/football/blog/2017/feb/13/arsenal-fan-TV-and-the-case-against-arsene-wenger. Last accessed 1/12/2017

Redmen TV (2015) *Ibe, Coutinho, Markovic & Sterling take dizzy pens for dizzy goals! | Redmen TV x Vauxhall football* at www.youtube.com/watch?v=5BTUd7cgRJk. Last accessed 1/12/2017

Smythe, N. (2017) Interview conducted by the author on 21/7/2017

Smythe, N. (2017b) Email exchange with author on 23–26/7/2017

Wagner, K. (2017) *Facebook is offering publishers money to create produced video* at www.recode.net/2017/4/21/15387554/facebook-video-deal-publishers-live-ads. Last accessed 1/12/2017

Wicken, O. (2013–2017) *Hornet Heaven* at https://hornetheaven.com/. Last accessed 1/12/2017

MAJOR PROJECTS

Longer pieces of sports journalism

CHAPTER 11

Podcasts

The word "podcast" derives from the iPod, the MP3 player that Apple launched in 2001 with a flashy advert soundtracked by U2. Six years later, Apple introduced the iPhone, which made the iPod more or less obsolete. After all, a smartphone could do everything an iPod could, plus it was a phone as well.

At this point, there were those who thought the word podcast would die out. The BBC, for example, started talking about "downloads" rather than podcasts. More importantly, what was the point of a podcast? It didn't have pictures – unlike a post on YouTube – and lacked the immediacy of radio. The podcast was beginning to look like something that had only existed because of the limited technological developments of its time.

That all changed in 2014 with *Serial*. The first series, which investigated the unsolved murder, 15 years earlier, of a high school student, generated 80 million downloads and led to a search for "the next *Serial*". While no one has laid claim to the title of "the sport *Serial*", all the podcasts referred to in this chapter have, indirectly, benefitted from the revival of interest in the format since 2014.

Sport has generated a wide range of different types of podcast. We've already looked at fan-based podcasts in Chapter 10. Other podcasts take an overview of a particular sport, such as the *Football Ramble*, *The Offside Rule* (football), *Effectively Wild* (baseball), *Full Contact* (rugby union) or *Sidepodcast* (Formula One). Others cover several sports like *Second Captains*, which discusses all things Irish, or tell the back stories behind sports, such as *The Narrative*. Then there are those that offer the kind of in-depth interview rarely found on radio, such as *The Offside Rule* (again) and *Move the Sticks*. Some podcasts are built around celebrities such as *Athletico Mince*, which features the comedian Bob Mortimer, or *I am Rapaport* with actor Michael Rapaport. ESPN's *30 for 30* demonstrates sophisticated production while *Radio Cricket* often consists of nothing more than presenter Nishant Joshi talking into a microphone. Large legacy media organisations like the BBC, the *Guardian* and the *Telegraph* all produce plenty of sports podcasts while there are also those like *Radio Cricket* and the *Rhoden Fellows* which have social or charitable objectives.

If you google "best sports podcasts", you'll come across lots of lists of top 10s, top 20s or top 25s. The remarkable thing about these lists is that they'll all include different podcasts; there won't be much duplication. That's a reflection of the vast number of downloadable shows now being produced. That's great for audiences but it does make it very hard for a new podcaster to make a name for themselves in an already crowded market.

One of the reasons there are so many podcasts is that they are very inexpensive to make – and require little or no specialist technical skills, such as photography or picture editing. But the fact that it's easy to create a podcast is also a reason for there being a great many very poor ones out there.

A very common format for a podcast is to have two or three men (it is almost always men) sitting around a table discussing the latest developments in football, basketball, motorcycling or whatever. You and your mates enjoy regularly talking about sport? Great, you think – record our conversations and release them as podcasts. OK – but there are people talking about sport in every school, workplace and pub the length and breadth of the country. How do you make yours different or special?

You could get great guests in. That makes a lot of sense early on as, if the guests post about their appearance on their social media feeds, then you can grow an audience quickly. But securing amazing guests week in, week out is very hard unless you are well-established. "The thing about having guests is it's very difficult to have guests on board and schedule them with the podcast and with your work schedule as well", says cricket podcaster Nishant Joshi (2017).

PODCAST VS RADIO

To understand the audience for podcasts, it's useful to examine how they differ from their most obvious "old media" relative: radio. Initially, the two platforms seem quite similar – in fact many podcasts are repackaged radio shows while some podcasts have made the journey in the opposite direction and ended up being broadcast on mainstream radio. But there are some important differences.

Radio is immediate; podcasts are in-depth or reflective

Before the advent of the internet, radio was the best medium for breaking news. Unlike print, which required type to be laid and paper to be printed, and television, which needed a producer, director, PA and presenters to all be on the same page, a story could be broken on radio in seconds. Anyone over 40 will have fond childhood memories of listening to important sporting events on radio with pictures painted by the likes of Brian Johnson, Ron Jones or Alan Green.

Podcasts are far less immediate. No one is going to listen to live commentary via a podcast because a podcast has to be uploaded by its creator and then downloaded by the listener which creates a significant time delay. The nearest a podcast comes to providing live commentary is probably *Test Match Special* who produce edited highlights of each day's play.

Twitter is perhaps closer to radio in terms of its effectiveness in breaking news while live blogs provide commentary.

TIP: A podcast is not primarily about conveying information. It's suited to analysis, reflection, speculation and humour.

Radio is not made to be time-shifted or shared; podcasts are not linked to any point in time

Since the mid-1970s, it's been possible to time-shift television programmes: first through VHS or Betamax recorders, more latterly through on-demand or catch-up services on the internet. But radio, traditionally, was never time-shifted. Cassettes typically recorded 45 minutes on each side and, so, were too short for most programmes; manufacturers didn't design tape decks that could be preprogrammed to record shows while you were out.

This helped give radio a curious ephemeral quality; you knew you were only going to hear it once. So, it wasn't very sharable. You could tell your friend that you heard a great programme but all they could do was catch the next episode – the previous one had disappeared into the ether.

Podcasts on the other hand are all about sharing. If your podcast is going to be a success, you need as many people to share it as possible; every podcast mentioned in this chapter has depended on word of mouth to develop a following.

TIP: What's special about your podcast? What jumps out that will make people tell their friends about it?

Radio is linked to places; podcasts are not

Similarly, radio is made for a particular geographic audience: generally local or national. There's no such limitation on podcasts.

This helps explain the popularity of *Second Captains*; there are plenty of people interested in Irish sport who don't live in Ireland. It also helps explain why *The Anfield Wrap*, which we've already looked at, attracts a massive audience.

TIP: Your potential audience is huge. What do you have that's going to appeal to someone in San Francisco? Or Sydney? Or Hong Kong? Avoid using terminology that only people in your part of the English-speaking world will understand.

Radio has to fit into a schedule; podcasts can be as long or as short as you like

Enter the name of a podcast like the *Football Ramble* or the *Offside Rule* into iTunes. You'll see the lengths of each episode. Note, they're not the same – some might be 51 minutes, some 48, some 54 etc. By contrast, radio programmes, even those that are pre-produced, have to fit proscribed time slots: typically, an hour or a half hour (or slightly less in order to accommodate advertisements, news bulletins or traffic updates).

When it comes to sport, each event is competing with other events on radio. Radio presenters don't have an hour to analyse the Lions rugby tests from New Zealand or Australia which finish mid-morning in the UK because a Premier League football match is about to kick off. That's not a problem for the podcasters of *Full Contact* who have as long as they like.

TIP: Don't set out with a set duration in mind; see how much interesting content you can generate.

Radio is broadcast; podcasts are narrow cast

Radio has to appeal to a fairly broad audience. If a presenter on Radio Five says "coming up an hour's discussion of clay pigeon shooting", they'd know that a lot of the audience is going to switch off. The beauty of podcasting is that you can make a programme just for a very niche audience: fans of a particular club or fans of a minority sport. (Yes, there have been several individual podcasts about clay pigeon shooting though not, as far I can find out, a *regular* one about the sport.) The BBC makes a podcast about mixed martial arts; it doesn't broadcast a regular programme about the sport because it knows that many of its normal audience, accustomed to hearing football or cricket discussed, would find it a turn-off.

The flip-side to this is that the audience has specifically sought out and chosen to listen to *your* podcast. They're not listening just because there's nothing else on other channels. So, you can explore a topic in more depth. Ollie Mann gives an example about when he interviewed a woman who travels the United Kingdom photographing brown road signs (the ones that direct people to tourist attractions or leisure facilities).

> She'd been interviewed by newspapers and radio stations and it was always a case of "oh aren't you unusual, you photograph brown signs, ha ha ha". Because we had more time, we could find the real story which was about the way all our towns are starting to look the same and identifying what makes them distinct.
>
> (Mann, 2017)

TIP: Ask yourself: what areas of sport aren't currently being covered by podcasters?

WHAT MAKES A GOOD PODCAST?

Having said all that – there is one important feature that radio and podcasts share: the personality of the presenter or presenters is crucial. Good radio presenters tend to make good podcasters because they are accustomed to working on a medium where there's much tougher competition for people's attention.

If you think about it, there are probably television programmes that you've watched where you don't particularly like the presenter. It doesn't matter because there are other things going on in the programme that compensate for your feelings about the host. But when have you regularly listened to a radio programme or podcast when you don't like the main voice? The one-to-one relationship between presenter and listener lies at the heart of a successful podcast.

Sidepodcast is a good example of this – and worth listening to even if you are not a fan of motorsport. The main presenters have clearly defined roles. Christine Blachford became a fan of F1 as an adult in the early noughties; she displays all the fervour and energy of a convert. Mr C, described on the podcast's website as a reluctant presenter, is calmer and more authoritative, drawing on a knowledge of the sport going back much further. The podcast works because of the balance, or chemistry, between the two.

If you are the presenter, stay true to yourself. Bear in mind, you're going to be talking for up to an hour and you may be making several editions of your podcast. So be yourself. It's virtually impossible to maintain an artificial persona for weeks on end – and listeners will soon smell a rat if you seem inauthentic.

Having said that, you are going to be very dependent on your voice if you are recording a weekly podcast over several years. So, it may be worth getting some advice on how to present; there are various vocal exercises you can do before going on air to ensure your voice is warmed up.

"Presenting a radio show influenced what we did with the podcasts", says Neil Atkinson (2017) who presents on both *The Anfield Wrap* and Radio City Talk. "It stopped them being a bit dry and creaky. The radio show went out on Friday night and our attitude was 'we want you to have the best Friday night you can possibly have'."

When you think of successful radio broadcasters, the *Test Match Special* team for example, they give the impression that they are talking to just one or two friends rather than broadcasting to thousands. This is an important skill to develop. Don't talk as though you are broadcasting through a tannoy. Think about how you can make individual listeners feel important.

Sports radio, such as Talk Sport, *606* on the BBC and countless local variants, makes extensive use of the phone-in. It's a great opportunity for individual fans to express their opinions. Because they don't go out live, podcasts can't do this. Instead, they often make sure they dedicate a section of their output to readers' emails, tweets or other communications. Some podcasts have an answerphone so that listeners can record their opinions or questions, which can then be played out during the next recording session. It's easy to see why this helps build an audience; the callers will be listening to hear if their contributions are used – and what they sound like "on air".

Whenever I've talked to people who *make* podcasts, it becomes clear that they also *listen* to podcasts; they are students of the genre. Before making your own podcast, it's worth immersing yourself in other people's to get a feel for what kind of style you feel most comfortable with.

The Football Ramble is a good example to study. At first it sounds like a million and one other podcasts. Three blokes, who all seem to be of a similar age, sit around talking about football. No guest interviews, no professional sports people, no celebrities. It could be very dull. Instead it's surprisingly slick and well-informed. Try this experiment:

Get a pen and paper and start listening anywhere in the show for five minutes. Every time one of the contributors says something that is either informative, amusing or thought-provoking put a tick on the sheet of paper.

My guess is that you'll get around 15–20 ticks in the course of five minutes. To me that makes *The Football Ramble* good value, in terms of what you get out of it compared to what you put in, namely your time.

To achieve this requires a bit of planning. Maybe there are interesting facts or statistics that the presenters have come across during the week; they'll note them down and think about how to work them into the podcast. Jokes might also be prepared. In one edition, they were reflecting on the versatility of the Brazilian defender David Luiz. "David Luiz is the kind of bloke who, if you said you'd got a bit of toothache, he's say 'let me have a go.' I think he'd be quite confident in any discipline", joked Pete Donaldson (The Football Ramble, 2017). I may be wrong, but I suspect that might have been planned in advance.

While a good podcast tends to sound spontaneous, there is a strong argument for being prepared to edit ruthlessly. Ollie Mann, the co-creator of *Answer Me This*, a podcast that's been running for more than ten years and has won a Sony Radio Academy Gold Award, describes making the early episodes of the show.

[Co-presenter] Helen [Zaltzman] would do a rough edit of the show, taking out some of the bits she felt were superfluous, and send it to me. Then I'd spend hours going for walks and listening to every bit of the recording and asking "do we need this bit?" before we got together for a final edit.

(Mann, 2017)

Now their podcast is well-established, they don't do anything like as much editing. But this is only because they've now developed an acute sense of what their audience enjoys, honed over the course of hundreds of shows.

YOUR TURN: MAKING A PODCAST

Pick your subject

Most sports journalists don't start out with podcasts. They regularly write about a particular topic, build up contacts and expertise and, then, graduate to a podcast. So, it would be logical to stick to something you know well. If you have 3,000 people following you on Twitter because of your coverage of women's rugby, then it's going to be easier to get them to listen to a podcast about women's rugby than one about downhill skiing.

Pick your personnel

Most of the podcasts we've looked at have at least one regular presenter. As we've seen, a major reason people listen to podcasts is because they feel they have a relationship with the presenters. So, make sure you have one or, preferably, two people who will be on air throughout the whole of every edition of the show. You'll find that sustaining 45 minutes is very draining if you're on your own so a co-host is a big help.

You may, however, also decide to include occasional contributors who take part in sections of your programme or pop up as guest presenters. If your podcast features a particular club, for example, you could have a guest who talks about the youth team. Or you could have a statistics corner presented by a club historian.

Think about the way the voices will mix with each other. *Sidepodcast* benefits from having a female and a male presenter – listeners can always tell who's talking. If you don't have a mixture of genders, perhaps you could get a mixture of accents.

Pick your equipment

Most podcasts are recorded in quiet surroundings where there's as little external noise as possible. Some are recorded *at* sporting events and benefit from the atmosphere. But these will prove hard to edit and you can easily get distracted, so, perhaps, aren't for beginners. Similarly, some are recorded in front of live audiences but, until your podcast is established, no one will turn up to be in the audience.

As a rule, using good quality studios should pay off. Maybe you have access to university equipment or know someone who works at a local radio station. The first editions of *The Anfield Wrap* were recorded at a studio used by professional musicians. "Because we took it on a Monday morning we got it cheap; you won't get a rock'n'roll band to record at 10am on a Monday morning," Neil Atkinson (2017) revealed. But Atkinson admits they can't always record in studios:

If I do a post-match show. I'll find a car or a hotel room and record it there. For Chelsea away we booked a karaoke room in central London, because we couldn't find a cheap hotel room and turned the karaoke off. We just use a small Marantz put it in the middle of the car and all talk into it. If you try to get the sound quality really good and you fail you do people's heads in. If you say "this is us, we've just been at the game, we're in a car, this is what this is, then people go okay".

(ibid)

(A Marantz is a brand of portable recorder which has been used by radio reporters for more than 30 years. A basic model will set you back around £300. Other leading brands include Roland and Tascam.)

If you don't have access to a studio, then it might be worth buying a recorder with several different microphone inputs. That way, if one contributor is much louder than the others, you can adjust the varying volumes in post-production. Rooms with soft-furnishings tend to make good ad hoc studios; avoid using bathrooms or toilets as they have a lot of hard surfaces which means the sound tends to bounce around.

If you are going to have guests on the end of a phone line, you'll find you tend to get better quality if you use Skype or Facetime rather than a normal phone line.

Plan your show

A podcast shouldn't be over-planned, because you'll lose your spontaneity. But it is worth following a rough plan. For example, you might start with the main presenters reviewing news from your chosen sport over the past few days. Then you might go into an interview. That might have been quite intense so follow it with something more light-hearted like a quiz. Then you could have a slot for readers' texts, emails and social media posts, etc.

I would suggest having a side of A4 paper outlining the schedule of the show and at least one other sheet of paper with some of the facts, statistics and jokes you plan to work in.

Most podcasts have some kind of sting or theme music at the start. On radio, this is very important because it alerts someone who may only be half-listening that a new programme is starting. You might feel it's less important on a podcast because the listener is in control.

Nishant Joshi (2017) explains why the theme music matters: "From my own experience of listening to podcasts, it's quite nice to have that sense of regularity. It's quite calming, quite therapeutic. In a busy world, it's nice to know that regular voice is there."

Try hard to think of original ways of covering topics. Using the format of a game often helps. For example, for years podcasts have asked contributors to predict the coming weekend's results. To make it more interesting, some now run some kind of predictions league where the contestants gain points for correct results. Others have turned transfer speculation into a game where the pundits are given a set budget and have to decide how to spend it.

Decide what your policy is going to be on swearing. Podcasts made by mainstream organisations like the BBC or the *Telegraph* don't allow any swear words. Some sports, such as golf or horse-racing tend to be inherently conservative and you could alienate listeners by swearing. On the other hand, many fan-based ones are quite happy if every second word is an expletive. So, it's important to be clear where you stand and to make sure all the contributors know the policy.

Make sure all the team have a copy of the schedule and know when you are going to move on to other areas.

Go for it

When you start recording, it's almost certain things won't go to plan. The fantastic interviewee you had lined up won't be on the end of the phone when you need her to be. One of you will have an uncontrollable cough or a fit of the giggles.

Go with it. This isn't going out live on the radio so, if things get too out of hand, you can edit it.

In the studio, you are a team. Some contributors may be disappointing and you may have to "carry" them – don't complain; on another day, they might have to carry you.

Be prepared to experiment or to diverge from your planned structure if something interesting and worth exploring crops up. But be careful not to slip into private jokes. If you're recording with friends, don't start talking about people or events that only you know. From a listener's point of view, there are few things more annoying than people laughing about something that you know nothing about.

Edit, edit and edit again

Obviously, if you are creating a post-match podcast which you are hoping to post an hour after the end of a game, then you won't have much time to edit. But, if you have more time on your side, then it pays to make sure that what goes up online is as strong as it can possibly be.

Remember the rule from Chapter 7: make sure nothing is any longer than it has to be. Ask friends who weren't involved in the recording to listen to what you've produced – do all the jokes work? Are all the anecdotes interesting?

Upload your podcast

This stage is actually more complicated than you might imagine. In order to ensure your podcast reaches as large an audience as possible, it makes sense to make sure it can be found in as many places as possible. Some people might download it from a store like iTunes; others may visit your website or a host site like SoundCloud.

Firstly, don't host your podcast on your own website – unless you're a large media organisation with unlimited storage. Podcasts tend to be quite big and take up a lot of space – so you may soon exceed your storage limits and the speed of download will be frustratingly slow for would-be listeners. You may also find that your host charges when people download your file – they may even take down your site because the bandwidth used when hundreds of people download a podcast is expensive.

Instead, you'll need to create an account with a podcast-hosting service. These include Buzzsprout, Libsyn, Blubrry and SoundCloud. Some of these are free; the others do not charge particularly high fees – the highly-rated Libsyn starts at $5 a month, for example. The advantages of the paid services include better workflows, the ability to analyse your audience and they won't change your content, eg by adding adverts.

Once you've uploaded your podcast to one of these hosts, you can embed the podcast on your website. So, it will appear as though people are downloading direct from your site but, in fact, it's coming from the host. Some of these companies also offer players that you can also embed on your site so people can stream your content.

The host will also give you a web address called an RSS feed. If you want to make your podcast available on iTunes or other audio apps, then you'll need to supply them with this address. For iTunes, you'll also need to create an image to go with your audio (you can find their requirements on the app).

FIVE TOP TIPS: PRODUCING AND PRESENTING A PODCAST

Nishant Joshi presents *Radio Cricket*, which ran for six years. Initially, he co-presented it with James Marsh but, later, he hosted the show on his own, often along with guest interviewees. He somehow managed to combine podcasting about cricket with a full-time job as a doctor in critical care.

1   Practise how you speak and be ruthless about how you speak.

2   The first 30 seconds they ever listen to you might be the last 30 seconds they ever listen to you; so, you'd better make it damn good.

3   Make sure your promotion and branding are on point. When we started, Twitter and Facebook were the only realistic ways of promoting it. It helped to get a guest on board. Especially after our [leading Indian cricket commentator] Harsha Bhogle episode and [South African pace bowler] Dale Steyn as well – they got us a lot of traction. Dale Steyn tweeted out to his audience of one million people.

4   Make sure your podcasts are regular. Cricket has a difficult schedule; it's very seasonal. It helps to have a regular job because I can say "ok, I'll pencil in this time most weeks to work on the podcast". There are some days when you don't want to talk for an hour but that's part of the fun: challenging yourself to sit down for an hour every week.

    Do you save up topics for weeks when you know there's not going to be much competitive cricket?

    No, saving up topics tends not to work – they'll often go stale. My approach is "all killer, no filler".

5   Make the length listenable. Anything longer than an hour is very ambitious. Don't make it any longer because very few of us have more than an hour to listen.

THE BUSINESS SIDE OF PODCASTS

As we've seen, some of the best podcasts are made by the likes of ESPN, the BBC, the *Guardian* or the *Daily Telegraph*. All of these are freely available on iTunes and other apps. Why do these legacy companies want to be involved in the world of podcasting?

The motives are probably slightly different in each case. ESPN produces a good deal of content, typically well-produced. Their podcasts normally start with an advertisement, so it sees them as a source of income. The licence fee-funded BBC, of course, doesn't make money from podcasts but probably regards them as part of its remit to produce interesting coverage across a wide range of platforms. Relatively few podcasts are paid for and even those that are tend to offer some free episodes as inducements to listeners to subscribe.

Independent podcasters can also make money. Advertisements can be scheduled before or during a show. Advertisers will pay more if the presenter him or herself reads the ad rather than an actor doing it. Of course, it's important that the presenter is convincing – there's no point asking a football fan to read an ad for a life insurance policy.

"We want to feel as though the product is one that we wouldn't have any problem saying to our subscribers 'we think you'd like this'," explains Neil Atkinson (2017) of *The Anfield Wrap*.

> We're working with a fantasy football game and I think it's great but [my co-presenter] Gareth hates it. And he's got full licence to say he hates it and he has done and I laugh at him. If you're listening it doesn't sound like a corporate message "play this fantasy football game, we all think it's marvelous"; instead everyone gets to be themselves. That's difficult for some brands, they need to get smarter and understand that that's an honest voice and an honest endorsement.
> (ibid)

Sports podcasts are attractive to certain types of advertiser because they know exactly what type of audience they are getting: typically, young men with a love of sport and disposable income. Nishant Joshi says he's turned down offers of sponsorship from gambling websites because they didn't fit with his "personal ethos". If you're sponsored by a betting firm, it may be difficult to discuss topics like match-fixing.

Joshi encourages listeners to donate "the price of a cup of coffee" via a website that manages donations and subscriptions; Ollie Mann similarly invites bequests of "beer money". Though neither of these generate an enormous income, they help maintain a down-to-Earth relationship between the presenter and the audience. They're not paying for a luxury jet; they're helping fund a well-earned drink at the end of the show.

SUMMARY

- At the heart of a good podcast is the relationship between the presenter and the audience. Broadcast as though you are talking to one person and think about ways of involving the listeners as much as possible.
- A good podcast should sound spontaneous, but it's the result of careful preparation and, often, a lot of post-production editing.

- Your first 30 seconds are vital.
- Make sure you know how to disseminate your podcast; read reviews and message boards for advice on the pros and cons of different podcast hosting services.

FURTHER READING (AND LISTENING)

The Podcast Host is an excellent guide to all aspects of producing and sharing podcasts at www.the podcasthost.com/.

Shout me loud also has several articles about podcasting. Go to www.shoutmeloud.com/ and search for "podcast".

All the podcasts referred to in this chapter can be found on iTunes and other podcast hosting services.

REFERENCES

Atkinson, N. (2017) Interview conducted by the author on 2/8/2017

Football Ramble (2017) *Circus for sale*, downloaded from iTunes on 20/10/2017

Joshi, N. (2017) Interview conducted by the author on 12/7/2017

Mann, O. (2017) *Talk at the University for the Creative Arts*, Farnham, Surrey, 23/03/2017

CHAPTER 12

Longform journalism

There is a really interesting challenge for the industry, namely that we don't go too short form; we don't say "people only want short form content therefore let's create everything in short form" because there is a place for all of it. I think YouTube would say they're seeing a significant interest in length of content consumed in that environment because people have chosen to take the time, to commit the time, to go and look for something and find a piece of content.

Alex Willis (2017), head of Digital Communications
and Content, Wimbledon

Longform has taken off over the last seven or eight years in a way that no one predicted. The *Guardian*'s longform stuff is hugely popular. I think they see it as one of the flagships of the paper. So, there's definitely an appetite for longform. People have realised there is something nice about being able to sit back and taken an hour reading something rather than skipping onto the next thing. You can get far more depth by doing that.

Jonathan Wilson (2017), editor, *The Blizzard*

Aged nine and encouraged by my history teacher, I started reading the football and rugby reports in *The Observer*. These were often extraordinary pieces of writing. While the paper's news writers were constrained by the requirements of objective, inverted pyramid-style writing, the sports team could let rip and show off their knowledge of language and culture. The writing was challenging to read but highly rewarding once you'd decoded it.

Early this century, the *Guardian*, who now own *The Observer*, reprinted some of these reports in a series of booklets. They still made riveting reading and were quite unlike any other contemporary journalism: in one report Patrick Barclay included a 77-word sentence (Barclay, P, 1978).

As we saw in Chapters 4 and 5, match reporting today is far more straightforward – aimed at getting information out as soon as possible rather than showing off the writer's dexterity. But does this mean there is no longer a place for longform sports journalism? For extended story-telling that brings out the scale of human achievement reflected in sport?

FIGURE 12.1 Photograph of Simone Biles, one of the subjects of the *New York Times'* Fine Line series, courtesy of Eileen Langsley

There are many who will answer "no". Millennials, so the argument goes, have short attention spans. If a story cannot be told on social media, then there's no point trying to tell it at all. People point to the statistic about the average length of time people watch a video on Facebook being ten seconds (see Chapter 7).

But, hold on: I know people in their teens or early 20s who are capable of spending more than 24 hours playing computer games or binge-watching six or eight episodes of a new television drama.

As we've seen, people are happy to spend an hour listening to a podcast. The 21st century has also been a golden age for books about sport; there are two leading sports book awards – William Hill and Cross, both of which seem to showcase an ever-higher standard of writing year on year. We've also seen some brilliant films such as *Fire in Babylon* about West Indies cricket, *Rush* about the rivalry between Formula One drivers James Hunt and Niki Lauda and the *Damned United*, which covered Brian Clough's short spell as manager of Leeds United.

So, it is my strong belief that not only is there a place for longform sports journalism but that, during the next few years, we will see it acquire more prominence. YouTube and Facebook are both already rewarding longer films – content that keeps eyeballs on their sites for longer.

In this chapter, I'm going to look at four very different types of longform journalism across four different media. Each, in its different way, is experimenting with new ways of telling longer more complex stories while, at the same time, drawing on older journalistic traditions. As befits experiments, they may not last. But they do seem, in different ways to offer a glimpse of where sports journalism is going in the future.

CASE STUDY: THE PODCAST

In 2009, ESPN announced plans to release 30 hour-long films about sport to commemorate the network's 30th birthday. The films proved sufficiently successful for ESPN to commission two further series plus a block of shorter films (typically 15 minutes or less) and a further collection dedicated to soccer. Finally, in 2017, it decided to branch out into sports podcasts.

The first point to make is that ESPN define sports in a broad sense. One 30 for 30 podcast is about casino gambling, another about a polar expedition.

Secondly, perhaps because of their experience of making filmed documentaries, the team seem to have an acute understanding of what works well on an audio-only platform. The casino podcast, *A Queen of Sorts* (30 for 30, 2017a), tells the story of Chung Yin Sun, a baccarat player with an unparalleled knack of making vast winnings. The programme talks to her and her past accomplices and explains her method. To do this in vision would be impossible: the gamblers would probably refuse to appear on camera unless heavily disguised and the casinos would not allow filming. You'd end up with a succession of blurred or pixelated talking heads. *The Fighter Inside* (30 for 30, 2017b) tells the story of a boxer who rose through the sport's ranks while serving time for armed robbery. Again, this would be difficult to realise on screen as it would involve securing access to a maximum security jail.

Finally, and crucially, ESPN is one of the world's largest producers of sports podcasts. So, they have extensive experience of distributing podcasts and attracting advertising or sponsorship. They could be reasonably confident that there'd be an audience prepared to give 30 for 30 a try. But there's a big difference between a topical podcast full of punchy opinions about the latest round of NBA or NFL games and a more considered documentary.

On the Ice (30 for 30, 2017c), presented by Rose Eveleth, covers the first all-woman expedition to the North Pole. It tells the story from the team's recruitment at an audition weekend at Dartmoor National Park through to the journey itself. This was in 1997 so smartphones with cameras and Go-Pros were still some way in the future. Perhaps some members of the team would have had some photographs, maybe even a bit of video, but clearly not enough to tell the story in any great detail.

As it's a podcast, you experience the polar region through the women's eyes, not your own. The scene where several of the contributors describe seeing the ice for the first time is very memorable, each grappling for adjectives to describe something well outside their previous experiences.

The group included Ann Daniels, a mother of three-year-old triplets. Early on in the expedition she comes unstuck – badly.

> Claire was in front of me and her foot broke through the ice and I knew I was going to go in. So, I just tried to ski as fast as I could in but I felt my skis go in. As my skis went in and I went down, it was very fast but it felt like slow-motion and I just felt sick.
>
> (ibid)

No one could see what had happened or hear her shouts for help. Running through her head was the advice of Matty McNair, her guide; "if you get wet, you die". Her only chance of getting out of the water was a boulder jutting out above her. "As I hauled myself up, the boulder of ice broke off. I tried a second time and the same thing happened again."

Even if the skier behind Ann had had a go-pro, she wouldn't have been able to film much, owing to the distance and the lack of visibility. At this point, ESPN are dependent on the radio programme-maker's greatest asset: the audience's imagination and ability to paint pictures in their own minds.

At 48 minutes, *On the Ice* qualifies as a piece of longform journalism. It would have taken several months to produce as it involves more than a dozen interviewees, some scattered around the United Kingdom, some in Canada. They would have needed careful coaxing to revive memories of an expedition 20 years previously. The documentary also incorporates sound effects and archive of news reports from the time.

CASE STUDY: THE VIDEOCAST

In the pre-digital age, the obvious home for longform journalism was magazines, which had the space to run 3,000–5,000-word features. Magazines enjoyed something of a boom in the 1990s and Simon Wear was part of that boom. He rose to the post of chief operating officer at Future Publishing, the company behind magazines as diverse as *Mountain Biking UK* and *Total Film*. "In its pomp, it had 150 magazines, 1,400 people and offices in five countries," he recalls.

Sports magazines have enjoyed less success this century. When the iPad came out (2010), it looked as though the tablet might be the saviour of the magazine. There were exciting ideas of producing online magazines that readers could flick through but then click to view match highlights or videos advising people how to improve their golf swing. These don't seem to have taken off as much as it was hoped and, as a result, haven't attracted advertisers – though some matchday programmes make use of this technology.

So, the question for Wear was this: where would the type of person who bought *Mountain Biking UK* in the 1990s, get their cycling fix 15 years down the line? His answer (Wear, 2017) was in the world of online video.

> The internet didn't really deliver on the revenue promise that we all thought it would. So, I went off and set up my own specialist media business at the end of 2010, beginning of 2011. Really my focus was always going to be how are the modern generation of consumers going to get their specialist information and I was always of the view that it was always likely to be video. So, in 2012 I pitched Google the idea for our first channel, the Global Cycling Network, and got about £1.1 million funding to help launch that channel.

Global Cycling Network (GCN) soon had two little sisters: the Global Mountain Bike Network and the Global Triathlon Network, which all come under the umbrella of the Play Sports Network. Interviewed in 2017 (ibid), Wear describes the qualities he's needed to build the network:

> You need really strong knowledge of that subject, number one, you need a huge amount of creative juices to generate new ideas and trial and test new things, you need business acumen to execute commercial deals to enable you to fund those projects, you need a deep understanding of how all those social and digital distribution channels work and then you probably need another 20% of single minded pig-headedness that enables you to battle through the difficult bits.

When you watch a show on GCN, Wear's background in magazines is apparent. The same kind of content you'd expect in a recreational cycling magazine is there on screen. There's recent news about cycling, quirky photos or videos, jokes, interviews, product reviews, readers' emails and features on various aspects of the sport – some serious, some more light-hearted.

But the shows don't simply resemble magazines in terms of their content – they are also similar in tone. A good magazine should be a bit like a cool older brother, or older friend. By reading the magazine, you're being introduced to the exciting things that your friend's mates get up to. You're being accepted and initiated into the group. So, the shows are full of comments like "we've all been there" or "we all remember"; phrases that break down the traditional barriers between presenter and audience. Global Mountain Bike Network, in particular, runs regular polls and makes constant use of viewers' contributions.

> The shows are scheduled and subscribers will tend to watch them in the week they come out. But the networks also release stand-alone films, such as How To videos, Top Fives and Top Tens, Essential Skills and Your Cycling Questions. These appear to attract higher numbers of views on YouTube and it's easy to see why, as viewers will return to them when they need to buy a new bike or repair something on their bike or to learn new skills before going on a cycling holiday. This sort of content makes the Play Sports Network very different to traditional scheduled (or "linear") television: "Our world is so much more flexible and so much more entrepreneurial compared to a linear television world. We live in a much faster digital environment."
>
> (ibid)

Wear feels the content of the shows is driven entirely by the audience.

> If you think of media over the last 80 years, something like that, it's all been about power and influence. Why do some of the most powerful people in the world own media property? It's because they wanted that influence. Now it's much more about the masses and the way they vote through social. So, if consumers vote something up, giving it likes, shares whatever, it has a huge amount of consumer influence on content that they didn't have in the past.

CASE STUDY: THE MAGAZINE

While Simon Wear felt that the future of magazines lay in online video, Jonathan Wilson believes that the traditional magazine has its place. Wilson is one of the most prolific sports journalists around, writing for the likes of the *Guardian, The Telegraph, The Bleacher Report* and *World Soccer*. He's written several books, including *Inverting the Pyramid: the History of Football Tactics* (Orion, 2008), which won best Football Book of the Year at the British Sports Book Awards, while the *Guardian's Fiver* email describes him as a "floating footballing brain in a jar". *The Blizzard* was born out of a love of longform journalism and a frustration with the click-driven journalism that was emerging by the end of the first decade of the 21st century. In the editorial for the first issue, which is now reproduced on the magazine's website, he wrote:

> I'd been frustrated for some time by the constraints of the mainstream media and, in various press-rooms and bars across the world, I'd come to realise I wasn't the only one who felt journalism as a whole was missing something . . . I became aware there were other writers so keen to break the shackles of Search Engine Optimisation that they were prepared to write for a share of potential profit, that the joy of writing what they wanted and felt was important outweighed the desire to be paid.
>
> (Wilson, 2010)

Wilson told me that a particularly decisive moment came when he wanted to write about a footballer called Steve Mokone, the first black African to play professionally in Europe. After his playing career was over, Mokone moved to North America, where he became a psychiatrist and an outspoken opponent of apartheid. But, in America, he was jailed for ten years for throwing acid in the faces of his ex-wife and her lawyer. Journalists who have investigated the story believe he may have been framed by the US security services working at the behest of South Africa's government.

> This was in the run-up to the 2010 World Cup, so it was a very apposite story. But I couldn't place that story [ie find someone willing to publish it] because it wasn't the image of South Africa that advertisers wanted. I ended up running it in the *Financial Times* in much shorter form.
>
> (Wilson, 2017)

So, his response, with two friends, was to set up his own magazine. *The Blizzard* is published quarterly on thick paper – it's deliberately designed to be collectable – and costs £40 for the year. Readers can also, however, buy a digital subscription for £20. Both forms of subscription include unlimited access to the magazine's archive. Wilson thinks roughly twice as many people take up the digital subscription as the paper version. Three free articles are available to non-subscribers.

Blizzard articles cover a wide range of footballing topics, but they tend to have certain common features. They all tend to be well over a thousand words long and to draw heavily on face-to-face interviews. The magazine values history – there are typically several features in each issue that draw on the game's past – and geography – no region of the world is out of bounds. Features are loosely grouped into themes: in issue 26, for example, there are ten articles in which well-known football writers talk about their favourite stadia; in issue 25, five diverse stories come under the heading "Revolutions".

Regular components include a crossword, a photo essay, Greatest Games and something called Eight Bells, in which a writer selects eight short goalkeepers, eight successful managerial careers that started badly, eight great performances by teams reduced to ten players or other footballing curiosities. Apart from the photo essays, none of the pieces carry photographs.

What would Wilson advise people planning to pitch ideas for *The Blizzard*?

Firstly, would you write this piece for free? We do pay – but would you write this piece for free?

Second, could anyone else in the world write this piece? We want something you've been burning to write for years and you are the only person with the requisite knowledge and experience to write it. . . [we're looking for] people who have this great idea that doesn't fit anywhere else, because of length, because of obscurity, because of whatever. And we, hopefully, find a platform for that.

We also have to have slightly more mainstream pieces. If it is about Barcelona or Messi, is this an angle I haven't seen before? Is this an angle that's different to what anyone else has done?

It's easier to say what's not a *Blizzard* piece than what is a *Blizzard* piece.

(ibid)

Since *The Blizzard* launched, there has been a distinct growth in longform writing – covering both sport and other areas of journalism.

Around about 2010–11, there was a very clear belief that bitesize is all we want and nobody is going to be bothered to read even 500 words on a screen, never mind 1,000 or 5,000. I think two things have gone on.

One is that technology has got better. It's more comfortable to read stuff on screen nowadays; that sense of "I've got a screen drilling into my head" isn't there anymore.

The other is that newspapers have struggled to find a role for themselves. In a world of bloggers where you have fans of a club who have been to every game for 20 years and who have a very specific knowledge – in what sense is a newspaper giving readers something that that fan's blog doesn't? The fan has been to every game, he talks about it all the time and picks up every bit of gossip in the pubs or from taxi drivers all the time.

Broadsheets have realised that one of the things they have is authority and the ability to put stories in context and the ability to interview people from a wide cross-section of football and the only way to do that in a meaningful way is in a longer form piece – or a book.

(ibid)

Other sports may follow Wilson's lead. In 2016, Caitlin Thompson and David Shaftel launched a tennis magazine called *Racquet*, crowdfunding the project through the Kickstarter website.

Like *The Blizzard*, *Racquet* is quarterly, though it's only available in print. Also like *The Blizzard*, it was born of frustration with existing journalism. "Former coaches are the people who commentate, and the columnists are married to the agents who represent the players," Thompson told Nieman Lab in 2017 (Lichterman, 2017). "It was just: Man, nobody is going to say anything interesting about this sport."

CASE STUDY: MULTIMEDIA PACKAGES

For a long time, a common criticism of new media was that it hadn't created any of its own ways of telling stories. It simply mimicked existing forms. For example, an online news story or match report, is simply a slightly different form of newspaper story, a podcast was a slightly different form of radio programme and so forth.

That all changed on 20 December 2012 when the *New York Times* published "Snowfall: The Avalanche at Tunnel Creek" (Branch, 2012). This was a 16,000-word piece by John Branch which told the story of how 16 skiers and snowboarders, including elite professionals and experienced skiing journalists, got caught up in an avalanche in Washington State. Three were killed. The story combines text with short video clips, interviews with the survivors, rescuers and meteorological experts and footage from the skiers' head-cams. It also includes maps, photographs, a complex graphic explaining the cause of the avalanche and audio clips of calls to the emergency services. Each time a new character is introduced, there is a short slide show which captures a bit of that person's history and wintersports experience.

"Snowfall" is split into six chapters. At any time, the reader can also refresh their memory by looking at a map of the area or a list of the group. As you scroll down a page, the photographs and maps expand. In short, "Snowfall" was a full-on multimedia experience – and Branch's gripping writing was part of that experience – for example:

> She had no control of her body as she tumbled downhill. She did not know up from down. It was not unlike being cartwheeled in a relentlessly crashing wave. But snow does not recede. It swallows its victims. It does not spit them out.
>
> (Branch, 2012)

It was also an interactive experience as it was up to the reader whether or not to play some of the video clips that offered insights into, for example, the weather conditions and the reasons the group ignored warning signs. In theory, readers could even choose what order to read the story in by selecting later chapters before earlier ones.

Inevitably, "Snowfall" produced a string of imitators, such as the *Guardian's* "Firestorm" (2013). "Snowfall" became a verb in some newsrooms: "Can we Snowfall this?" But it proved hard to emulate, partly because of the NYT's resources and range of skills which made it almost uniquely capable of producing a story of this kind and partly because the story of Tunnel Creek was itself unusually well-suited to this kind of story-telling.

The *New York Times* sports desk was involved in the production of "Snowfall". Branch credits sports editor Joe Sexton for the idea of expanding "Snowfall" into something bigger than a basic text story (*New York Times*, 2012). And, so, unsurprisingly, the sports desk attempted to use similar techniques to tell other sports stories.

An early effort was "The Jockey" (Bearak, 2013). This was a study of Russell Baze, the US's most successful jockey in terms of race wins (11,839 at the time of the piece) and, yet, because he devoted his career to the minor league tracks of northern California, not a well-known figure outside racing experts. Over eight chapters, Barry Bearack looks at Baze's career from different perspectives, such as Baze's family background, the injuries he's suffered and his impact on local gamblers. The final chapter tells the story of Baze's 50,000th race (yes, *four* noughts). The first few chapters are illustrated with lushly filmed videos but, while easy on the eye, these add relatively little to the story.

Just before the 2016 Olympics, the NYT produced a series called the "Fine Line", which took a scientific approach in its study of four of the US hopefuls: a swimmer (Ryan Lochte), a high jumper (Derek Drouin), a triple jumper (Christian Taylor) and a gymnast (Simone Biles). None of these sports are well understood by the general public and so the pieces act as explainers, identifying why these particular sports stars have discovered ways of gaining slight advantages over their competitors. For example, we saw how the swimmer, Ryan Lochte, had developed a new way of turning at the end of each length of freestyle (*New York Times*, 2016a). Rather than hitting the end of the pool with his legs and then turning back on to his stomach immediately,

FIGURE 12.2 Photograph of Christian Taylor, courtesy of Mark Shearman, Athletics Images

Lochte stays on his back five feet below the water, only turning and surfacing later. This means he avoids the turbulence caused by his competitors and benefits from his powerful kick off.

The use of video and text explains Lochte's technique better than mere words alone could. Traditional television *could* explain his method, but the advantage of the NYT's approach is that it puts the viewer in control. You can take as long as you like – and as many replays – to help you to understand the techniques involved.

The technique works best on the Simone Biles piece (*New York Times*, 2016b). It looks at her signature move, the double layout with a half-twist and a blind landing. I found it useful to be able to watch the manoeuvre repeated several times before I clicked to move onto the next section. I was also able to go back to recap on earlier bits. A more knowledgeable gymnastics fan might not have needed to do this and could have moved through the piece more quickly. That's a luxury that traditional television doesn't permit.

The piece explains that Biles is able to get away with an unusually short run up which, in turn, gives her more room on the mat to execute the move itself. This, it goes on to explain, is down to her natural "air awareness" and, to illustrate this, we are shown what looks like a home video clip of her at a young age doing a series of aerial forward rolls in her family home. The piece also includes footage of her competing on the vault and beam at a young age.

The "Fine Line" pieces are all fairly short: around 300 words each; you could watch all four in ten minutes. But, like "Snowfall", they make extensive use of video, of graphics and of graphics overlaid on video. Twenty-three people are credited as working on the collection. They certainly helped me better understand aspects of four sports about which I knew very little. That said, I find the NYT's habit of combining a clip of the athlete or their coach speaking with the same text appearing on screen annoying: I can read, I don't need both components. I also dislike having to click "next" every ten seconds to move through the different sections of the stories. So, the "Fine Line" looks like an experiment in online story-telling rather than an established format.

One of the most prolific producers of multimedia longform journalism is *L'Equipe*, the daily French sportspaper that has been around for more than 70 years and created the European Cup. Visit *L'Equipe*'s Explore page and you will see a diverse range of "grands reportages and interactivité" covering mountaineering, tennis, football, rallying, cycling, yachting (a piece on the Vendée Globe race, entitled "Suivez-les en enfer": Follow them to hell) and, interestingly, eSports. Almost all run to four or five chapters and include text, video, illustrations, tactical graphs and the kind of scrolling images seen on "Snowfall".

A piece entitled "Guardiola: La Loi des 32 minutes" (L'Equippe 2016) is worth reading in detail. The piece was written when Pep Guardiola, former coach of Barcelona and Bayern Munich, had been in his new job at Manchester City for a few weeks and had just won the undying affection of the club's fans by beating rivals Manchester United at Old Trafford. The title, which translates as "the 32-minute law", refers to Guardiola's assistant Manuel Estiarte's claim that his friend could only go 32 minutes without thinking about football. Unlike some *L'Equipe* Explore stories, it hasn't been translated into English but it can be viewed using Google Translate.

The piece, which is the work of more than 15 people under the authorship of Grégoire Fleurot and Dan Perez, runs to around 8,000 words, split over four chapters plus an introduction. If you read the story on a phone or tablet, you'll find that, part of the way through the introduction, you come to a timeline of Guardiola's career. At this point, you can either scroll right to see an overview of the Catalan's career or scroll down to continue with the story. Later, you are presented with the option of listening to video clips of some of his former players talking about him. So, the reader has a degree of control: interactivité.

Much of the piece looks at Guardiola's tactical philosophy, unsurprisingly as he's regarded as one of the most innovative coaches of his era. The tactical diagrams are animated so the little red and white hexagons which signify players move around on the screen. There are also boxes showing other managers who've influenced Guardiola's thinking, going through his match-day routine (apparently he's too nervous to eat for eight hours before a game) and illustrating some of his trademark gestures.

YOUR TURN

Why undertake a major piece of longform journalism? After all, it's unlikely that anyone is going to commission you to write a 10,000-word epic until you've been working as a journalist for many years. And it's a big undertaking in terms of time; you'll need a large cast of interviewees who may take some time to track down.

The answer comes from Jonathan Wilson: you've been burning to write this piece for some time. If you want to be a sports journalist then, I suspect, you have stories you want to tell. Maybe you support a small football club with an interesting past? Maybe you know of an athlete whose exploits are now forgotten? Maybe you feel strongly about the way a sport is reported or mismanaged?

If you are a student and you are required to produce a piece of longform journalism as a final major project, then I'd really urge you to look on this as a great opportunity. You won't get another chance to write a story that only you can tell for some time. Even when you do, you will have to deal with editors or producers or other figures who will try to shape your work, sometimes in ways you don't want it shaped.

It is impossible to write a "how to . . ." guide for longform sports journalism. It would require a lot more space than is available here and, in any case, part of the joy of longform writing is that no two pieces are the same. What follows are some ideas to make a major project more manageable. They are designed to apply whether you are trying to tell your story using text, audio or video.

1   Think of an audience

As with any piece of communication, *who* you are talking *to* is often as important as *what* you are saying. The way you'd tell a story to your mum is different to the way you'd tell it to your best friend and, similarly, the way you'd talk to readers of *FourFourTwo* is different to how you'd talk to readers of *The Blizzard*. Once you're chosen a publication, try to read, watch or listen to it – a lot. Get a feel for the kind of language it uses and the references it expects its audience to understand. You should be able to clearly explain why your piece is suitable for a particular outlet with reference to stories that it's carried before. For example, as we saw in Chapter 7, Copa90 made a film about what it saw as the mismanagement of Leyton Orient Football Club. That suggests it might also be interested in other stories of struggling teams in the lower leagues.

2   Nail your interviewees first

A piece of longform journalism will need different voices to keep it interesting. Sure, you could write 10,000 words based on information you find online – but so could anyone else.

"Someone pitched an idea [for *The Blizzard*] about [Juventus and Argentina striker] Paulo Dybala", Jonathan Wilson (2017) recalls.

> I thought "great". I don't think his background is very well known in Europe. He's from Polish stock and his grandfather moved to Argentina just after the Second World War. Sounds an interesting story. What's his background? And the piece we got back was one that anyone could have written by googling "Paulo Dybala". We needed someone who had spoken to half a dozen people who'd known Dybala as a kid, someone who can inform us on Dybala in a different way.

But persuading people to be interviewed takes time, particularly if you're hoping they'll set aside an hour or more and be prepared to open up a bit to you. So, even if you have two months to complete your project, get your requests in early.

Don't assume that you have your interview in the bag until you've actually spoken to the person. You will find that some people will say yes in response to your initial email or social media request but then go silent on you. Be persistent; if they said yes, then they probably do want to help, but it may have slipped to the back of their list of priorities, so be prepared to chase them up – on the phone if necessary.

I'd also recommend you don't conduct your interviews over social media, which isn't conducive to getting people to open up and feel as though they are engaging in a one-to-one conversation.

3   Split your project into chapter headings

A really big project can seem unmanageable unless it's broken down into smaller chunks. Very few of the stories we've looked at in this chapter are told in chronological order. The stories of Russell Baze and Pep Guardiola were both split into chapters that we might term "thematic". That is to say, they looked at general themes throughout the central character's career rather than having a chapter devoted to childhood, one to their early career and so on.

It's hard to know how long it will take to write 8,000 or 10,000 words, but it is possible to say "okay, I'll set aside the next three days to write this 2,000-word chapter". You'll also feel much better once you know you have one or two chapters finished. Try to set yourself mini-targets based on chapter completion.

Of course, your chapter headings don't have to be fixed in stone. If you're writing a feature on a manager or coach, you might decide to have a section on your subject's relationship with players. Fine – but maybe you collect a lot of interviews for this section. There's no reason why you couldn't, later on, split it into relationships with up-and-coming players and relationships with star names.

4   Be prepared to draft, redraft and redraft again

When I look back at TV reports I produced in my early career, I'm normally pretty uncomfortable as they seem pretty awful. That's probably a good thing; I've developed as a journalist, and the fact I now wince at these old pieces shows that I've gotten better.

Over the course of your project, you will develop as a journalist, and when you look back at something you wrote a month earlier, you'll probably want to change it.

It can, however, be difficult to view your own writing objectively, so it's always a good idea to get other people to look over it. Try to find friends who will take the time to read it in detail but who also won't hold back but will be totally frank. For your part, you need to be receptive to their criticism.

LONGFORM JOURNALISM: THE FUTURE

It's interesting and certainly not a coincidence that print, audio, audiovisual and web-based sports journalism have all started experimenting during the 2010s with longer narratives. It suggests that there's a real appetite for exploring sport's rich history, its complex tactics and sometimes contradictory lessons it tries to teach us about life.

No one in the future will be going back to those *Observer* football and rugby reports of the 1970s and 1980s. That style, rich in classical allusions and martial metaphors, would be meaningless to most audiences today. The language used in *The Observer*, and its sister publication the *Guardian*, today owes more to fanzine culture and the snappy, ironic writing of the turn of the century.

During the next few years, I expect the generation that grew up in the 1990s and early years of this century to get more involved in longform journalism. It will be interesting to hear the language they'll use and how they'll cover sports stories.

REFERENCES

30 for 30 (2017a) *A queen of sorts* at https://30for30podcasts.com/episodes/a-queen-of-sorts/. Last accessed 3/12/2017

30 for 30 (2017b) *The fighter inside* at https://30for30podcasts.com/episodes/the-fighter-inside/. Last accessed 3/12/2017

30 for 30 (2017c) *On the ice* at https://30for30podcasts.com/episodes/on-the-ice/. Last accessed 3/12/2017

Barclay, P. (1978) 'Tottenham's defence were as open-mouthed as the rest of us' in Hills, D. (2012) *Liverpool: 20 Defining Matches*, ebook: Guardian Books

Bearak (2013) *The jockey* at www.nytimes.com/projects/2013/the-jockey/#/?chapt=introduction. Last accessed 3/12/2017

Branch (2012) *Snowfall: The Avalanche at Tunnel Creek* at www.nytimes.com/projects/2012/snow-fall/#/?part=tunnel-creek. Last accessed 3/12/2017

Guardian (2013) *Firestorm* at www.theguardian.com/world/interactive/2013/may/26/firestorm-bush fire-dunalley-holmes-family. Last accessed 3/12/2017

L'Equippe (2016) *Guardiola: La Loi de 32 minutes* at www.lequipe.fr/explore/guardiola-loi-32-minutes/. Last accessed 3/12/2017

Lichterman, J. (2017) *"There's almost no journalism in tennis," but the print quarterly Racquet is trying to change that* at www.niemanlab.org/2017/05/theres-almost-no-journalism-in-tennis-but-the-print-quarterly-racquet-is-trying-to-change-that/. Last accessed 3/12/2017

New York Times (2012) *Q. and A.: The Avalanche at Tunnel Creek* at www.theguardian.com/world/interactive/2013/may/26/firestorm-bushfire-dunalley-holmes-family. Last accessed 3/12/2017

New York Times (2016a) *The fine line Ryan Lochte swimming* at www.nytimes.com/interactive/2016/08/05/sports/olympics-swimmer-ryan-lochte.html. Last accessed 3/12/2017

New York Times (2016b) *The fine line Simone Biles gymnastics* at www.nytimes.com/interactive/2016/08/05/sports/olympics-gymnast-simone-biles.html. Last accessed 3/12/2017

Wear, S. (2017) Interview conducted by the author on 7/9/2017

Willis, A. (2017) Interview with the author, 14/9/2017

Wilson, J. (2010) *Editorial* at www.theblizzard.co.uk/about. Last accessed 3/12/2017

Wilson, J. (2017) Interview conducted by the author on 14/11/2017

Glossary

As it happens report — see *live blog*.

Aspect ratio — the shape of television pictures. For most of the 20th century, television pictures were 4:3 (four by three) meaning that if your TV screen was 40 centimetres long, it would be 30 centimetres high. Modern TVs have an aspect ratio of 16:9.

Blog — a contraction of "web log". While the terms website and blog are sometimes used interchangeably, a blog typically takes a diary format with little capacity for the reader to navigate between sections.

Camcorder — a contraction of the words "camera" and "recorder". Traditionally, video gatherers for television news and sports programmes used camcorders though there is now a case for using a DLSR (see Chapter 7).

Dark social — Content that is shared by email, text message or private messaging apps, such as WhatsApp, Facebook Messenger or Viber. The sharing is, therefore, invisible and cannot be recorded by the content creator.

Dashboard — Websites and social media accounts will all have a dashboard. From there, you can design the look of your pages, order content and look at the data that shows how your site or profile is performing.

Digital native — someone who has grown up surrounded by the world wide web, personal computers and social media. Several people interviewed in this book say they prefer to work with digital natives rather than digital immigrants (broadly speaking, anyone born before 1990) as they have a more intuitive understanding of digital technology.

Domain — the place where a website "lives" on the world wide web. When setting up a website, you can either purchase your own domain or use a sub-domain owned by a company such as WordPress, Weebly or Blogger. From the Latin, *domus* meaning house or home.

Download — the process of pulling a file (such as a document, a video or a piece of music) from a location online down onto your computer or phone. This is an alternative to streaming, which involves playing the file from its original location.

DSLR — Digital single-lens reflex camera. In short, a traditional-style camera that uses digital storage, normally an SD card, rather than film.

Landscape — a term to describe pictures that are wide and long, as on television or in cinemas, as opposed to portrait images which are tall and thin.

Legacy — companies that make "old media" products such as newspapers, magazines and radio and television programmes are described as legacy media or legacy businesses. These organisations have to produce content for the web and smartphones at the same time as maintaining the, often expensive, infrastructure needed to print or broadcast their journalism.

Live blog — A report made up of a series of short posts produced while an event is in progress. Also known as a minute-by-minute or as-it-happens report.

Minute-by-minute — see *live blog*.

Multimedia — covering more than one media form. For example, a multimedia journalist refers to some-one who can work in television, radio and online journalism. A multimedia project might refer to a piece of work that includes audio, video, maps, graphs and text.

Native advertising — content that is designed to look like normal journalism but is, in fact, paid for.

Native video — video that is designed to be hosted on social media sites such as Facebook, rather than on a media organisation's own website.

Owned channels — Channels that an individual or company own themselves, ie their own website, as opposed to feeds they set up on other channels such as Facebook or YouTube.

Podcast — a programme or show for audio only. The name derives from Apple's iPod.

Portrait — a term to describe pictures that are tall and thin as opposed to landscape images that are wide and long. Footage shot by citizen journalists on their phones is often shot in portrait as this is how people tend, instinctively to hold phones.

Preroll — a sequence added to the start of a video clip. The best examples of this would be advertise-ments that play at the start of clips on YouTube.

Search engine optimisation — the art of trying to push your posts higher up Google's search rankings.

Shovelware — An IT term to refer to software that is not being used for its original purpose. When applied to journalism, it means content designed for one medium (eg print or television) that is shovelled up and plonked online without being modified to suit the new medium.

Social media — An online platform that permits peer-to-peer communication (as opposed to those that simply allow communication to and from the platform's owner) and enables people to group into commu-nities based on shared interests.

Streaming — a process of playing a piece of audio or video directly from a website. Streams can stop and start if you have a weak connection to the internet. In this case, it may be preferable to download the file.

Uniform resource locator (or url) — the link or address that leads someone to a website.

Upload — the process of pushing a file (such as a document, a video or a piece of music) from your computer or phone up onto a website (including social media sites).

User-generated content — content, generally pictures or video, which has been sent in to a media organisation or uploaded to its servers by members of the public or people caught up in dramatic events.

Index

Note: page numbers in *italic* indicate a figure on the corresponding page.

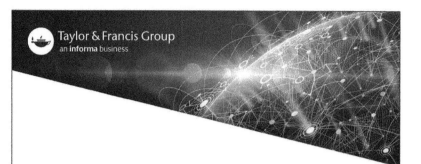